THE HOSPICE
MOVEMENT

THE HOSPICE
MOVEMENT

REVISED EDITION

*A Better Way of Caring
for the Dying*

SANDOL STODDARD

*With an Introduction by
William M. Lamers, Jr., M.D.*

VINTAGE BOOKS

A DIVISION OF RANDOM HOUSE, INC. · NEW YORK

FIRST VINTAGE BOOKS EDITION, JANUARY 1992

Text copyright © 1978, 1991 by Sandol Stoddard
Introduction copyright © 1991 by William M. Lamers, Jr., M.D.
Appendix copyright © 1991 by Hospice Education Institute, Inc.

Grateful acknowledgment is made to the following for permission to reprint
previously published material:
THE AMERICAN JOURNAL OF HOSPICE AND PALLIATIVE CARE:
Excerpts from "Hospice, Entropy, and the 1990's: Toward a Hospice World
View" by Douglas MacDonald. Reprinted with permission from THE
AMERICAN JOURNAL OF HOSPICE AND PALLIATIVE CARE.
Harvard University Press: "Pain—has an Element of Blank—" from THE
POEMS OF EMILY DICKINSON edited by Thomas H. Johnson, The
Belknap Press of Harvard University Press, Cambridge, Mass. Copyright
1951, © 1955, 1979, 1983, by the President and Fellows of Harvard
College. Reprinted by permission of the publishers and the Trustees of
Amherst College.
Macmillan Publishing Company and SCM Press Ltd.: Stanza entitled "Death"
from "Stations on the Road to Freedom" from LETTERS AND PAPERS
FROM PRISON, revised, enlarged edition by Dietrich Bonhoeffer, Copyright
© 1953, 1967, 1971 by SCM Press Ltd. Reprinted by permission of
Macmillan Publishing Company and SCM Press Ltd.
NOVA LAW REVIEW: Excerpts from "AIDS Discrimination: Its Nature,
Meaning and Function" by David Schulman. Reprinted by permission of
NOVA LAW REVIEW.
THE PHAROS: Excerpt from an article by Dr. Martin G. Netsky from the
Spring, 1976 issue of THE PHAROS. Copyright © 1976 by Alpha Omega
Alpha Honor Medical Society. Reprinted by permission of THE PHAROS.

Library of Congress Cataloging-in-Publication Data
Stoddard, Sandol.
The hospice movement: a better way of caring for the
dying/Sandol Stoddard.—Revised ed.
p. cm.
Includes bibliographical references.
ISBN 0-679-73467-8
1. Hospice care. 2. Hospices (Terminal care) I. Title.
R726.8.S74 1992
362.1'75—dc20 91-4530
CIP

Book design by Stephanie Bart-Horvath

Manufactured in the United States of America
10 9 8 7 6 5 4 3 2 1

This new edition of *The Hospice Movement* is dedicated to all who watch and wake by night, especially the care-givers.

ACKNOWLEDGMENTS

This updated and greatly enlarged edition of *The Hospice Movement* could not have been written without the generosity of many friends, old and new, who have not only supported its creation but offered, in many cases, parts of their own lives to readers of the following pages.

Above all I need once again to thank Dame Cicely Saunders and the staff of St. Christopher's Hospice in London who so kindly allowed me to work there as a volunteer thirteen years ago while gathering material for chapters 6 and 7. The inspiration of these good people and of the patients I learned to love at St. Christopher's has been a steady guide and comfort to me in the intervening years, and I was not surprised to discover that these chapters were almost the only ones in the original book that did not need reworking for a new edition.

To all hospice people who have welcomed me more recently, and especially to my new friends on the AIDS frontier, and in Southeast Asia, I am deeply grateful for their trust, their unfailing graciousness, and their invaluable assistance.

Michal Galazka, director of the Hospice Education Institute in Essex, Connecticut, has done more than to supply the wholly new Clinical Appendix; he has been a source of comradeship, insight, and information for this edition. However, it should be said that I alone bear responsibility for any error or misstatement in the text.

Warm thanks are also due to the many individuals who have contributed to the book by adding to my own well-being during the research and writing of three entirely new chapters. Obviously, they cannot all be named here, but I cannot neglect the opportunity to mention at least the following: Robin Straus, peerless agent and friend; Joe, Michael, and David Kanon, peerless house-sitters; Luann Walther, my fine editor at Vintage Books; Fr. John Engelcke, the Rev. Canon Roswell Moore, and Maggie

Ross, who have helped to keep mind and soul in order while June
Vieth and Peggy Sankot helped to keep the rest of the plant in
operation; Priscilla Lord, who has never failed me; Bessie, my
computer that has, but is beloved anyway; people who have
prayed with me, including especially Cynnie Salley, June Kerr,
Meris and Brad Farwell, Sylvia and Cullen Tendick, Petey Sei-
bold, Cynda Unger, April Weiss, Joan Focht, Jasmine Locatelli,
Lee Fierro and Bo Hamilton; Maynard Mack, ever present in the
memory of Amazing Grace; Laura Ashton, helpful source at Hawaii State Library, Hilo; Natasha Lamers, sterling defender; and
most of all, members of my family, especially my sons Andy,
Peter, Gerry, and Jason Warburg, and their wives and children
who have given me so much, and my lovely stepdaughter and
friend, Stephanie Goethals; but first and foremost (for the first
shall be last) my husband, Peter Randall Goethals.

CONTENTS

INTRODUCTION

*A*t the time Sandol Stoddard wrote this definitive and enchanting book, hospice was more a memory and a vision than a movement: there were no more than a handful of newly organized hospice programs in the United States and Canada. That there are well over a thousand solidly functioning hospice and palliative care programs in the same area today is tribute to the timeliness of the first edition of *The Hospice Movement* and, in part, reflects the impact of the earlier work. This new, expanded and updated version of the classic comes at a time when a new generation of hospice workers needs to know both the recent and remote history of an approach toward life and living, dying and death, that transcends science and technology and speaks to the human spirit. At the same time, a new generation of health care consumers needs to learn about positive alternatives in the face of prolonged, catastrophic illness.

For most of recorded history, dying was a brief process that usually took place in the company of one's family, usually in the home. The physician had little to offer to change the course of the injury or illness. Secondary infections brought a quick and often peaceful end to life. In the pre-antibiotic era, for example, pneumonia was known as "the old man's friend." But the remarkable achievements of this century brought an end to the premature death suffered by former generations. For many, dying is now largely a matter of advanced age coupled with degenerative, incurable illness. Dying persons are usually the benefactors of complicated technology and expensive care. The natural "care by family" has yielded to care by professionals in an institution. The current economic and bioethical dimensions of protracted, impersonal, institutionalized dying confront us daily in the media.

"Death," Norman Cousins tells us, ". . . is not the ultimate tragedy. The ultimate tragedy is depersonalization . . . dying in an alien and sterile arena, separated from the spiritual nourishment that comes from being able to reach out to a loving hand."

Hospice is a positive response to the depersonalization Cousins alludes to. Yet, as Stoddard clearly describes in this book, hospice is more than mere hand-holding. It is, in the words of Dame Cicely Saunders, "hard medicine with a human face." It is the best of traditional medicine blended with an awareness of the complexity of the human spirit, with careful and caring attention to the multidimensional needs of patient, family, and caregivers.

Since the publication of the first edition of this book, hospice has found even broader application in response to the challenge of the HIV (AIDS) epidemic. Hospice philosophy and practice have become an accepted part of care for patients not only with cancer and HIV infection but with a broad range of problems including advanced cardiorespiratory and renal disease, as well as a number of neurologic disorders.

This is not a book about dying and death. It is a testament to life, to joy, and to the warmth and richness that can result when one person reaches out to another to soften the impact of disease and loss. It contains a message that will never be outdated. Re-reading it evokes memories of those "hid in death's dateless night" who have taught us important lessons about life.

In health sciences, we have found limits to our technology. There is no limit, as Lois Wheeler Snow pointed out, to our humanity . . . save by our own making. *The Hospice Movement* is a guide for those who believe that dying can be, as one of our patients told me, ". . . the experience of a lifetime."

William M. Lamers, Jr., M.D.
Malibu, California
April 27, 1990

A PERSONAL FOREWORD

Some years ago I lay in the large maternity hall of a respectable old Boston hospital, laboring to give birth to my first child. The name of the institution was world famous, and the care given its lying-in patients was considered exemplary.

All around me in this vast, echoing room were criblike beds where rows of women lay still as death, or tossed and moaned, or shrieked like victims on the rack. In accordance with the system of the day, the majority were heavily sedated. Few had any real understanding of what was happening. Pregnancy itself was rarely mentioned in polite New England circles in those days, and the actual process of getting a baby born was a mystery known only to the Olympian, grave-faced, and uncommunicative (male) physician. It was generally assumed that the women involved could do nothing about it one way or another—except to submit, and try not to disgrace themselves any further by being a nuisance. Husbands, family members, and friends had no part in this arcane procedure beyond delivering the unfortunate victim to the hospital door.

Under these circumstances, babies arrived slowly. Most were taken by instruments at the obstetrician's convenience, for he was a busy man. My own obstetrician was one of the finest. He was so busy that it cost one thousand dollars every time he crossed the street from his office, washed his hands, and pulled a baby out of its mother's body with a pair of forceps. A thousand dollars was a very large sum of money in those days. But of course, in matters of life and death, nothing but the best would do. Our babies arrived smelling of ether, listless and bruised, their heads dented like windfallen fruit.

In the bed beside mine all this long day and into the night, a young woman wept for her mother. I could see her long, dark hair lying in a tangle on the pillow. I remember thinking that she must be a visitor from some exotic land—France or Spain, or Italy, perhaps—because when she was not crying out for her mother, she was sobbing, "Jesus, Jesus."

Eventually her cries became piercingly loud and incessant. The two nurses on duty shrugged at one another in distaste, inspected her briefly, and decided to wheel her bed into a soundproof anteroom.

"Why don't you do something to help her?" I asked. "She is frightened out of her wits, and she is in terrible pain."

The nurses stared at me in consternation. "What are you doing awake?" asked one. "She isn't feeling anything. She is very heavily sedated."

"But listen to her," I insisted. "If she is not suffering, why is she screaming and begging for help?" The two nurses looked at one another, and looked away. "She'll forget about it soon enough," I was told. Then I was given an injection; and after that, I don't remember anything that happened to me for fourteen hours.

Several years later I lay resting comfortably in a very different sort of hospital, an institution also highly respected, and noted for its enlightened maternity care. My airy room overlooked the grassy, moonlit spaces of northern California on a summer night. Wide awake that afternoon, I had given birth to another child.

In a round mirror I had watched the crowning of the small, dark head. I had seen the eyes of the doctors and the nurses in attendance—caring, helping, encouraging, congratulating me. Family and friends had come to embrace me. Now I had flowers, music, wine, perfume, and the silence of the night around me as I lay in a state of happiness so profound that sleep was irrelevant.

The day had been hard. The birth had been complicated and dangerous. I had been badly frightened, and had felt at times a great deal of pain. Yet with the help of those around me, I had been able to obey the enormous demand of that primal event. And in doing so, I had experienced a new dimension of reality. Claiming a birthright of my own, I had journeyed that day to a place beyond pain or death. Heaven, some would say, had opened itself to me.

A mystical moment, others might call it, or "a peak experience"—that glimpse of a joy beyond joy or grief, of a great reconciliation shining at the heart of things. At any rate, I knew that as long as I lived I could never be afraid of dying again. Dying and giving birth, being born and dying: in some inexplicable way, I had come to know that they are the same.

As I lay there, perfectly comforted and at peace, I began to hear on the other side of the wall beside me the voice of a woman weeping. *"God! Oh, God,"* she cried, and then began calling for her mother. I could hear her struggling for breath, grappling, laboring. Another child coming into the world, I thought—the wonder of it, the mystery! She began to scream, "I can't do it! I can't!" Oh, my dear, I thought, yes you can—but why on earth doesn't anyone come to help you? I rang my own bell.

Footsteps. Doors opening and closing. Voices. A telephone ringing. Beyond the wall, the sobbing and the moaning, on and on.

I tried to get out of my bed, and found that I was too weak. Through the wall, then, I tried somehow to lend her what energy I had. *Don't be afraid,* I thought. *Just breathe, in and out, and then, let go.* "Oh, God!" she began to scream again. *Let go,* I thought, *let go.*

Footsteps again, and the night nurse was standing over me. "What are you doing awake?" she scolded. Beyond the wall, the screams continued. "Don't worry about her," the nurse said hastily. "She isn't suffering. She is very heavily sedated."

"But why . . . ?"

"Don't worry about it," said the nurse.

"But no one goes to her," I said. "Why doesn't anyone go in there and try to help her?"

"It wouldn't make any difference," replied the nurse, giving me an injection. "She doesn't know what she is doing. If it bothers you, dear, just turn up your radio."

Early in the morning I awakened and crept out of my bed. I made my way to the room next door. It was empty, and the bed was stripped. It took me two more days to find out what had been happening in that room. Everyone I asked about it was either disinterested or embarrassed.

I made a nuisance of myself until at last it was explained. There had been an administrative error. The person in question, a female aged thirty-seven, Caucasian, single, had not been giving birth; she had been dying. She had no business being in the maternity section. She was cancer, terminal.

The patient had been in the hospital many times before, they told me. There was nothing more anyone could do for her. They had already given her every test imaginable; they had cut out her breasts, her ovaries, her uterus. She was blind; she had bedsores; she was incontinent; and even when fully conscious, she was not altogether in her right mind. She belonged in medical-surgical, obviously.

For nine days before the birth of my child, they had been trying to get her moved. At first her papers had been mis-filed, and then there had been a problem about insurance. After that, there had simply been no other place for her to go. Under ordinary circumstances they would have put her, when she was being so noisy, into the little isolation cubicle behind the nursery. As it happened, even that room at the time had been filled.

They were terribly sorry. The whole thing had been very unfortunate. They apologized to me for the inconvenience I had suffered, having to lie awake next door to her and, due to the poor quality of the soundproofing of that wing, having to listen to her die.

The faces of the individuals who said these things to me were somewhat puzzled and distracted, but they were not cruel or even unkind. In fact, I have rarely found medical people—or people of any sort—to be deliberately stupid or consciously mean and enjoying it. Still, it is hard to reply to well-intentioned people who are, in matters of life and death, so very far off the mark. It has taken me some time to find a useful way of responding to the experiences I have here described.

In part, this book is my response. And although it con-tains a good deal of history and many facts about death and loss, it is nevertheless a celebration of life.

"After a long illness . . . at a local hospital . . ." is what the newspapers so often say. Someone anonymous, it seems, is always dying while the rest of us turn up the radio or look the other way. And yet, having accepted the realities of birth as a natural process to be celebrated and respected, we are now bound, I think, to have a clearer look at the process of death.

In medieval times, dying persons were seen as prophetic souls, voyagers and pilgrims valuable to the community in a number of ways, not least in the opportunity they provided those around them for service and spiritual growth. It is a modern and ignorant prejudice to consider death a failure. It is a modern superstition to avoid knowledge of it, to treat it as if it were something unnatural, shameful, or wrong.

It is time for us to root out the fears and misconceptions that lie behind this distorted view. We must begin to honor the labor of those pilgrims who journey on before us; and in being present for them during the part of their living which is called dying, we must learn better to honor life itself.

This is what the hospice movement is all about. If my dying neighbor, Caucasian female aged thirty-seven, had been cared for in a hospice instead of a general hospital, she would not have been forsaken and she would not have been in agony at the hour of her death. She would in all probability have been spared some of the medical degradations she was made to suffer in the name of "cure"—and she would have had a name. She would have been surrounded by people who knew and loved her. Her pain would have been honored and skillfully relieved. She would have mattered as a person, not as the anonymous receptacle of a disease. With hospice care, the woman whose name I will never know would have had safe lodging, and love, and peace at the last.

No one in a civilized society should have to die as she did. The emergence of the modern hospice in our world today brings with it the hope and, potentially, the promise of a far better way than this for all of us.

THE HOSPICE
MOVEMENT

1

THE CARING HOST

Hospice (ho'spis) [a.F. *hospice,* ad. L. *hospitium* hospital-ity, entertainment, a lodging, inn, f. *hospit-em:* see HOST sb²] 1. A house of rest and entertainment for pilgrims, travellers or strangers . . . for the destitute or the sick.

Oxford English Dictionary

. . . For the ayde and comforte of the poore sykke, blynde, aged and impotent persones . . . whereyn they may be lodged, cherysshed and refreshed.

From a petition by the citizens of London to Henry VIII (1538)

*I*t is 3:00 A.M. and the television set of the ordinary householder is turned off. Downtown, however, in the newest wing of the university hospital, a skilled R.N. scans another set of screens. In the sophisticated purlieus of the intensive care unit, the drama is complex, intense, continu-ous. Here the humblest, least conspicuous of human signals is translated instantly into a series of extraordinary, elegant mechanical events. The ICU is a supercomputer, a biochem-ical celebration, a sound and light show. It is also something like a launching pad. Disconnected from every familiar form of human contact and every ordinary support system, the patients lie one by one, espaliered, wired, and tuned like astronauts. In the silence of the night it might be asked—where are they going? But in this place there is no silence, and there is no night.

In places of transit—bus stations, train stations, space stations, airports, hotels, hospitals—lights blaze twenty-four hours a day. Surfaces are hard here, cold and glittering; there is a smell of disinfectant in the air. People in such environs experience loneliness, anxiety, disorientation, a loss of the sense of personal identity. They become part of a mechanical situation, an observed and measured event.

Bus stations, space stations, hotels, hospitals. Question: does the word *hotel* belong in this group? If you have felt the urge to cross it out, then you may be one of the fortunate—one of the lucky few—who remember what the deliciously intimate hotels of the world used to be like before they, too, began wrapping the facilities in paper and the drinking glasses (for your protection) in plastic. Or perhaps you remember with delight those little places in Paris that until recently, that is to say, until a century or so ago, were private homes. The curtains hang in shreds, there are mouse-tracks under the armoire, and the bed squeaks—but the hospitable concierge slips you a wink and an extra croissant with your morning chocolate; and every room is filled with roses.

The Latin word *hospes* meant both host and guest. This in itself is interesting, since it puts the spotlight on a process, an interaction between human beings, that was once perceived as simple and mutual. In terms of our present medical models, both as promoted in the media and as experienced in professional practice, it is even more fascinating to consider the development of the word *hospes* into *hospitium,* into *hostel, hôtel-Dieu,* and *hospice;* also, of course, into *host* and *hostess,* into *hotel, motel,* and *hospital.* It is a sort of litany we have here, recording subtle shifts in value judgments, and in the differing relationships people have chosen, over the centuries, to have with one another. It is a litany perhaps worthy of some contemplation.

Certainly it is a measure, for example, of the split between mind and heart in the modern consciousness that we have needed a dictionary to help us recover the ancient connection between the objective thing, *hospital,* and the embracing act, *hospitality.*

It is a strange embrace, the one we now find welcoming us into the place called *hospital.* It is one that neutralizes instantly whatever life force it is that makes each one of us into a unique individual. *Hospital* welcomes my body as so many pounds of meat, filled with potentially interesting mechanical parts and neurochemical combinations. *Hospital* strips me of all personal privacy, of all sensual pleasure, of every joy the soul finds delight in; and at the same time seizes me in the intimacy of a total embrace. *Hospital* makes war, not love.

Let us leave sentimentality out of it, by all means. My need, if I am very ill, and especially if I am dying, is not for sappy get-well cards and background music. If there is a chance of mending me, so much the better. For example, that flesh wound I picked up during a difference of opinion with a would-be mugger: I very much appreciate having my host, the intern, sew it up for me. I am delighted to have my heart started up again by technicians of any sort, using whatever means they may have at their disposal, if my heart has quit simply because I overburdened it with carrying packages on a hot day. I will gladly be their guest, and I am grateful for their assistance.

And yet, ruthlessly realistic as we in the modern medical situation may imagine ourselves to be, is it not incredibly *sentimental* for us to imagine that we are engaged all this time in conquering an enemy called Death? Our young medical warriors in the media are so brave, so attractive, one wants them always to win. There is a mystique about this war against death that makes us turn our heads away from those who are hopelessly, incurably ill; and also from those who are quite consciously ready to die. These are the ones who disturb our picture of the way things ought to be. From *hospes* to *hospital,* the psychology has changed from one of love to one of war, and in the psychology of war, force is imperative. Therefore we arrive at the strange, new embrace that pins the inert body of a man or woman, terminally ill, to a machine that forces that person's body to breathe without even knowing its name.

It is our attitude toward death, I believe, that has so badly skewed and spoiled our contemporary sense of how persons who are well ought to relate to persons who are sick. In America, for reasons having to do with the development of our own culture, the problem is particularly acute.

"Death is un-American," Arnold Toynbee once remarked. It denies our power to conquer the globe with know-how and muscle, with science and machinery, with the youthful vigor and hope that conquered the frontier. Mocking what we have unconsciously believed was our inalienable right to live happily ever after, the Grim Reaper still awaits us at the end of every path we launch into the wilderness, or into space. The death of a patient is perceived as a humiliation and an outrage by the average physician in our culture; to the nursing staff in an acute care hospital, it feels like a personal defeat. To the patient's family it may very well represent the occasion for a malpractice suit. For indeed, why should such an untoward thing as death be allowed to happen in our society? The very look of a modern hospital identifies it as a fortress, an armory, a place of battle. The doctors dressed for combat with their engines and their weapons of cold steel—are they not the knights-errant of our modern Crusades? If death succeeds in storming such walls as these, who has been at fault? Who has slept on watch? Or has there been a traitor within?

Omnipotence is what we have expected for too many years from our physicians. Omnipotence is what they have too often claimed, and demanded of themselves, as well. It is not surprising that we have all been bitterly disappointed. And so we call regularly these days upon attorneys to punish our former idols in the courts, much as natives of Polynesia during the eighteenth century beat their tikis to a pulp, when these objects of worship failed to perform as expected.

What is needed now, however, rather than wrath, is a better grasp of the mortal realities on the part of physicians and public alike. We might then approach death together, not as adversaries, but as compassionate and enlightened friends. Many physicians, as we shall see in this study, are at the forefront of a movement toward this very outcome.

The unadorned truth is that of 5.5 billion human beings alive on this planet at the moment, some 80 million of us will die this year despite the best and the worst that the medical profession can do. Yet all of this tends to take place, as Lewis Thomas reminds us, ". . . in relative secrecy. We can only really know of the deaths in our own households, or among friends. These, detached in our minds from all the rest, we take to be unnatural events, anomalies, outrages. We speak of our own dead in low voices; struck down, we say, as though visible death can only occur for cause, by disease or violence, avoidably." But death will happen to us all, and it will happen because, in the natural order of things, it is supposed to happen. This itself may be perceived, with humility, as a *hospitable* fact: moving on, leaving space, time, and materials for others. Why shouldn't it be required of us all?

Unfortunately, just as we have lost the conscious connection between the word *hospital* and the word *hospitality,* we have also managed to lose a sense of the proper, necessary, and positive continuity between life and death. For too long a time we have maintained a really unfortunate illusion that one can exist without the other.

A new wave of awareness is beginning at last to change all of this in some positive ways. Pioneers such as Dame Cicely Saunders in England and author Elisabeth Kübler-Ross in the United States have brought the subject of dying into the open, and have helped us to learn more about the reality of it. Hundreds of books and articles have appeared in the past twenty years, describing and analyzing the processes of death, dying, mourning, and bereavement. Courses are now being given in universities and many nursing and medical schools to help young people reach a better understanding of a subject that was, until very recently, taboo. Films have appeared (notably, Michael Roemer's magnificent documentary, *Dying*) that treat the subject sanely, with decent concern and respect, and with none of the mawkishness that has served so often in the past as a mask for fear. Even in the commercial marketplace we can find a film such as *Rocket Gibralter,* designed for family viewing, which deals with terminal illness in a sensible and straightforward way. Improved communication with the dying and enlightened care of their needs has become a topic of great and ever increasing public concern.

We have begun to realize, I believe, that the enemy all along was not death, but our own unwillingness to incorporate its reality into our consciousness. There are a number of reasons why we have been able to do such a good job of deceiving ourselves over the past hundred or so years on this particular subject. In our present culture, more and more people are living a great deal longer than they used to. The dying are now more or less automatically removed from their traditional position as protagonists in a communal drama: the deathbed scene. They are whisked away to the medical fortress where machines instead of human beings will be their companions at the last. Even nursing homes for the aged and incurably ill tend to maintain the myth that no one actually dies there. They are called, as a rule, "convalescent homes" and bodies of dead inmates are whisked out the back door so as not to give the place a bad name. We have also the current worship of youth and youthful life-styles to contend with in a culture that has forgotten—temporarily, one hopes—how to nourish itself upon the experience of its elders. Last but not least, we have the chilly Puritan attitude that loss of individual power, vigor, and self-control is somehow disgusting: the same attitude that in the past has buried sex in the unconscious or else turned it into pornography, manageable because plastic and fake. In the Puritan system, orgasmic experience involving personal surrender of any sort must be denied, and therefore, after the late Middle Ages, says Philippe Aries, ". . . like the sexual act, death was henceforth increasingly thought of as a transgression which tears man from his daily life, from rational society, from his monotonous work, in order to make him undergo a paroxysm plunging him into an irrational, violent and beautiful world."

Beautiful though the world of death may be—and we have some rather astonishing evidence on this score, which will be taken up in a later chapter—the experience of dying can be a very difficult one.

"Dying is hard work," says Dr. T. S. West of St. Christopher's Hospice in London. The woman who gives birth instantly and unexpectedly, in a taxicab, perhaps, or in a public rest room; the man who, looking the other way, is smashed to bits by a truck; or, feeling a little overtired one morning, leans over to tie his shoes and is dead before he finishes—these, fortunately or unfortunately, are the exceptions among us. In most cases, dying, like birthing, is a process requiring assistance. It is an event that asks us to be present for one another with heart and mind, bringing not only practical help as necessary, but also attentive awareness and appreciation of the individual involved. At its finest, it elicits from us the frankly and fully offered human companionship that brings positive benefits, and a kind of joy, to any shared venture.

Oddly enough, most of this was known long ago, when the early medieval *hospice* was in operation throughout Europe, not only in England (where some seven hundred fifty were counted at a time of minimum population), but in major towns and cities across the map (forty in Paris alone, thirty in Florence); at monastic hermitages in wilderness areas; and in particular, at the mountain passes and river crossings that presented the greatest hazards to travelers on their way to the Holy Land. It was natural enough in those days to see death as a venture, for life itself was perceived then as a journey, a pilgrimage. Man was not expected, in the days before the Renaissance, to be omnipotent. The ancient *hospice* differed from the modern *hospital* in many ways. It offered an open door of welcome not only to the sick and dying, but to the hungry wayfarer, the woman in labor, the needy poor, the orphan, or the leper with his bell. The common base or denominator of the offering was *hospitality* in its original sense of protection, refreshment, "cherysshing," and fellowship, rather than the demand of a patient for a cure.

Powerful herbs grew in the gardens of medieval, monastic hospices. Medieval medicine—and Greek, Egyptian, Indian, and Babylonian medicine long before it—provided many a wise prescription for the healing of the body and the soul. Many are turning out today to be as effective as those

we have discovered since. But it is the view of human value
and of the human relationships involved that makes it most
intriguing to study the development of the hospice from its
earliest beginnings to the present day.

Endings and beginnings. Where does any idea or created
thing ever really end, and where does it begin? "What are
the Middle Ages?" asks medical historian David Riesman.
"For all we know we may be living in them." The hospice
idea did not begin with the work of Dr. Saunders in the
1960s, nor with the Irish Sisters of Charity in Dublin a
hundred years before. It was not invented by the White
Cross Knights of the eleventh century, nor by the Benedictines, nor did it have its beginnings with the rescue dogs of
Saint Bernard in the Alps. The concept antedates the magnificent hospice of Turmanin in Syria, A.D. 475, and the far
more modest one founded in the port of Rome much earlier
than that by a disciple of Saint Jerome named Fabiola to care
for pilgrims returning from Africa. Pilgrims returning from
Africa—almost two thousand years ago! People traveled
tremendous distances in those days, perhaps more boldly
and freely than we imagine.

It must have been a great nuisance at times—people wandering in, as it would have been said in the old language,
per ager, which means, literally, "across the field." Life was
a struggle in those days. If you live in a village with wild
animals in the surrounding forest, you are likely to have
your hands full building and mending your fences, shearing
your sheep, trying to raise a little barley and oats, and
keeping some chickens and a goat alive. You don't need
foreigners and strangers peregrinating across the field, arriving tired, dirty, and hungry just as your stew turns tender
in the pot.

Or do you? After all, it does get lonesome here from time
to time. If only we knew whether in some way or another

this fellow might be useful, we might let him in. And so we do—and he likes it, and he stays. "Three days gast," says the ancient Anglo-Saxon law, and after that, *agen hine* (after that, he waits on you). Plautus in 205 B.C. put it more definitively: "After three days, a guest and a fish begin to stink."

And yet, with incredible persistence, the stranger kept coming over the field. We discovered that he often brought interesting news, or helped us with our own chores, or taught us some new skill. If the one who had come *per ager,* that is to say, the *peregrina* fell ill while staying with us, we nursed him as best we could. If he died, we were sorry, and we buried him and placed a marker by his grave.

In the centuries that followed, there were times when we ourselves found reasons for leaving home. Then we discovered firsthand what it is like to be a *peregrin,* a *pellegrino,* or a *pellegrin.* In the fourteenth century the English word for all this activity became—in time for Chaucer's pious and bawdy crew to capture it as their own on their way to Canterbury—simply, *pilgrim.*

People were not any "better" in ancient days than they are now—or so I believe. Yet we of the twentieth century begin only now very gradually to emerge from a period of intense materialism during which personal relationships, like our relation to the earth itself, have suffered a devastating loss of richness and grace. Perhaps we needed to begin running out of material things, and thus to become in some sense primitives again, before we could stop to wonder whether things were really what we wanted most of all. We are tired and confused today about matters as basic as our right to be alive and to inhabit the planet at possible cost of despoiling it altogether. We mourn our loss of innocence and grace, as we grieve for those now scourged by the twin plagues of drugs and AIDS.

It is an adventure of the heart and a recovery of our own humanity at such a time to read the statutes for care of sick pilgrims by the Knights Hospitallers of the Order of St. John of Jerusalem in the twelfth century A.D.:

> How our Lords the Sick Should be Received and Served:
>
> When the sick man shall come . . . let him be carried to bed and there . . . each day before the brethren go to eat, let him be refreshed with food charitably according to the ability of the house.
>
> The beds of the sick should be made as long and as broad as is most convenient for repose, and each bed should be covered with its own coverlet . . . and each bed should have its own special sheets. . . .
>
> Little cradles should be made for the babies of women pilgrims born in the house. . . .
>
> The Commanders of the houses should serve the sick cheerfully, and should do their duty by them, and serve them without grumbling or complaining. . . .
>
> Moreover, guarding and watching them day and night . . . nine serjeants should be kept at their service, who should wash their feet gently, and change their sheets. . . .

Throughout the history of the hospice (or of the *hospitium, hôtel-Dieu* or "hospitall," for these concepts were for a number of centuries interchangeable) one finds again and again the sense of life itself as a sojourn among strangers—a journey, a pilgrimage toward some future state of rest and blessedness. In a time of reexamination of material values and of renewed spiritual questing, it is no coincidence that we find hospices once more appearing on the scene. At the present time in somewhat different guise, aided by every advantage of modern medicine, psychology, and clinical pharmacology, the hospice concentrates its energies upon dying individuals, their families and friends. If they are alone in the world, the hospice community becomes their own.

In Great Britain there are some four hundred such hospices now in operation. A rapidly increasing number of hospice teams and facilities is appearing today in widespread locations, particularly in Northern Europe, Japan, Australia, and other Pacific Rim nations, and throughout the United States; many of the best of these are using as their model of excellence St. Christopher's Hospice in London. Of the modern hospice concept, Dame Cicely Saunders (founder and director of St. Christopher's) says, "This is indeed a place of meeting. Physical and spiritual, doing and accepting, giving and receiving, all have to be brought together. . . . The dying need the community, its help and fellowship. . . . The community needs the dying to make it think of eternal issues and to make it listen. . . . We are debtors to those who can make us learn such things as to be gentle and to approach others with true attention and respect."

The modern hospice: a place of meeting, a way station, a place of transit, of arrival and departure. And yet how different from the airport, the hotel lobby, the hospital. It is the difference in the quality of human life assumed and provided for that makes for the contrast we shall see in the chapters to follow. People in hospices are not attached to machines, nor are they manipulated by drips or tubes, or by the administration of drugs that cloud the mind without relieving pain. Instead, they are given comfort by methods sometimes rather sophisticated but often amazingly simple and obvious; and they are helped to live fully in an atmosphere of loving-kindness and grace until the time has come for them to die a natural death. It is a basic difference in attitudes about the meaning and value of human life, and about the significance of death itself, that we see at work in the concept called *hospice.* The reasons for that difference are worth looking at, in some detail.

2

NOT LIKE YOU AND ME

[In sixteenth-century Spain] the sick became the precious possession of the community. . . . The incurably
sick had the love of the people and the royal favor, for
heaven was open to them.

Dieter Jetter

Each one thought or felt, "Well, he's dead but I'm
alive! . . . He has made a mess of things—not like you
and me!"

Leo Tolstoy

Will *you* turn me out if I can't get better?

Patient entering
London hospice, 1960s

G reen-black against the twilight sky and echoing with
birdsong, the pines of Epidaurus still stand, guarding
the cool and flowery valley sacred to the healing god Asklepios. Here, only twenty years ago, Maria Callas sang
Medea before a wildly cheering audience of twenty thousand in an amphitheater whose aesthetic grace and acousti-
cal perfection have yet to be surpassed. The theater was
built as an integral part of the patient-care system devised
by Greek physicians of the fifth century B.C.

The history of medical practice in the Western world is,
of course, a subject far beyond the scope of the present
study; however, there are a few key spots and a few moments in time worth examining closely in the process of

centering down upon the hospice concept. Contrast and comparison are useful in helping us to understand exactly what a hospice is, and what it is not.

Epidaurus was not a hospice. Actually, it resembled in many ways one of our vast, modern medical centers, though it differed in some respects from such places as the Columbia-Presbyterian Hospital in New York or the University of California Medical Center in San Francisco. Modern diagnostic machinery was not available and a great many useful curative procedures had yet to be invented. However, Epidaurus was definitely a place of healing, with a powerful mystique and system of its own. Temples of the most exquisite design stood near the amphitheater, decorated with the finest carvings of the day and sheltering statuary of ivory and gold. Here also were a superb gymnasium, hygienic lavatories, treatment rooms, and baths of the sort one would expect to find now at an elegant spa. The best of contemporary medical treatment was available, including a number of procedures such as hypnotherapy and behavior modification, which are only being rediscovered at the most enlightened of hospitals today, such as the Pain Management Center of the Mayo Clinic, and the City of Hope National Medical Center in Duarte, California.

Twenty-five hundred years ago in the history of the universe as we know it is merely the blink of an eyelid in time. Let us suppose that you have some ailment that has not responded to a day or so in bed with a hot-water bottle and a dose of good herb tea. The thing to do, obviously, is to proceed to Epidaurus for a cure. You are a retired soldier, let us say, or a courtesan out of favor this season. You suffer a devastating pain in your lower back, and you arrive feeling dreadful.

You lie down and are bathed, first in mud baths, then in

steam, and last in fresh tubs of water—first very hot, then tepid, then cool. Now you are gently anointed and massaged with fragrant oils. The attending physician arrives, examines you, and prescribes a careful regime of physical exercise. In particular, you are urged to take long, quiet walks in the beautiful countryside around us. A sense of well-being and peace begins to descend gently upon your consciousness, and seeps through all your muscles and nerves.

Next you are questioned about your eating habits and placed—alas—upon a sensible diet. Hot milk and honey, fruit juices, and water alone it will be for those of us who have been overindulging of late. Others will have fresh vegetables and cheese as well, along with bread, olives, nuts, and other wholesome fare. We are required, as a part of our cure, to go to the theater regularly, there to witness the most hilarious comedies and the most horrifying tragedies of the day. Now we experience *kátharsis* of the emotions that have kept our bodies tense, rigid, defended. We laugh, we weep, we scream, we shout. We listen to glorious music by the hour, and we feast our eyes upon the beauty of the landscape, the art, the sculpture, the architecture around us. Thus the healing process begins. But the best is yet to come; for the greatest curative power to be found at Epidaurus is in a long portico of marble facing the temple of Asklepios and known as the *abaton.* On the open porch of the *abaton* we lie visited by moon and by wind, by birds and by starlight, not only to rest and to sleep, but most significantly, to dream. Our dreams—even as in the most ancient of Egyptian healing temples and as in the offices of psychoanalysts today—will be interpreted as messages, as ways and means of completing our diagnosis and our cure. Messages from the gods, they were called in those days,

rather than messages from the unconscious: a bit more flat-
tering, put that way, and leaving less doubt as to whether
they should be acknowledged.

The rate of cure at such a place as Epidaurus was apparently excellent. The pain in the old warrior's back went
away, as such pains are apt to do, without a spinal disk
operation. The businessman's ulcer, the migraine of the
nervous politician, and the dyspepsia of the bon vivant all
vanished here in due course. So did the psychosomatic tics
and paralyses of the anxious, the vague arthritic aches of the
lonely and the bereaved, and the simple boils of the un-
bathed. Epidaurus was a magnificent medical happening,
rather as if in our own time Dr. Freud, Dr. Jung, and
Elizabeth Arden had managed to collaborate with Hollywood in a vast project designed, simply, to make people feel
better. Anyone who surrendered to such an environment
and followed such a delightful and sensible regime would
be certain of improvement; unless, of course, he or she
were quite hopelessly, incurably ill.

And that, in this particular situation, was their Catch-22.
The rule at Epidaurus was that people who were incurable
were not admitted. Terminal cases had to go somewhere
else to die; and if they had no other place to go, then the
field or the side of the road would have to do.

The Greeks were a hardhearted people, of course—not
like you and me. On the other hand, any efficient administrator of a medical facility nowadays would be likely to
understand the problem. The reputation of the staff—the
image of Epidaurus as a place of healing—is at stake. Imagine trying to operate such a place on a pay-as-you-can basis
of remuneration from grateful patients—in other words,
from patients who have been cured! The overhead is incredible. The local farmers are always overcharging us, the
politicians are breathing down our necks. The doctors are

making a fuss about conditions, the playwrights are constantly quarreling among themselves, and meantime, the actors steal our drugs. We can't keep an operation such as this going if people come here and die. If anything of the sort does manage to happen, we'll simply have to load the body out the back way and someone else will have to bury it.

Crossing the field now, appearing over the horizon at the most awkward of all possible moments as usual, comes our old friend, the pilgrim. She has come by ship this time, from one of the Aegean Islands, perhaps, or up from Africa. She has walked the long, dusty road up from the port of Nauflion knowing that she is very ill but having no coin left in her purse to buy or rent a donkey to carry her. At dusk she arrives, limping, hungry, frightened, and in desperate pain. She has reached the sacred precincts at last. The lamps are being lit beside the holy temple, and the smell of fresh-baked bread is in the air. But our friend the pilgrim unfortunately has a cancer and the hour of her death is now upon her; therefore, she will be turned away.

The classical world differed in many ways from ours. However, they did admire the perfectly formed, beautifully groomed, and healthy human body with as fervent a passion as we in America do today. Everyone wanted to be thin. Men did a great deal of jogging in ancient Greece. Women of Athens dyed their hair, painted their faces, plucked their eyebrows, and used depilatories. One method commonly used for improving the race was the practice of "exposing" infants who were ill or unattractive and letting them die upon a mountainside. Superfluous girl children were also eliminated in this convenient way. Thus the survivors were apt to be healthy as well as handsome, and useful to the state.

Very practical, all this—and yet one wonders whether

these marvelously accomplished people were missing something. It must be admitted that Epidaurus and similar centers of healing throughout the ancient world offered better cures for many common ailments of mankind than are to be found at the average hospital today. And after the fashion of what is now reappearing as "holistic medicine," they treated emotional and physical problems as an integral unit. However, the view of the *value* of human life per se is here curiously limited, lacking in dimension, as if the figures involved turned out, after all, to be cutouts made of cardboard. The ordinary Greek of the day was no Socrates. He believed that he and his fellows were moved about hither and yon, from place to place by the mischievous company of gods who pulled the strings and watched it all from their gallery on Mount Olympus. When the gods were no longer amused, human beings were simply abandoned. In such a system a glittering aristocratic superstructure may be maintained, without a second thought, upon a base consisting of the labor of human slaves. In such a world as this, the basic concept of hospice is as yet unborn.

Hospitals there were, in the fully modern sense of the word, only a few centuries later, under the rule of Rome. Interestingly enough, they were constructed for the purpose of mending three classes of people considered particularly useful to the empire, and therefore too valuable to be cast aside to die: warriors, gladiators, and slaves. In a powerful yet vulnerable military state, the soldier was an important unit. Gladiators were prized after the manner of modern rock stars or professional football players for their entertainment value to the populace. Slaves, even in those days, were apt to be expensive. The Romans were fine, solid builders, and great efficiency experts as well. Two thousand years of hospitals following theirs in the Western world have reflected the Roman way of housing those in disrepair, and effecting their reentry into the system.

Soldiers, gladiators, slaves. Again, it was a supremely practical way of looking at things. None of these had the power or the means to summon the private physician to his home—if indeed he had anything he could call home. Yet each was a member of a class judged indispensable to the welfare of the body politic, and thus, if hurt or diseased, must be mended if possible.

One can easily imagine the atmosphere in these *valetudinaria,* as they were called: wooden barracks set on the square with small rooms and symmetrical corridors around four sides, stark and well scrubbed. The model, both architecturally and tactically, was strictly a military one with a highly rational, hierarchical division of labor. In the bare, echoing halls one could hear at all hours of day and night the hurrying feet of the attendants cleansing wounds, sewing them up; and of others, more highly skilled, setting bones and performing surgery. One would hear the cries of the wounded, the voices begging for water, for wine, for opium; and the consultations of the various caretakers and surgeons among themselves.

The skills of the Roman physician were indeed extraordinary, but it is difficult to find much of anything else to applaud in a place so coldly cynical in its intent. No patient here has control over his own present situation or his own future; he is merely a tool of that society's war against chaos, an object broken and needing to be fixed for other people's convenience. The slave, when mended, takes up his function as a unit of mechanical energy. The soldier is off to battle again as soon as he is able. And the gladiator with mended wounds goes once more into the arena to provide entertainment for the howling masses. Who, in such a hospital as this, might one day stop and think, *Here lies a human*

being before me, living, dying, feeling, suffering? How might any
"well" person in such a place even begin to consider the
reality of the situation: that the sick individual being "cared
for" here is a person with a mind, a heart, and a soul?

Setting these questions aside for the moment, let us turn to
a description of the treatment received by a dying patient
of our own time, in a large, modern teaching hospital that
prides itself upon the excellence of its patient care. The
individual in question was the mother of a professor of
medicine at one of our Eastern universities, with full access
to what we are accustomed to considering the finest of
medical expertise:

> What happened was a nightmare of depersonalized
> institutionalization, of rote management presumably
> related to science and based on the team approach of
> subdivision of work. . . . Different nurses wandered in
> and out of my mother's room each hour, each shift,
> each day, calling for additional help over a two-
> way radio. . . . They were trained as part of a team
> "covering the floor" rather than aiding a sick human
> being. . . . Laboratory studies of blood and urine con-
> tinued to be performed, fluids were given, oxygen
> was bubbled in, antibiotics were administered; the
> days went by but seemed to be years. The patient was
> seen occasionally by large groups of physicians mak-
> ing rounds, presumably learning the art of practicing
> medicine properly. . . . The chart was enlarged regu-
> larly with "progress notes." These hastily scrawled
> writings always dealt with laboratory data, never
> about the feelings of the patient or her family. . . .
> One report stated that occult blood had been found in
> the stool. Someone responded by writing in the chart
> that in view of this finding, sigmoidoscopic examina-
> tion and a barium enema were indicated. I suggested
> to the author that his conditioned reflexive act was
> not warranted in the care of an unconscious 80-year-
> old woman who wanted to die gracefully. . . .

Marvelous and, indeed, almost miraculous as the performance of our acute care systems may be; much as we need and appreciate the heroic efforts of modern physicians to cure us when cure is possible; much as we admire the diagnostic and curative powers of present-day technology *when these powers are appropriately used;* this is the sort of situation that can only be called intolerable. If the patient's body has become merely an object, a public commodity, and a pawn in our irrational war against death, then it is time to call a halt to such proceedings.

Attorneys, judges, politicians, clergymen, and professors of medical ethics all over the country are even now engaged in a lengthy struggle to redefine the circumstances under which one may properly "pull the plug" for patients whose lives in fact have already ended. The moral issues involved are extremely delicate, and it is fitting that they should be studied with great care. Indeed, the questions we are forced to ask one another in this respect may not have any answers that are always, and everywhere, and in each possible circumstance, morally right. Still, we must ask them and do the best we can with them. Technology now demands this service of us, since we are able to keep people technically alive under conditions that were not dreamed of by those who first set forth to heal the sick. Living wills, euthanasia, and suicide have become, for the same reason, topics of increasingly anxious public concern.

What is not so well known is that we have already available a better model for the care of the terminally ill than any that is to be found either in the institutional world of classical antiquity or in the conventional medical center of the present time. The ancestor of this model has been available to us, in fact, for nearly two thousand years. While the *valetudinaria* still labored to mend their servants at the borders of the empire, rather quietly and inconspicuously the first of our modern hospices were born.

Exactly where and when this happened, it is of course impossible to say. Ancient monastic ruins give us hints, and there are other signs in certain heaps of rubble here and there, beside old village walls. Every now and then some delightful scrap of written record has a way of turning up, usually in Latin, Spanish, or French, telling us the rules of such and such an establishment, or listing the medicines, the loaves of bread, and the jugs of wine that have been provided during the past twelve months for the sick. The Knights Hospitallers of St. John of Jerusalem were great compilers of information about what became, in their case, an organized network of hospices and hospitals throughout the civilized world. However, their flowering was not until the time of the Crusades, whereas we can hear at least one voice out of history speaking quite clearly on our subject, at a time many hundreds of years earlier.

It is the voice of the Roman emperor Julian the Apostate speaking in A.D. 361, and essentially he is complaining, not only to the populace at large, but to himself. The Christians are making an intolerable nuisance of themselves in Rome. Julian passionately wants his people to pay proper attention to the gods of their forefathers, but it is reasonable to assume that military power, as usual, is the ultimate issue at hand. His borders are overextended, the German tribes are threatening from the north, and it is impossible for the emperor to cope with such a situation while things are getting more and more difficult at home. They have tried, over the past few hundred years, feeding these rebellious people to the lions, burning them alive, and nailing them up by the thousands in the Colosseum. Nothing, however, seems to work. More and more of them keep appearing on the scene and refusing to pay homage to the gods and the authorities, or to behave in any reasonable way whatever.

He asks himself, why do the masses flock to this strange new faith, knowing full well what the penalties may be? Why is it that this weak, unruly, and essentially undefended group of individuals has become a political power that simply must be reckoned with? Emperor Julian watches them. They are a queer people indeed. They wash the wounds of lepers, and give them food. They embrace the most utterly useless members of society—the poor, the orphans, the prisoners, the dying, and the blind. Every human wreck and stray mendicant in Rome—Christian, Jew, pagan, believer or nonbeliever—is in some mysterious way their friend. (This stubborn and motley crew would have been giving tender, nonjudgmental care to AIDS sufferers, no doubt, had there been any wandering the byways of the empire during the fourth century.) Furthermore, a wealthy and influential matron named Fabiola, having embraced Christianity, has now opened her own home to strays and pilgrims. If they are ill, she nurses them; if incurably so, she cares for them until they die. This puts her into close contact with every sort of riffraff imaginable. She sees some value in them, apparently.

Why this is happening, the emperor does not quite know; but he is an able politician and he understands the danger of it. He issues a proclamation. It is time, he says, for all good pagans to change their ways. Something is stirring in the land that may defeat us. Unless we co-opt it, we shall have our old gods and goddesses losing the last of their power before very long. "What makes these Christians such powerful enemies of our gods," says Julian, "is the brotherly love they demonstrate toward the sick and the poor." He urges Roman citizens to begin imitating them.

In every religion there are saints, and among people of every culture on earth there have been those who perceived something of holiness or ultimate worth in their fellow human beings. It would be foolish indeed to suggest that Christians invented compassion, or that they alone stand witness to the transcendental dimension of life. However, the coming of Christianity to the center of Western political power does represent a turning point in the moral life of the classical world. From this time on it was no longer possible for a civilized society in the West to ignore, in good conscience, the needs of its helpless or afflicted members. The greatest humanitarian movement in world history was now in progress, and with it an expansion of the human consciousness that continues today.

"It was so strange," said a patient entering a London hospice recently, after being discharged from an ordinary hospital. In other places, she explained, "no one seemed to want to look at me." She was dying of cancer and to look at her might have meant to see, in a place where only successful cure was acceptable, that she was incapable of being cured. To look at her might have meant to see failure, and with it the terror of one's own inescapable death. To look at her, in fact, might have meant, to see *her.*

"The hospice teaches a new attitude," says Leonard M. Liegner, M.D., "with the realization and conscious acceptance of dying and death as part of being born and part of the struggle of life." If the dying patient can be perceived first as a person, an individual accomplishing an important part of a full life cycle, then care-givers can concentrate upon giving what is really needed in the situation. They can actively prevent the interference of mindless technological tricks, and can instead provide surcease from physical and emotional pain. They can offer, instead of mechanical resuscitation, a hospitable place in which the personal and spiritual growth of the individual can continue during the process of dying.

In the medieval Christian world, the offer of hospitality to the hopelessly ill and the dying was based upon a literal interpretation of the text, "inasmuch as ye have done it unto one of the least of my brethren, ye have done it unto Me." The names of many modern hospices now operating in England give evidence that they, too, are instructed by the New Testament command: St. Joseph's, St. Christopher's, St. Ann's, St. Margaret's, St. Luke's. However, the doors of these hospices are open to persons of every faith and creed, and from any true hospice, no atheist or agnostic will be turned away.

> Oh, let me e'er behold in the afflicted and the suffering, only the human being.
>
> Rabbi Moses ben Maimon

> [When the Chinese came] with the personal—the person put foremost, Ed was no longer "a case." . . . The doctors' tact and tranquility generated ease and there was no feeling of secretiveness or estrangement. A community had formed, and we were an integral part, no longer outsiders waiting in an impersonal corridor for piecemeal information, hesitant to intrude in an area beyond our ken. . . . Our meetings were microcosms of what I had seen and read about Chinese society. . . .
>
> Lois Wheeler Snow

> To be with a person who is dying, to share consciousness with him, and to help him die consciously is one of the most exquisite manifestations of the Bodhisattva role.
>
> Baba Ram Dass

Perceptions such as these span the centuries and reach around the globe. In the United States today the hospice movement appears to take its energies from a more secular or at least a more broadly ecumenical base than in the

United Kingdom. However, it was a Jewish patient who gave the first five hundred pounds toward the founding of St. Christopher's in London, saying to Cicely Saunders at the time, "I want to be a window in your home." While under the care of Dame Saunders, who is a deeply committed Christian, this young man, who had escaped from the ghettos of the Hitler regime, experienced a rebirth of his faith in Judaism. And this is what the hospice concept is really all about, for this is true "cherysshing"—true hospitality.

3

LEST STRANGERS SHOULD LOSE THEIR WAY

The truth knocks on the door and you say, "go away,
I'm looking for the truth. . . ."
> R. M. Pirsig, *Zen and the
> Art of Motorcycle Maintenance*

Thus King Stephen gave the Yorkshire manor of Steyn-
ton upon Blakhommer ". . . to receive and entertain
poor guests and pilgrims there, and to ring and blow the
horn every night at dusk lest pilgrims and strangers
should lose their way."
> M. R. Clay, *The Medieval
> Hospital of England*

The healer has to keep striving for . . . the space . . . in
which healer and patient can reach out to each other as
travelers sharing the same broken human condition.
> Henri J. M. Nouwen, *Reaching Out*

*I*n his immense, gleaming white, air-conditioned cruise
ship, the twentieth-century traveler docks at dawn in the
port of Rhodes in the Aegean Sea. The "package deal"
offered seven islands in eight days, or eight islands—was
it?—in ten. By now he is in a state of exhaustion that prevents him from remembering quite how many, or what all
the names of them were. He has paid his fare in advance—a
good deal more, counting extras, than he could comfortably
afford—and yet, despite luxurious food and drink, and blue
seas and harbors fulfilling the glossy promise of the bro-

chure, the trip has been, for him thus far at least, curiously unsatisfying. *Too many damn tourists,* he mutters to himself, waiting in line for the narrow approach to the gangplank. *No matter where you go these days, they're always there ahead of you.*

Inching forward in the crowd, clutching his camera and his guidebook, he passes a mirror and for a moment fails to recognize himself. He looks again, then takes out his comb and runs it through his thinning hair, worrying about the sunburn beginning to blister on the end of his nose, and about how much to tip the cabin steward at the end of the journey. Trapped in place for the moment, he gazes into his own eyes. Here he is, packed into a swarming mass of people, with his wife nearby and the well-loved bodies of his teenaged children pressing close against him; and yet, in some awful way he cannot fathom, he is utterly alone.

Ten minutes later, they are on the dock. A brown-skinned man, half naked and wearing a yellow turban, is pounding a small octopus with rhythmic strokes on a worn stone block. *Local color.* Older men squat, ignoring the new arrivals, mending yellow nets. *Natives.* Automatically, he stops to take a picture of them.

The traveler looks up at the city of Rhodes. He sees tremendous medieval walls, battlements, towers, banners, gates, and beyond the walls, the tops of cedars and palms, and the graceful minarets of mosques. He is surrounded now by odd, spicy odors and the cries of hawkers from the bazaar, but looking up at the battlements, something else stirs in him like the memory of a dream from long ago, and he shivers, standing in the fierce sauna-heat of the morning sun.

Hesitantly the traveler moves away from the rest of his family, looking up a street inside the gates, a narrow passage slanting upward, paved with disk-shaped stones set on edge

in cement and sure to hurt his feet. He has worn the wrong
shoes for this. "Where are you going?" the others ask.
"Well, I don't quite know," he answers humbly—a modern
pilgrim without a destination. "I just had a feeling. I'll look
for you later, at the ship. I just thought—well—that I'd
wander around for a little while." With these words, a
vague wave of the hand, and an apologetic smile, he stuffs
his guidebook into his pocket and sets off alone, up the
Street of the Knights, in search of his past.

In the deep shade of early morning, the narrow street is
comparatively quiet and cool. Beside him on doorways are
the elaborately decorated shields of the various national
orders of the Knights Hospitallers of St. John; beyond iron
palings he glimpses inner courts filled with blooming olean-
ders, oranges, geraniums; he sees fountains and hears the
sound of splashing water. At the end of a long climb he
reaches the *castella,* but it is not a place of mystery and
enchantment as he had rather romantically supposed. It is
a brute of a castle, meaning business of another sort—
wealth, intelligence, and a tremendous concentration of
military power. The rooms above, he finds, are vast and
echoing, set about with hulks of carved and gilded furniture, tapestries, urns, mosaics. He feels distinctly uncomfortable here, knowing that it is art but not being sure
whether or not it is the kind of art he is supposed to like.

The order was founded, he is told by the keeper of the
castella, in Jerusalem in the eleventh century A.D., when
some merchants from Amalfi obtained permission from the
caliph of Egypt to build a way station there for sick and
weary pilgrims. One Brother Gerard managed the original
place, and his band called themselves "The Poor Brethren
of the Hospital of St. John." Thereafter the Hospitallers,
pressed by the advancing Saracens, moved on to Tyre,
thence to Acre, and eventually to the island of Cyprus. At

Cyprus they first became a naval power of sorts, in the process of providing galley ships for pilgrims to the Holy Land and arming them against the pirates of the day. Year by year, gifts from the wealthy nobles of Europe increased their power. The military order was first recognized by a papal bull of 1113, and the knightly brethren who took charge of it during the Crusades were sworn, as was the custom of the day, to vows of poverty, chastity, and obedience.

The guide moves on, telling of the battle in which the Knights Hospitallers stormed Rhodes in 1306, and of how they held it then, heavily fortified, for two centuries against the full weight of the Muslim onslaught, and, incidentally, how they founded here in the meantime one of the finest institutions for the care of the sick and the wounded that the world has ever known.

Pondering the disquieting question of chastity, the middle-aged tourist is moved to look closely at a massive table in one of the upper rooms. The legs of the table, he discovers peering underneath, are carved upward into the forms of voluptuous female busts, so that the knees of those saintly knights—how long ago was it?—must have pressed and rubbed as they sat in conference against them, just so. All of this is very, very strange, he thinks. *Fighting and sanctity, jewels and poverty, cannonballs and naked breasts.* He looks around him. *Well, what next?*

An hour or two later, he is even more thoroughly confused. He has wandered about the Old City with the sense that nothing much has changed here for hundreds upon hundreds of years: streets no wider in places than a man is tall, private houses shut tight against the heat and against the swarm of human traffic on the paving stones, shops beside them open wide, people roasting meat an arm's length away, people making sandals, belts, jewelry, bags, sewing shirts. Old men, toothless and grinning, spitting, hawking vegetables. Women, children, cripples selling fruits, pastries, sweets. A man with one arm. Flowers blazing everywhere, the smell of incense and ginger, garlic and dust. Laundry hanging out red and yellow, mustard-gold, personal laundry in the streets. A ragged pair of underdrawers, pale blue, hanging like a flag, and an urchin in a doorway underneath, naked, sucking a half-cucumber. Women sweating, shouting in a language he cannot begin to understand, and the sour smell of baking bread, and the dark eyes of women watching him go by. The intimacy of it staggers him—the richness and the openness of it all to casual view, as if he were moving around all this time in the hallways of a single house where everyone lived together in a seething mass of contradictions and cross-purposes, not minding it— yes, that was it—not minding it at all. *Life,* he thinks. *Everyone here is alive. I am a ghost.*

Sore-footed, tired beyond reason, and feeling more than ever alone, our friend the traveler finds himself standing at last outside what seems to be a palace, or an art museum. He consults his book. No, this was the famous hospice- hospital. He goes in. The tumult of the marketplace is left behind him. The light falls into the central courtyard here in such a way that every line in space around him seems caught in a sudden stillness. The soaring arches of the infirmary speak to him of an old form, an old order filled with blessedness and peace. *This is beauty,* he thinks. *I always forget what it is, until I see it again.* He climbs the steps slowly, on his aching feet, and sits by an urn filled with fresh mint, and reads.

In the great hall here, "Our Lords the Sick" were received. They were gently washed and carried to their beds, each with its own curtain around it, and there they were served by the noble knights themselves, who brought them (in vessels of solid silver!) none but the best and most delicate of foods and drinks such as a royal prince might desire. The wiŝest of physicians visited them daily, diagnosing and prescribing for their ills, and the director of the hospital himself was ordered twice each day to speak to each and every patient, giving comfort and encouragement. After the evening services, "Our Lords the Sick" were entreated by the priest to join in the great prayer, dating back to Acre in the twelfth century, in which they made special intercessions to God for the rest of the world, since heaven was now so directly open to them: "My Lords the Sick, pray for the peace of heaven, that God may bring it to earth; pray for the kings and the cardinals, for the bishops and for the soldiers; pray for the Pope, and pray for all poor, weary pilgrims who are now lost on land or at sea; and pray for us who serve you here, that we may all be brought in time to the great repose."

All personnel here, the traveler reads, were under the oath of poverty, and even the acceptance of gifts from grateful patients was forbidden. The knights and attendants ate, in their own quarters, far plainer fare; and if they were unkind to patients or if they neglected their needs in any way, they were put on bread and water for a week, and whipped. Whipped? Yes, flogged, twice a week, Wednesdays and Saturdays.

But wait. Here is something equally odd and interesting. "At the hospital at Rhodes," the traveler reads, "for the first time, patients with incurable diseases were separated from all others." And where were they put? In a group of eleven small rooms clustered around the second-story balcony, which were also reserved for pilgrims and travelers.

Our twentieth-century pilgrim stands on the balcony, looking in. The little rooms are quiet and airy, golden-hued, filled with the sweet smell of old stone. Swallows flit in and out, silently. *Travelers and incurables,* he thinks. What does that mean? It means something that catches him at the heart like the sight of beauty, unmistakable when it suddenly arrives, no matter how long forgotten. *Travelers and incurables,* he wonders—*Which am I? I am both, I suppose, always searching for something, I never know quite what. Feeling always a little foolish, a little out of place with the dreams I can't name, and the hopes—always wanting to go somewhere, longing for another place, another time, another chance to figure out the meaning of it all. There must be a meaning somewhere, in another language, perhaps, a different way of being, a level of consciousness I can't quite grasp—But it is always there, just around the corner waiting for me, waiting to receive me. And now I know how they must have felt, lying here wondering, waiting to move on, travelers—incurable travelers—living, dying here in these little rooms, moving on always into the unknown. Yes, here am I.* He touches the cool stone wall beside him and in that instant, fully recognizing himself, he puts down the burden of being a self separate from all others, and with it the pain of his aloneness.

So the Poor Brethren of St. John must have felt a thousand years ago in Jerusalem, looking bare-hearted and undefended into the eyes of the sick and the dying, finding their own spiritual substance reflected there. The political and military power that came eventually to surround this primal experience with battlements, and to decorate it with banners and jewels, never succeeded in destroying or engulfing it entirely, even within the order of the knights themselves. Six hundred years of their records show a constant struggle within the organization to maintain the discipline of its origins, despite the acquisition by gift and by conquest of tremendous wealth.

By the time the Knights Hospitallers were driven from

their last great outpost on the island of Malta in 1798, they had such a treasure in silver that Napoleon was able to melt their plates, their goblets, and their artifacts down to 3,449 pounds of bullion; with this, he paid his entire army for his Egyptian campaign. Some two hundred years earlier they had already become a power so awesome that Henry VIII felt obliged to steal most of their English holdings for himself. Their rise from obscurity, from Cyprus to Rhodes and Malta, to Italy, Germany, England, and throughout the West, was a stunning event, particularly in view of the fact that it was begun barefoot and in rags, and that the impulse behind it was a perception so simple that it can be shared by a somewhat shy and confused, camera-draped and sunburned tourist today.

If the same man—let us call him Smith—were to waken from his reverie in Rhodes and find himself not on his cruise ship, nor in the great hall of the Knights Hospitallers, but instead in a small town in fourteenth-century England, he would find it strangely familiar. Having seen Rhodes, having walked through the streets of the Old City, he will immediately recognize a similar quality of life in medieval Devon or Kent. Again, he moves with a swarming crowd through narrow and cobbled streets, seeing people at either side of him making belts, bags, shoes, shirts, measuring out oil for lamps, sharpening tools, roasting nuts and offering them for sale. Their manner of dress is somewhat different, tuned to a cooler climate, of course; the colors about him are not so exotic, and yet the sense of tumbling richness and variety and vibrancy is there. The people are shouting, laughing, sweating, gossiping, haggling at the produce wagons (it is market day) over cabbages, peas, leeks; arguing the merits of fresh eggs, hens, eels, oysters, pullets, partridges, and, unfortunately, swans. The price of a swan in the London market in 1338 was three shillings, but you could eat a peacock cheaper if you liked.

Our friend John Smith begins to feel rather uncomfortable. He has a notion that he should at least be able to understand the language. It seems to be English, of a sort. He catches a word here and there, in the flat, nasal accent of the twentieth-century American Midwest. But it is all larded through with other sounds (French? German? Latin? Dutch?) that confuse him. Being among strangers, not understanding what is happening, reminds him of the time he had a heart attack. At the hospital they gave him all sorts of frightening tests, then someone put him onto a gurney, wheeled him down to the end of an empty hallway, and forgot about him. It all came out right in the end, but by that time he was almost too exhausted to care.

Stop being a fool, he tells himself firmly, and gets up. *This is obviously a dream, and I will wake up soon.* He reaches for his money, points to a keg of barley brew, and tries to indicate, rather loudly, to the owner that he wants to make a purchase. Immediately a curious crowd gathers around him. *I guess they don't understand this kind of money,* he thinks. *Maybe they want coins.* He takes out his coins: Greek, Turkish, American. Closer and closer around him people press, talking *about* him to each other, never *to* him. They smell strange and their hands are clammy. Now they start feeling his arms and legs, poking around his belly to see what he is made of, how strong he is. *In a minute,* he thinks, *they are going to take my camera away from me, and they are going to start taking off my clothes.* "Let me alone," he shouts at them. "Get off me, for God's sake." He is very weak and dizzy now, and he sinks down on his knees on the cobbled roadbed, very much afraid that he is really going to be sick.

"Pellegrin!" he hears someone say. Then a woman's

voice, ringing and firm: "Be off with you, let be! The holy man, he calls for God! You there, for shame! Take him to the hospice now, let be!" John Smith is lifted up and carried through the streets. A woman walks beside him, holding his hand. Into a small stone building they go now, beside the village wall. Gently he is laid onto a pallet made of straw, resting in a bedstead of rough, brown wood. The light falls from a small, high window past a wooden cross on the wall to the dirt floor beside him. He hears the clucking of hens and pigeons, and sees them, walking around, pecking at the dirt inside the little house. The woman leans over him, covering him with a blanket made of wool and tucking a soft scrap of sheepskin under his head. He had thought she must be older—that voice of command, and the hand holding his so rough and gnarled—but her face is very young. "Sleep," she says. "You are safe."

He sleeps. When he awakens, she is there. Three other men, he sees, are lying in beds nearby him, and a child is playing with a bit of yarn in the sunlight by the door. The man closest to him is very old, and he moans as if he is in pain. The woman is bathing his forehead with a damp cloth that smells of roses.

She looks at Smith and sees that he is awake. Without saying anything, she brings him a small, round loaf of brown bread, washes his hands and face with the same sweet-smelling cloth, and indicates that he should eat. The bread has a nutty flavor, rich and sour. When he has eaten, she hands him a steaming mug of something powerful to drink. It resembles wine, or beer, but there is honey in it too, he thinks, and something else—he cannot tell what. She watches, evidently with great satisfaction, while he drains it to the last drop. Then she turns to the old man next to him and begins to rub his withered old arms and shoulders, bare under the blanket, humming something like a nursery song as she rubs. The old man breathes deeply, and grows quiet.

John Smith realizes that the potion he has drunk was something very powerful indeed. It had nourishment in it, as well as the heady quality that makes him feel like rising up to see if there are any dragons in the neighborhood needing to be slain, or any maidens needing to be rescued from a dastardly fate. On the other hand, he thinks, it might be just as pleasant to turn over and sleep for a week.

"Is this a hospice?" he finally asks.

"Yes," she answers, smiling. "It is."

"Is a hospice something like a hospital?"

"Oh, yes, this is a hospital, a *hôtel-Dieu*. You are in God's house now. No one will hurt you here."

"I don't understand," he says, "but you are very kind. I don't know that I belong here, however. I am not really sick, you see. I was only lost for the moment, and a little confused."

"Yes," she says. "I know. You have come on a long journey. Now you are safe."

"But I am not like that poor old fellow there," says Smith, lowering his voice. "I mean, I can see that he is not long for this world; but I am all right—I am not dying."

"Not dying?" Her smile has a hint of mischief in it now. "Not dying! Well, that is strange indeed. Were you not born of woman, sir? I was." She turns to the child and asks her to fetch a pitcher of water and a cup.

"What about the child? What is she doing here? Is she sick?"

"Her parents did not want her. Therefore she belongs to God, and she stays here with me and the other sisters. Now, my dear . . ." For a moment, John Smith thinks she is talking to the little girl, but she is talking to him. She pours a cup of cool water for him and gives it to him, looking with her young-old face and her smiling eyes deep into his own. He takes a sip of the water and wonders what will happen now, as she sits quietly, watching him. Evidently she is ready to sit here peacefully beside him as long as he wants her to stay near, not saying anything or expecting anything of him, simply being there, paying attention to him without intruding, offering him her presence.

After a little while, he begins to talk. He tells her at first about the sense of fear that came over him in the village, and then about the strangeness of his experience in Rhodes. He tells her about his childhood on a farm in Indiana, and about a number of things that have happened since that never, until this moment of telling them, seemed to hang together in any way, or to make any sense. Scenes and memories form themselves into patterns as he talks all the long afternoon, shapes that really cannot be conveyed in words, but he senses them there, and in the pauses between, the silences becoming longer seem themselves to take a kind of shape; and words and silences together come at last to form a kind of shining whole—his life. It is the first time that he has ever seen these things, these thoughts and hopes and fragments of experience that belong to him, in such a way. After a while, pausing at length, he decides that there is nothing more to say.

"Except," he adds, "that I still don't really know how I came here, and who you are, and what a hospice is." Holding the old man's hands between her own again, she looks around the bare little room, with its stone walls and wooden rafters, its rough cross pegged to the stone, and the pigeons moving about in the sunlight on the earthen floor, and then she smiles once more at him, a smile radiant with affection and merriment and says, "But you do know. Hospice is just this—what you know now, what you see here."

It may be something rather worse than a death sentence,

I am afraid, to send poor John Bunyan Smith III back to vodka martinis, rock music, and Valium on an air-conditioned cruise ship after an interlude such as this. Go he must, but perhaps he may be allowed to take with him a prescription from the Franciscan master of medieval pharmacology, Roger Bacon (ca. 1214–1294). If he looks at it from time to time and takes it seriously, he may manage to survive his allotted portion of life on this planet in reasonably good shape. Brother Roger's own favorite medicine was fresh rhubarb, and his prescription for good health and long life was: "Joyfulness, singing, the sight of human beauty, the touch of young girls, warm aromatic water, the use of spices and strengthening electuaries, and bathing on an empty stomach after getting rid of superfluities."

Superfluities, of course, are what we fill our lives with when we exist in a state of emotional poverty and spiritual starvation. The medieval world we have glimpsed here, in its simplicity and in its splendor, in England and at Rhodes, had a centered and intentional wholeness about it that we do not often allow or even perceive as a possibility in our own lives. In our society, the child does not play in the corner of the room where the old man is dying, and she is not asked to help with the nursing of the sick. If she is a waif, she is sent to an orphanage; if her parents are wealthy and conscientious, she is packed off to boarding school and then, on holidays, to camp. The old person is wheeled to the end of the hall in the general hospital, and there forgotten. (Recent studies have shown that nurses take, on the average, twice as long to respond to the call bell of the dying patient as they do to those of patients who are apparently recovering; and doctors themselves, feeling helpless in the situation, tend to avoid visits to the terminally ill.) If the old man has no obvious symptoms requiring immediate treatment, or if he is mentally disabled beyond repair, then he is put away in a home for the aged, out of sight. When we walk down the street, we try not to look at the man who has only one arm; cripples are invisible to us. Our own wounded condition as ordinary human creatures living in the midst of a mystery we cannot fathom, yearning for something better, becomes a matter of shame to us, like a set of ragged underwear that must at all costs be concealed. In the process of thinking this way we ourselves become partially invisible to ourselves, partially lobotomized, so that we walk the streets of our own cities like ghosts and trespassers, feeling—as indeed we often are—a little less than human.

It would be a mistake to return to all known procedures of medieval medical care, of course. In all probability the village we have just visited in England was about to be ravaged by bubonic plague, which carried away one fourth to one third of the population of Europe in the fourteenth century, and which can now be cured by a simple course of antibiotics. We have learned about bacterial infection, and we know that the young hospice-keeper (who was a lay sister of the local priory, trained and skilled only in the simplest nursing procedures of the day) should not have used the same perfumed cloth to wash the hands of John Smith that she had used to wipe the spittle from the face of the dying man. These are good and useful things to know, for we cannot hope to improve the quality of life without paying attention, in the meantime, to appropriate ways and means of preserving life itself.

Still, we may learn an important lesson in humanity from the great hospice-hospital at Rhodes, and from the simple hostel for the sick and weary in our nameless English village. From Turmanin in Syria, St. Gall's in Switzerland, from the Hospice de Beaune in France, and from the hundreds upon hundreds of way stations established on similar principles in medieval days, we who now approach the twenty-first century can take renewal and refreshment. Such places of welcome remind us with great force and power that we are all one family, all seekers and wanderers on the face of the earth. They also help us to remember that what happens to the mind and the spirit at any given time is at least as important as what happens to the body. *L'hygiène physique et morale des malades* (the physical and moral hygiene of the sick) was attended to at Beaune, where a treasure of art and architecture and a fine library, as well as clean linen and wholesome food, were provided for the ill and the dying. Monastic attendants throughout Europe in the Middle Ages not only heard confessions and offered spiritual comfort to sufferers, but gave them fellowship in the acknowledgement of our common, broken, and imperfect human condition. The dying were seen as individuals useful to mankind, not as objects of medical manipulation, but as beings moving forward, more rapidly than others, on the metaphysical plane.

At the farthest frontiers of modern science, physics now begins to meet again something that can only be called metaphysical. Moving beyond the structural limitations of medieval thought, we find evidence at quite another level of the permanence of energy, and of the insubstantiality of matter. Less and less it becomes possible for us to state that the medieval view of dying as a form of transformation was wrong. In taking the name *hospice* for a newly intelligent and compassionate mode of caring for the dying, we reclaim what was best in the vigor—both physical and spiritual—of village life long ago.

Nothing that is human is excluded from the premises of hospice life, or from the consciousness of hospice thinking. Beauty here is not a superficial matter. Rather, it pertains to those relationships and exchanges between people, living and dying, who value one another exactly as they are, each one unique, honored, irreplaceable.

Part of our coming of age in the past century has been the dawning realization that our entire planet has become one village, badly in need of healing. Our experience of time, as well as space, has undergone a transformation recently, for it was not so long ago that we scorned the scientific ineptitude of our forebears, and a cure for that complacency of ours has arrived with the HIV virus. Millions around the world are suffering from an immune deficiency that, we now realize, is in some ways even more to be dreaded than bubonic plague, for AIDS does not kill quickly, but lurks and dissembles, only gradually forcing the once wholesome body to become a walking repository for disease. The measure of each of us, and of our civilization, may well be taken in the way we respond to the AIDS challenge. In a world swarming with potentially dangerous bacteria, how severely will we punish those without the ability—*for whatever reason*—to summon up defenses? And inasmuch as we judge, scorn, and reject these fellow human beings, what will be the cost to the rest of us? "Caring in the AIDS crisis," writes Maggie Ross, "means caring not only for people infected with the virus, but for everyone in the human community. . . . Fear and hate may kill more people spiritually, and even physically, than AIDS."

And so, yet again into our lives, comes the stranger. Crossing the field ragged, filthy, and weary—arriving, as usual, at exactly the wrong moment, just as it seemed that the world was turning sweet for us—for some of us, that is.

Why is this happening? Why now? Will this perpetual stranger, this immortal intruder, bring us news that we need to hear, remind us of something, perhaps, that we had forgotten in our eagerness to enjoy our newfound peace and prosperity? But most of us by now are quite well defended. We know all about germs and cleanliness, about dangerous drugs, about sexuality—don't we? We know by this time all that we need to know in order to live The Good Life—isn't that so?

Of course, it is entirely the stranger's fault, all of this, and yet there is something about it that tears at our hearts, something we really do not understand, something demanding all over again to be recognized. And this "something" occurs to us from time to time in the form of a question: Why is the homeless one still homeless, defenseless, why is the wanderer still on the road?

For Maggie Ross, a Christian writer and theologian, the answer to this question is to be found within the riddle of existence itself; and she offers a stunning insight into the anguish of the continuing AIDS epidemic:

> While AIDS may seem to present a new crisis without precedent, Britain and Europe faced a similar epidemic when in the 16th century syphilis spread silently through the population. The famous Isenheim altarpiece by the artist known as Matthias Grunewald, now to be seen in the museum at Colmar, was painted during this time, and the tortured figure of Christ in its crucifixion scene is covered with syphilitic sores. There is some reason to believe this altarpiece was painted for a hospital [hospice/*hôtel-Dieu*] for terminally ill syphilis patients. Whatever its history, it is clearly an icon for our times.

God has AIDS, she says, *as long as any one of His children suffers from it.* Those who die of AIDS, tortured and disgraced in the eyes of society as His Son was, have the assurance of such an icon as this that they do not die alone, or beyond the reach of God's mercy. Can those of us sharing a brief time, a small space, with these children of God offer less? The truth is that not only must those stricken by the virus be healed, but society itself must be healed in the years to come, healed of despair and division, hatred, resentment, scorn—healed, above all, of pride and complacency.

The uninvited guest who has come this time will not go quickly. We must live together now, perhaps for many years. Have we the courage to love and serve one another under the circumstances? I believe that we do. Established hospices in this country are responding to the epidemic, in general, with great devotion and generosity. AIDS support networks all over the United States are modeling themselves, to a large degree, upon the earliest of our hospices. "The hospice concept came along just in time to show us how to take care of one another," says an AIDS network leader in California. "Sometimes I think that was a miracle." The immortal intruder may indeed teach us, this time, a great deal worth knowing, for as long as we continue to treat any part of the human family as "the other," as "those people who are different from us," they will continue to be strangers. And in that very strangeness will continue to exist a breeding ground for despair and disease. But miracles do happen. Sometimes we are enabled to look without flinching into our own darkness, and to take responsibility for it. No longer estranged from ourselves, we may then gain the power to reach out to others. And in doing this, as all "hospice people" know, we discover our own wholeness. This may be part of the essential riddle, the mystery: the dying individuals we care for so very often teach the rest of us how to live.

4

TURNING POINT

The First Law: Do it! Money will come when you are
doing the right thing.
             Michael Phillips, *The Seven Laws of Money*

... While we look not at the things which are seen, but
at the things which are not seen: for the things which
are seen are temporal; but the things which are not seen
are eternal.

                            II Corinthians 4:18

*A*fter the long drought of summer, a cold gray rain is
falling steadily in Marin County, California. At 7:00
A.M. it is still quite dark, but in the small town of Belvedere,
St. Stephen's Episcopal Church presents a parking problem
even at this hour. Like a medieval village under one roof,
this is a place of widely varied communal activity; the
church bulletin mentions not only frequent services here
throughout the week, but workshops and seminars in everything, it seems, from dance, hatha yoga, and printmaking to
the theology of Dante, Thomas Merton, and Kierkegaard.
On the kiosk in the courtyard, I note an invitation to the
men of the parish to come on Saturday morning and learn
to make bread.

A fire is blazing today in a Franklin stove in the small
redwood room adjacent to the parish hall. In the vestibule,
the fragrance of good food and coffee mingles with that of

wet raincoats and overshoes. Members of the board of Hospice of Marin are arriving for a discussion-breakfast.

Marin's hospice came into being late in November 1975 when a small group of individuals made the decision to offer their professional services free of charge to dying members of the community and their families. The existence of the modern English hospices was not unknown to them. They were familiar with the work of Elisabeth Kübler-Ross, and had taken note of the home care program operated by Hospice, Inc., in New Haven, Connecticut. However, it was out of personal experience and in response to the needs of friends and neighbors that this small, non-profit corporation was quietly founded.

Since 1975, because such needs within the community have long existed and now are at last beginning to be met, the original group of four has doubled and twice again redoubled its number of volunteer workers, board, and staff. Standards of care have proved not merely acceptable, but enlightening and a welcome boon to the local medical establishment. Public notice now begins to focus upon Hospice of Marin with an eagerness that threatens the young organization with a serious identity crisis. The meeting this morning, in fact, represents a turning point that may be typical in the life of any group that sets out to offer the public with open hands something that it very urgently needs.

The small room begins gradually to be filled with quiet laughter and conversation. Father John Thornton, rector of the church, is also president pro tem of Hospice. Grave and correct in clerical garb plus a red canvas apron and hiking boots, he serves coffee from a pewter pitcher in front of the fire, welcoming each new arrival with a penetrating glance deep into the eyes, and a quick, warm smile. An instructor of advanced nursing is here from the state university south of San Francisco, and now a young doctoral student of medical anthropology comes in from the University of California campus in Berkeley across the bay. Both must have risen long before dawn and driven an hour or more in the dark and the rain in order to be here. The president-elect of the county medical society hurries in, a distinguished internist who must leave the meeting early to attend to his own practice. The director of the Department of Aging of the State of California is here, and a San Francisco attorney known to have a good head for business—and also for medieval studies, Tibetan lore, and classical Greek. He stands chatting with a charming lady in proper tweeds, noted locally for her somewhat miraculous skills at fund raising, while the executive director of Hospice of Marin, weary from a recent bout with major surgery herself, pulls up a cushion to sit before the fire.

At seven-thirty the state senator of the district comes loping up the path, casually elegant in regimental tie and rumpled raingear. Humanitarian, conservationist, and raconteur par excellence, he is the newest member of the board; he has recently spent many hours nursing his brother through terminal cancer. The room is filled now, nearly to its manageable limits. The door is closed, but is almost immediately opened again to admit an explosion of human energy, blue-eyed, Viking-sized. Despite armloads of notebooks, the new arrival somehow manages to envelop each person present in his immense and exuberant embrace before settling down to the solemn duties of breakfast. This is William M. Lamers, Jr., M.D.—psychiatrist, writer, lecturer, inventor, fisherman, fisher of men, and philosopher—in whose fertile brain Hospice of Marin was conceived, and who now serves as its medical director.

The conversation at breakfast is noisy and full of enthusiasm. I am here as a guest, saying little, listening a great deal, and am aware of being in a sort of time warp just now that includes much that is unseen. Two days ago I was a pilgrim in fourteenth-century England, lying in a little hospice beside a medieval priory. Last night I pored over the ground plan of the magnificent ninth-century monastery of St. Gall's in Switzerland, noting with delight the "Hospice For Pilgrims and Paupers" tucked in beside the "Brewer's Granary" and the "House for Horses and Oxens and Their Keepers." Yesterday a letter came from a friend in Geneva with pictures of the Hospice of Saint Bernard, which after eight centuries is still functioning, sheltering travelers and wayfarers of every sort, and rescuing victims of avalanches at the heights of the alpine passes. My head is filled today not only with facts and figures about Hospice of Marin, but with the music and snows of other ages: odd scraps of chivalry, banners and bandages, homespun and barley brew, swans, the laundry hanging in the cobbled streets of Rhodes, and the shields of the Knights Hospitallers.

The history of hospitals is one thing, it seems, and that of hospices quite another. Since the closing of the monasteries during the Reformation, the two concepts have split away from one another; and until recently, the hospice process has been relatively invisible. The St. Bernard dog with the keg of brandy under his chin now figures in cartoons and comic strips—familiar enough, but unless one is actually up there shivering in the snow, rather a joke. Governments and corporations have assumed the function, once purely personal and religious, of caring for the sick. Scientists have been busy discovering germs and naming diseases, while medicine itself has become entangled in a bureaucratic procedure demanding so much paper work of most nurses and physicians that the time and energy they can give to patients is sorely limited.

Looking around me in the little room, I think of money,

which is tangible and material—and of human energy, which is not. Hospice of Marin has happened simply because a certain number of people in a rather unusual, though small, California county felt that it was the right thing to do. History, in fact, has come full circle here. Once again we are in the realm of *hospitality,* where people are willing to labor unrewarded, to see that their neighbors do not die without grace, and that the families of the dead do not mourn uncomforted. We are in the presence here of an existential force as powerful and yet as invisible as electricity.

What is the source of this energy? Without presuming to speak for each member of Hospice of Marin, I do sense that the source, whether perceived as metaphysical or merely humanitarian, is something partaking of that realm which is eternal, and abides. Because of the nature of what is being done here, these people, board and staff and volunteers, are immediately related to a great family of individuals whom they may never meet. I think of Fabiola, who opened her home to sick and weary pilgrims in Rome in the fourth century; and of Jerusalem's Poor Brethren of St. John; and of the nurses of the Hôtel-Dieu in Paris who knelt by the icy banks of the Seine in the eighteenth century washing sheets, without soap.

The problem under discussion today is a crucial one. Hospice of Marin began by pooling its members' skills in medicine, pharmacology, nursing, counseling, psychiatry; learning from St. Christopher's Hospice in London; sharing information with Hospice, Inc., in New Haven, with the Palliative Care Service of the Royal Victoria Hospital in Montreal, with the hospice team at St. Luke's in New York, and others. In the process of development it has deliberately avoided publicity, fearing premature expansion of its commitment to the community at large.

Now the word is out. Small amounts of money have been arriving in the form of donations and grants. At the same time, the number of physicians, patients, and families requesting Hospice aid has suddenly doubled, then tripled. Approximately six hundred people can be expected to die of cancer in the county this year. A few months ago, Hospice of Marin was caring for only four or six patients at one time. Now there are eighteen, and only yesterday three more urgent calls were received. Some of these patients will require intensive nursing care by Hospice-trained specialists. All must have expert medical and pharmacological supervision. Many will need counseling with therapists, psychiatrists and/or members of the clergy, not only for themselves, but for their nearest of kin. Meantime, people from Hospice stand by the families of those who have already died, offering continued fellowship and support as needed. Somehow all of this must be managed, and managed right. It is inconceivable to the people here that anyone who comes for help to Hospice of Marin should be turned away. The only restriction that, at present, is tolerable is the concentration upon cancer, simply because this is the area of greatest need, and the disease most dreaded.

How, then, to organize properly, without losing the esprit that has already developed? The spirit is strong—stronger than ever, now that Hospice of Marin has shown what it can do. But the flesh is weary, and local banks have a way of reminding people rather regularly when their accounts are overdrawn. Obviously a core group of workers must be put on salary in order to free them from other responsibilities. No one here really wants to talk about money; but under the circumstances, money in quantity has become a necessity.

One of the ironies of the situation is that in the material sense, Hospice of Marin does not exist at all. It does not own so much as a hut or a bed in which to put a patient. *Hospitality,* in this case, is offered wherever the patient is. The state has certified Hospice of Marin as a home care agency, and this will definitely help. Medicare has certified Hospice of Marin for reimbursement; however, they are not yet seeking these funds, pending development of contracts with all medical insurance carriers. The office now runs on small donations, mostly from grateful friends and families of Hospice patients. Two modest grants, *acceptable because congruent with the nature and purpose of the work,* have been received, and the news now is that a larger grant, equally appropriate, is a distinct possibility.

A distinct possibility, someone remarks, is very nice, but it is not a horse. True enough, it is agreed—not a horse, nor even a unicorn. Nevertheless, enthusiastic plans are made for parceling out this excellent and ethereal animal when it arrives. Simultaneously, it seems, the creature is going to be ridden, raced, put into harness, and caused to pull a wagon; it is also going to provide steaks and soup for the entire staff before getting up to race again; and from there, no doubt, it will be let out at stud. The discussion rambles on until Father Thornton quietly interrupts with a motion, seconded and passed, of a compromise sort. This is a group quite obviously dissatisfied with compromise. In fact, Senator Peter Behr remarks wryly that the whole situation rather reminds him of the man who rushed to the river and tested the depth of the water with both feet at once.

There is a restlessness in the air as an attempt is now made to redefine the proper relationship between staff and board, and to chart the course of the future in view of rapidly multiplying commitments. The young doctoral candidate voices it: "Until now, Hospice has been a family group, a close community. After a while, if this sort of expansion goes on, I am afraid we will become just one more cold, impersonal institution. I don't like it. I don't feel good about it at all. But what can we do?"

It is a proper question, and indeed an important moment has arrived, one representing a turning point for many young hospice groups. From the records of the Knights Hospitallers to the progress reports of St. Christopher's Hospice in London today, one can see again and again the eternal struggle to combine efficiency with grace, financial sense with intimacy. Like the tension between spirit and flesh, that between the individual and the institution is a human constant, a part of the very delicate balancing act of staying alive and in motion. Here, in hospice work, the balance must never become precarious. The élan that launches a small, brave craft upon the waters needs to be cherished at every moment if disaster is to be avoided, the greatest disaster imaginable in hospice work being an easy, mindless slide into mechanical behavior, uncaringness, and ultimate depersonalization. *We will try our best,* they say, *to remember what this work is really about—and we will keep on trying.* Their faces are filled with eagerness and determination; and I think of a story told by Thomas Merton. "What do you do, there in the monastery?" an old friar was asked. He replied, "We fall and get up, and then we fall again, and get up again."

The meeting has ended. We stand now in front of the church, watching red and yellow leaves stream past the storm drain at the bottom of the hill. During their brief passage they give off their own light, it seems, into the gloom of the day. The human condition: there it is. Nothing in the universe is ever really wasted, I believe. And yet it becomes very important for me, just at this moment, to stand in the rain looking at red and yellow leaves.

The following day I have an appointment with Dr. Lamers to discuss the beginnings of Hospice of Marin, and to learn more details about its methods of patient care. Again we meet in front of a blazing fire, this time at his home some twenty-five miles north of San Francisco. In a book-lined room filled with plants of every description, with the largest dining table I have seen since my visit to the castle of the Knights Hospitallers at Rhodes, we sit on enormous floor cushions and talk.

In a way, he tells me, it all began with a man named Ed. He goes into his study and brings me a picture of a handsome middle-aged man standing at the edge of a dock or a boat with the water behind him, smiling, not knowing—because no one knew that day—that he was dying of cancer. "Ed was a friend of mine," Dr. Lamers says. "He told me that he wanted to die at home, and so that is what happened. I didn't know then all I now know about medication, but I was sure that he would be more comfortable in an atmosphere of good, loving care and support. Ed had a large family—wonderful people—and I worked with every one of them. We dealt with the realities of it, day by day. And they all came through it beautifully, even the youngest boy, who felt so gypped compared to the others, that he would never have a chance to know his father while he was growing up. I still keep in touch with them, of course. That was ten years ago."

In time, other families in the community began calling upon Dr. Lamers to help in similar situations. Colleagues, too, turned to him more and more often for aid with the emotional difficulties of terminally ill patients and their families. He responded by giving his time, evenings, weekends, whatever he could spare from his regular practice of psychiatry. Meantime, his sister died very suddenly, leaving six young children. Dr. Lamers went immediately to work with them, helping them to comprehend the reality of the situation and involving them as responsible members of the mourning process. He felt that it was important for them to see their mother dead, and to have a chance to say their own good-byes to her. When the youngest could not reach high enough to look into the coffin and asked to be lifted up, Dr. Lamers did this for him, allowed him to touch her face, and answered his questions truthfully and matter-of-factly, about why her skin felt different now, and why she lay so still.

By the late 1960s, he says, he was exploring the idea of setting up, with some other physicians, a "Center For the Reaction to Loss." He had found in his practice that more than 60 percent of his patients had emotional difficulties directly related to experiences of bereavement or abandonment. These situations had not been freely acknowledged or worked through creatively at the time, and were often buried deep in the unconscious. By now, he was lecturing throughout the country on grief and mourning, the cyclical stages he had observed, first of denial, then of anger and despondency; and finally, in healthy cases, a healing stage bringing with it recommitment to life and the courage to love again. If only, he felt, these processes could be brought to the consciousness of grieving individuals *during the experience itself,* then they might not turn up in psychiatrists' offices fifteen or twenty, even thirty years later, with lives essentially crippled by unfinished emotional work.

In the course of his lectures, Dr. Lamers often crossed paths with Elisabeth Kübler-Ross, who was speaking to many of the same audiences about death and dying. Kübler-Ross, by now a figure of considerable renown, had noted in her own patients similar cyclical stages of reaction to the prospect of death, and sought to emphasize creative potentials for personal growth in the lives of the terminally ill. It was not until the spring of 1974 in Ogden, Utah, however, that the two met for the first time. After sharing a platform at Weber State College for a lively question and answer session on their mutual concerns, they met again at a small dinner party and continued their discussions. Dr. Kübler-Ross confided a wistful ambition: she felt a great desire to ride horseback across the plains above the city and into the Wasatch Mountains. It was impossible that she should ever do such a thing; yet here in the American West a sense of spiritual connection with Indian life and lore was powerful.

Bill Lamers immediately made arrangements. Up toward the mountains they rode at dusk, in a sharp, cold wind with rain clouds hovering. While he struggled with his own unruly mount, Dr. Kübler-Ross suddenly took off at breakneck pace. "I will never forget that scene," says Dr. Lamers. "It was incredible. She is such a tiny little thing, her feet wouldn't even reach the stirrups, and there she was riding like a demon straight across that wild, enormous space with the dark mountains looming above and the wind blowing, and it was beginning to rain. I thought she was going to fall off and break her neck. She was completely unafraid, having the time of her life. Finally she came back absolutely beaming and said, 'Thank you, that was marvelous.' On the way back she was very quiet, and then suddenly she said to me, 'Bill, I think you should start a hospice in Marin.' "

Hospice? At that point, Dr. Lamers says, he was not even sure exactly what a hospice was. "I had been so busy doing what I was doing all that time, I had never stopped to find out." In 1973 he had been invited to hear Dr. Cicely Saunders speak at Grace Cathedral in San Francisco but had not been able to attend. "Now I began to do research on it, wrote to St. Christopher's, read all of their material, and held extensive discussions with Dr. Arthur Lipman of Yale. Lipman gave me a great deal of helpful information, particularly about the system of medication he had developed with the hospice team in New Haven. John Thornton and

I talked about it—he has always been deeply involved, of course, in parish counseling and in his ministry to the sick and the dying—and then in the autumn of 1975 four of us sat down together. We decided to incorporate, and get on with it."

Several important tasks immediately confronted the original Hospice team. First, they had to identify and adopt a fully effective system of pain control. Hospice policy demands that patients be kept comfortable—in their own homes, if they wish to be there—and this is a problem that had not, in general, been solved satisfactorily by the medical/surgical establishment. Second, the community had to be informed, even before Hospice of Marin would begin its formal operation, as to exactly what a hospice program can do. There must be no mystery or sensationalism about it. Standards of patient care must be legally and medically correct, appropriate, and clearly understood. Special training of volunteer nurses and therapists was the next priority; and only then would come the beginning of full-fledged hospice care.

The following year was a time of education for the growing Hospice of Marin team, and for the larger community as well. Fortunately, Dr. Lamers's background in clinical pharmacology was extensive. Together with Dr. Frederick Myers, professor of pharmacology at the University of California Medical Center in San Francisco, he had set up a notably successful program of nonnarcotic withdrawal from drug addiction. He had directed and helped to found well-known local programs for treatment of drug abuse. Thus he was in a good position not only to set up the medication program for Hospice of Marin, but to do the work of explaining it to local physicians, pharmacologists, nurses, hospital administrators, and the general public.

In 1975, at St. Christopher's Hospice in London, an oral medication known as Brompton's Mix was providing excellent pain relief for cancer patients. Brompton's contained some ingredients, such as diamorphine (heroin) and cocaine, that were illegal in the United States and other countries, and this at first was a matter for concern.* However, legally acceptable versions of the mix were soon developed here; and by 1976 Dr. Bill Lamers was prescribing a "Hospice Mix" that was proving "amazingly effective." This mix consisted of morphine, alcohol, and usually one of the phenothiazines (Thorazine, Phenergan, Compazine) in a water solution with cherry syrup to partially offset the bitter taste of the narcotic.*

In order to establish full relaxation, which is so helpful in the management of severe pain, initial doses of a Hospice Mix might be large. Nearly always, however, they can be reduced, and then maintained in a holding pattern. It is of *great* importance, according to Dr. Lamers, that every prescribed dose be taken, round the clock, night and day. This is done to prevent pain from having the opportunity to build up again. It is also important in the hospice system of medication that patients dispense and administer their own medicine and keep their own "comfort charts." Pain becomes far more manageable when patients themselves have a sense of control in the situation.

Pain control, it turns out, is not so much a matter of what is in the medicine as it is of how and when it is administered. In a short-term, accident, or acute care situation, analgesics such as codeine tablets or morphine injections as needed (PRN) may be entirely appropriate. However, terminal

---

* Brompton's and the earlier "Hospice Mixes" are no longer in general use. See Clinical Appendix, pp. 341–363, for improved pain-management systems.

care, when severe and chronic pain is involved, presents an entirely different set of demands. Morphine shots and heavy doses of tranquilizers, administered in a clockwork pattern in an automatic and impersonal atmosphere, tend to make screaming addicts or deeply depressed or helpless "vegetable" cases out of dying people who, with the right kind of care and medication, might otherwise be quite serene, clearheaded, and comfortable. The fear of pain increases pain itself by geometric proportions. When severe pain is experienced and is expected to continue indefinitely, even to get worse, the patient enters into a world of horror and hopelessness that for many treated by conventional methods ends only with death. *This is not necessary, and with good hospice care it simply does not happen.* Knowing that it is not going to happen is an important part of the comfort offered to hospice patients and their families.

Severe pain is, of course, not always present in cases of terminal cancer. However, other sorts and degrees of physical discomfort are all too apt to appear, such as nausea, vomiting, muscle spasms, headaches, difficulties with bladder or bowel function, anorexia, and other problems that may or may not even be directly related to the presence of the disease. Hospice of Marin personnel are trained to consider seriously and to cope creatively with all such symptoms. Sometimes rather sophisticated medications are necessary, and the literature on these methodologies grows very rapidly of late. At other times, however, procedures for relief of distress can be rather surprisingly simple. Gentle massage, a soft pillow placed just so, a subtle change in diet, a tempting drink, or time taken simply to be present, quietly caring and listening, recognizing the person as a unique and valued individual—these things can truly heal the dying, even when cure has become impossible.

"How do you decide when a patient has come to the point of needing hospice care, rather than active treatment of the disease?" I ask.

"Most of our referrals thus far have been from physicians themselves. If there is any element of doubt, of course, we can always ask for an additional opinion. We only work in situations where an attending physician is directly involved. Our work is comfort control, patient and family education and support, total hospice care during the dying process itself, and bereavement counseling. In some cases, we ourselves have recommended further intervention, such as chemotherapy. We have cared for patients who were having chemotherapy at the time, and suffering from the side effects of that. The changes in appearance, loss of hair, and so forth are often very distressing to patients and to members of the family. Our therapists have been able to help people to recognize and to manage the feelings they are having, not only about death and loss, but about the difficulties experienced during the course of illness and treatment."

"This is all very different, then, from the work of an ordinary nursing or convalescent home?"

"Yes, and except for bereavement counseling, which may continue for some time, it is a comparatively short-term operation as well. We come in where there is a limited life expectancy, usually no more than several months."

"Do people sometimes not want to know or admit that they are dying?"

"They know. We don't press the issue. We try to work with whatever they are able to encompass at the time. In some situations, the family enters into a conspiracy to pretend it isn't so. But we are certain, and there are statistics to prove it, that this kind of deceptive attitude causes serious difficulties in the lives of everyone involved. We work very hard, in such an event, to help the entire family unit face the truth together."

"How do the local hospitals feel about Hospice of Marin?"

"We have their complete support. And this is because we didn't rush into it. We took the time, hour after hour, month after month, to go around and talk with all of them, and to let them know exactly what we were going to do, and why. Let me tell you one story. When we were just beginning to work as a team with patients, less than a year ago it was, I was called in to one of the local hospitals by a physician. He had a woman there with cancer who had become completely unmanageable. She was heavily sedated, crying out hour after hour, and disrupting others on the ward. No one had any idea what to do for her. When I walked into her room, she was curled up in a fetal position, hallucinating, reaching around in the air for things that weren't there. I changed her entire medication system immediately, and as soon as she cleared up a little, began trying to get in touch with what was happening in her head. On the second day, quite free from pain, she sat up, looked me straight in the eye, and said to me perfectly calmly, 'I don't want to be here. I know that I am dying. I want to go home.' So we enabled her to go home, and in a short time, she died there very peacefully."

"Have you met situations where the family, even with help from Hospice, is simply unable to cope? I am wondering specifically whether you see a need at the present time for a special Hospice building, an inpatient facility?"

"Yes, we would like to have a small freestanding unit with several beds for certain kinds of circumstances. Sometimes the medical and nursing problems can become temporarily rather acute. Or a family may be in need of a rest from the situation. As it is, we go into the nursing homes and the hospitals and do what we can, but the dying have the right to a great many things that such institutions simply cannot provide. They need life around them, spiritual and emotional comfort and support of every sort. They need 'unsanitary' things, like a favorite dog lying on the foot of the bed. They need their own clothes, their own pictures, music, food, surroundings that are familiar to them, people they know and love, people they can trust to care about them. Hospices can provide this, in their inpatient units; and yet, for many individuals and their families, it is much better for it to happen at home."

I have heard by now of some rather extraordinary instances of personal and spiritual growth among dying people who have received hospice care, both in Britain and in America; before the interview ends, I ask Dr. Lamers to comment on this. The process of dying, as he approaches it, is clearly something to be looked at, felt, admitted, shared, and fully brought into the scope of conscious human activity. *Ars Moriendi,* it was called in the medieval Christian text. I am reminded also of the ancient *Tibetan Book of the Dead,* not a book about ghosts, but about how to die consciously, in a state of spiritual enlightenment. Hospice of Marin evidently offers its patients this opportunity, and I wish to know more about how people are responding to it.

The story Dr. Lamers tells me in reply is one of a young boy, fourteen years old, who was suffering from leukemia. When Hospice of Marin was called in, the situation was a desperate one. The boy was at home after extensive treatment that had won him some time without being able to effect a cure. He was very feeble and utterly withdrawn, hostile to a degree that had alienated him entirely from family and friends. The family situation was one of chaos and misery. His mother, in fact, had suffered from depression because of the strain, and was currently in a local hospital. For months previously, she had not been able to communicate with her son, and he had not been willing to speak to her, or even to look at her.

The Hospice team came in. Therapists worked with all members of the family, hearing their feelings and helping them with their immediate, practical difficulties. Dr. Lamers worked with the mother, giving her the psychological support she needed in order to come to grips with reality. Soon she was home again, working courageously with her own grief, caring for her family, learning to accept help from concerned and loving neighbors, and beginning at last to open up communication with her son. The boy, in turn, sensing the new strengths around him, was able to move out of hiding. The anger and the shame, the misery and the disappointment he had experienced throughout his illness had prevented him from being able to give or to receive love.

The last weeks of his life were made physically comfortable for him; but even more significant was the adult commitment he was finally able to make to those who cared for him. If the quality and not the quantity of life is important, then this boy achieved more than many an octogenarian; and if death at any age can be beautiful, this one was. On the day of his death, when his mother came into his room in the morning, the young boy spoke his last words. She asked him what he wanted for breakfast, and his reply was, "A kiss."

5

NIGHT FLIGHT

In the Vulgate, [the Greek word for "love"] is sometimes rendered by *dilectio* (noun of action f. *diligere,* to
esteem highly, love), but most frequently by *caritas,*
"dearness, love founded on esteem."
                              Oxford English Dictionary

Describing hospital procedure during the period from
the sixteenth century almost to the twentieth century
requires a strong stomach.
                              Mary Risley, *House of Healing*

"*T*his is your captain speaking. We apologize for the
delay, ladies and gentlemen," says the voice on the
ever so slightly faulty loudspeaker system, while the overhead lights blink off and on. "We have had a bit of trouble
with our electrical wiring, but that is now mended. The
reason for continued delay at present is that we are very
heavily loaded tonight, and we must wait our turn for the
longest of the jet runways. Relax, please. Make yourselves
comfortable. Do not leave your seats. No smoking. Keep
your seats in the fully upright position, and keep all seat
belts securely fastened."

The lights now go off entirely. Silence. Dark. The frail,
white-haired stranger sitting beside me sighs quietly, clears
his throat, and coughs. Something like a deeper sigh stirs
in the heavy air around us, but no one speaks. Four seats

abreast down the center of the aircraft, plus two or three on either side, times twenty, thirty—how many rows? Three hundred bodies at the least, pressed together arm and shoulder, elbow, knee, and thigh, each sensing the thickness and the heat of the other's substance, breathing in the invisible droplets of each other's sweat, the garlic, mint, and whiskey of one another's breath. Footsteps, running. A door ahead, opening into a half light, closing.

The old man beside me coughs again. His chest rattles. Is he ill? Is he dying, perhaps? Are we all about to die? *Illness creates dependency,* say the sociologists. Illness—well, yes. Being strapped down in such a spot as this creates dependency too. One hundred years ago (have we forgotten it so soon?) English-speaking people on both sides of the Atlantic called their sick *the impotents,* strapped them down in madhouses if they were strange, gave parties to come and laugh at them through the bars while they screamed, locked them up, if they were poor and sick, in workhouses, fifty thousand of them at a time in the city of London alone. At Bellevue Hospital in New York, in April of 1860, rats ate the nose, the upper lip, and half of the left foot of a newborn infant. The young mother, lying alongside in the same bed, was too ill and weak to prevent it; she was a charity case. The derivation of the word *charity* is the Latin *caritas,* which means *love.*

The lights come on again now, steady and full. Music plays loudly, a cheerful Strauss waltz. The plane begins to move. We all smile at one another a little sheepishly. Such things—such things as we were thinking about a moment ago—do not happen to us. They happen only to people who are poor and sick, or in another country long ago. The engines roar and the plane plunges down the runway; we laugh and chatter, powerful again, healthy and strong. Soon we will be on our way to London, eating steak and drinking

gin. There isn't a person on the plane at this moment who
does not believe that he or she is going to live forever.

And yet the runway is long, longer than any runway has
a right to be. We are nightmare-heavy, far too slow, it
seems, ever to get off the ground. There must be some
mistake. We are wallowing along, wings shuddering, everything swaying, lights blinking off and on and off again,
broken. Again and again the lifting moment fails us—will
there be fire?—then suddenly we are up, we have mastery
of it, the corridor to freedom, safety, space, and air.

What gods we are now, what power we have! Nothing
can touch us. We are safe. It is we who are still now; earth
swings away from us. Furthermore, like gods we now own
time: nine hours of it, belonging to us alone. The people we
left behind us are part of yesterday—too bad for them—and
the ones we are going to see will not be real until tomorrow. The elderly gentleman beside me pats his lips gently
with a clean, folded, white linen handkerchief and orders
sherry. Cities and towns lie sprawled below us, but their
business is none of ours. Distance it is that does it. However, you must be sure not to look down. If you do, and
actually believe what you see there, then the plane may fall,
and crash, and burn. Lit by the moon, vast plains of snow
and ice slide by below: we are approaching the Arctic Circle. Mountains of snow, pain, loneliness; sure death, slow
and terrible. If you must look, see it as mere background
decoration, stage design. This is how we do it—how it has
always been done, in fact. During the winter of 1868, when
the London workhouses were packed to their utmost limits
with the destitute and the dying, the president of the Poor
Law Board was on holiday in the South of France.

But what has that to do with us? We do not treat the
helpless and the dying—rich or poor—in our own society
in such a way. Or do we? Was there in fact a change in the

way we regarded human beings, particularly the incurable members of the community, during the period we have been taught to admire as the Age of Enlightenment? And does this change still linger as an unacknowledged prejudice in the modern mind? One hundred years ago, my own grandfather's grandfather was growing roses in New England, reading Shakespeare to his children by candlelight: a gentle country doctor, a kind and courteous man. Did he know, I wonder, about the workhouses, the concentration camps for the unemployable and for the chronically ill, which in England—the land of his own cousins and his forefathers—had become the Dachaus and the Belsens of the day? Poor because they were sick, sick because they were poor, these were the ones who, if judged beyond cure, were turned out of the best London hospitals and sentenced to die in the workhouse. My grandfather's grandfather died in his own bed, at home. People did, in those days, if they could afford to.

But why the workhouse? Medical history suggests at least one answer. Doctors and hospitals were struggling day by day in England for the economic right to exist. And indeed, "what opinion would the public form of the skill of the medical attendants in the hospitals if upon looking at the annual reports it should appear that the cases of death were to those of recovery as three to one?"

Not a very good one, true. But doctors and hospitals were not having much success at curing people in those days; and in industrialized, Victorian England, disease was rampant, particularly among the poor. It was a dark time, a dark passage in medical history, the hygiene of Greece and Rome forgotten, the medieval knowledge of healing herbs and anodynes generally ignored. Polite people of the Victorian age took themselves very seriously indeed; they spent a great deal of time congratulating themselves and one another (if they had solid bank accounts) on their respectability and their superior moral virtue. Propriety so smug has its demonic side. Surgeons operated then not only without anesthesia, but without washing their hands or their instruments. One London doctor, famous and much admired at the time, was proud to own a surgical coat so encrusted with blood where he had wiped his scalpel over the years that when taken off, it would stand alone. A wiser physician named Semmelweis, who insisted upon hygienic procedures, was driven mad by the mockery of his colleagues, and died in an asylum, disgraced. It was a great age of medical discovery and scientific experiment, but the comfort of the patient was no longer a main issue; and the Protestant work ethic had transformed the incurable poor into a scorned and unwanted class.

It was not only doctors who formed the public opinion of the day. There were few of them, and in their sometimes hideous fashion, they surely tried to serve society's interests as best they could. The question really was, what were the interests of society? Here, as usual, a clue can be found in the vocabulary of the day. Individuals sentenced to workhouses were commonly referred to, in print and by respectable citizens, as *objects* or, on occasion, as *miserable objects.* The solid, well-fed members of society died in comparative comfort at home while their fond families gathered around for the parting solemnities, waiting eagerly for the will to be read. Those who were mere objects, broken tools no longer able to serve the new mercantile system, were put away out of sight and, as much as possible, out of mind. Life in the workhouse was designed to punish the offender for the crime of dying slowly, in a conspicuous state of disrepair, without funds.

How did this change come about? We know, for one

thing, that Protestant clergymen since the Reformation had been preaching with great vigor the message that pain and sickness were a punishment for sin. The Puritans who migrated to America did not, unfortunately for England, manage to bring quite all of their savagery on this subject with them. Part of the transformation was religious: it represented a collapse of the medieval system of belief. Those who suffered were not seen now as holy, and no longer represented in their persons the suffering of Christ. Another reason for the change was economic and political, growing out of the circumstances of the Industrial Revolution. To be rich and dying in Victorian days was to languish in an entirely acceptable fashion; while to be poor and incurable was a sin. You could die of consumption or even of an unattractive social disease and, if you had money enough, expect deep sympathy, plus a marble monument over your tomb, draped with limp-wristed angels weeping; but if you were poor it was a different story. Disease in the rich was glamorous. In the poor, it was a sign of moral degeneracy.

We voyagers now being carried so lightly through space in a machine of the twentieth century, we who are so highly favored—what has all of this to do with us? Nothing, if we do not realize how precarious our position is, and how much of what we want out of life cannot be bought with money. How delicate is our balance, even at this moment—and the old man beside me coughs again, unconsciously, poring over the book he has brought with him—so that the simplest journey we make must weave its way always in and out of the real possibilities of instant darkness, present death. Each society chooses its own outcasts. Ours demands health and beauty, talent and power. Tonight we have it. But what about tomorrow?

And what about yesterday? Yesterday it was London,

1866. Snow on the ground, no heat, stone buildings pressing upon their inhabitants the cold of centuries, a pall of coal fumes in the air. Not in a plane but in a workhouse, people as real as we are lay crushed together with stone walls on four sides and windows too high ever to open on any view. At Paddington (say the records of the day) one small towel was provided for thirty-one inmates—people with heart disease, syphilis, typhus, tuberculosis, and rickets, "the English disease." At Kensington forty were forced to share thirteen beds with iron strips across their frames— no mattresses. At Castlebar the diet was water pottage, with a sheep's head boiled occasionally for soup. At Maryborough . . . at the Strand . . . rats and lice, babies crawling on the cold stone floors, whimpering. But, stop! We are not strong enough to hear any more of this, even to think of it. How could such things have happened, in a solidly progressive "Age of Reason"? What, in this world, has become of *hospitality*? Where are the clean, soft linens, the coverlets and the cradles, the goblets of silver, the sweetmeats and the wine that were given so gladly in the old days to the dying: *the precious possession of the community, for heaven was open to them*? Where are the hospices of medieval times and where is *caritas*?

We are astonished and confused, because we have believed so thoroughly the myth that human society moves in a steady, upward thrust as time goes by, toward freedom and enlightenment. Our schoolbooks taught us that Victoria's England was full of petticoats and parasols, a little absurd, perhaps, in its solemn propriety, but at least reliable and solid in its basic values. And we were taught that people in medieval times were cruel, superstitious, and quite barbaric; whereas we and our immediate ancestors, of course, have entered the Age of Enlightenment and of Technology, and thus have been able to accomplish such marvelous things as the Industrial Revolution, the rise of nationalism, the mercantile society, intercontinental missiles, napalm, DDT, and the Bomb. Hitler's regime, almost fifty years after its downfall, seems already to many an anomaly, one of those odd little aberrations that need not be explained, except perhaps as a footnote in some future textbook of history.

But it was during the Age of Reason that Napoleon melted down the goblets of the Hospitallers' patients to pay his armies for a megalomaniacal war of conquest. And in purportedly elegant nineteenth-century England, the cakes and the wine were in the mansions and private homes of people who quite honestly believed that they were better than others, purer of blood, more sensitive, deserving, and morally worthy, simply because they had more money. The reasons why they had more money were probably thought of as infrequently as they were mentioned; and to the proper Victorian, a great many facts of life were unmentionable. The theft of monastic properties by Henry VIII and his cohorts; "enclosure," which is to say, systematic, legalized robbery over the years of peasant agricultural lands; these, of course, were among the main reasons why there was now a huge class of vagrants and unemployed. Industry exploited these demoralized members of society who had once been yeomen, hardy, independent, and proud; it separated them not only from their land but from the parish communities of their birth in its demands for labor pools at factory locations. Poverty seen from a distance can seem like mere background decoration.

Polite Victorians ignored conditions in the mine pits until they heard that women were working naked from the waist up, beside their men, in tunnels eighteen inches high. Then they were horrified—by the suggestion of sexual indulgence that this scene implied. In the parlors of London, they knew better: they draped shawls over piano legs so that the sight of these naked appendages would not arouse their men to "beastly" behavior. Meantime, the factories and the mine pits of the day used men, women, and children less fortunate like machine parts, kept them unspeakably poor, and made them sick unto death. In this condition they were useless, and a blazing reproach to the moral consciousness of their "betters"; and thus, the dying poor became the American slavemaster's niggers and the Hitler's Jews of England, little more than one hundred years ago.

The movie is over now. It was something cheerful, evidently, about pirates. The moon has moved below the horizon, or we, perhaps, have moved away from it; encapsulated now in our own night thoughts, we are surrounded by nothing but darkness. We know what time it is in San Francisco and what time it is in London, but here we have no way of measuring it, not knowing anymore exactly where we are. Most people are sleeping, but not the elderly man beside me, who is so frail that his bony arm feels nearly weightless beside me, seems to take hardly any space at all inside his sleeve. He has large hands with long, thin fingers holding a worn, leatherbound volume of something— Homer, surely?—written in Greek. Slowly he turns the pages; each page, edged in gold, gleams briefly as it turns and settles lightly. His shoulders give a little shake and for a moment it seems that he is coughing again, but a quick glance tells me that he is only enjoying a small paroxysm of private amusement. Is it, I wonder, *The Iliad* or *The Odyssey* that he finds so refreshing? My own journey on this particular night, a breath away from him, must be a darker one. Tomorrow I will walk in at the door of St. Christopher's Hospice in London, and I am not sure yet how to find my way there. It is not simply a matter of locating a number 12 bus, or of hailing a taxi once we are on the ground again and giving an address. In order to be present at St. Christopher's one cannot come from San Francisco via the Arctic Circle; it is necessary to come there from the medieval *hôtel-Dieu,* via the workhouse.

History, I am thinking, does not work at all the way we were taught, does not rise in triumph like a rocket or a plane into space. It works like an accordion, perhaps, expanding and then collapsing on itself; or like a loom with its shuttle riding back and forth, in and out of the threads already set: circumstance in a constant process of enmeshing itself with necessity. Most of its threads are thick and dull, but here and there are some with a curious brightness and a stubbornly shining quality about them. These we must trace if we are to perceive any pattern to the whole.

Reaching back once again, it is London, 1538. The monasteries have been shut down, their lands, their goods, and their means of hospitality parceled out, in the main part, among favorites of the king. The nursing orders are dispersed and no relief has been provided for the wayfarer or the needy sick these past two years. People are dying in the streets and in the fields, untended. The citizens of London draw up a petition to Henry, entreating him to establish some place of refuge where the outcasts and the helpless may be "lodged, cherysshed and refreshed." These are shining words. They have life in them, the rustle of fresh linen, the smell of spice, the joy of bread and wine, and the warm promise of a human embrace. From these words we can tell that the citizens of London are asking, not for a house of correction, nor for a hospital in the modern sense, but for a place of hospitality—a *hospice.*

They ask, but from the state they do not receive. People who are irresponsible enough to be poor, it is thought, can be whipped into shape; and they are, by statute of Edward

VI's coalition in 1550: whipped, beaten, chained, and branded for the crime of not owning the land that has been taken away from them and of being, therefore, unemployed. The weary stranger coming across the field in search of shelter at sundown is no longer a *peregrino* or a *pilgrim*. The state has a new name for him now. He is a vagabond, and such persons, says the new law, "should be adjudged the slaves, for two years, *of any person who should inform against such an idler* . . . and the master shall cause his slaves to work by beating, chaining, or otherwise in such work and labor how vile so ever it may be, as he should put unto him. . . ." The weighty self-righteousness of Victorian England, it seems, has begun in an outburst of fury, three hundred years earlier, at those who do not fit into the new economic scheme of things. Better laws than this do appear later, and in time, a number of "voluntary hospitals" are founded to mend the bodies of the sick. However, for the time being a light has gone dim, and an essential grace has been lost. *Hospice* is no more.

Hospitals during the seventeenth and eighteenth centuries express the desire of society for order, efficiency, and social discipline. As medical historian George Rosen says, it was "a humanitarianism of the successful, tempering sympathy with a firm belief in the sober and practical values of efficiency, simplicity and cheapness." Incurables were discharged from Westminster Hospital, founded in 1719 for the relief of the sick poor of that parish; and the governing board of Guy's Hospital took only eight years in finding a loophole in the will of Sir Thomas Guy that would allow them to do the same, although he obviously meant to offer shelter, in the name of Christian charity, to those very citizens. "Improving" tracts were left by the bedsides of the ill, and they received, whether they liked it or not, a good deal of moral instruction, for the religious and spiritual care given in the early "voluntary hospitals" was "not that the dying body should give up a peaceful spirit, but that the recuperated body should possess a spirit less likely to fall a prey to idleness, drunkenness and other uneconomic aberrations."

The new unit of society was economic man. The purpose of hospitals in an industrial society is to mend machine tools, or to lock up separately those such as orphans, the insane, or the contagious, who may prove useful at some later date: hospitals as storage bins for society's spare parts. By the mid-1800s another purpose for hospitals is being mentioned. Approximately eleven thousand patients in the better hospitals of London are now "beginning to be more carefully selected to meet the needs of teaching and research." Individuals fortunate enough to find a "sponsor" to recommend them for such purposes (and guarantee funeral expenses) are required to express public gratitude in the most humble of terms, for the exquisite generosity of their benefactors. The language of love itself is now corrupted. Sweet *caritas* has become cold and condescending *charity,* cautiously dispensed by the righteous to those who are clearly "deserving." *Dilectio,* drained of all joy, survives only as *diligence*—industriousness, imitation in one's daily, human life of a machine.

The golden thread is lost. How can we find our way? In fact we know that a way has been found, for attitudes toward the sick and especially toward the dying have changed radically of late; and hospices are springing up once more, in the United Kingdom, in the United States, and in other locations worldwide. And we can find traces throughout the darkest of ages of a work that was being done, quietly and patiently, by hundreds upon thousands of individuals, in the simple name of love.

While seventeenth-century New England Puritans re-
joiced in the spread of fatal diseases, which they had
brought with them, among the Indians (the better that good
Christians such as themselves should inherit the land), Prot-
estants of a different sort went out into the streets of London
offering goods and services to their suffering fellow citizens. Guilds already active in medieval days turned their
wealth to the purpose of caring for their own sick and dying
members. Conscientious individuals, such as Sir Thomas
Guy, instituted a tradition of humanitarian philanthropy
that crossed the waters later and became the basis for the
American hospital system. Quakers risked and suffered per-
secution on both sides of the Atlantic in order to pursue
their stubborn policy of treating all men and women, of
whatever condition, as if they were indeed sisters and broth-
ers. Augustinians, Benedictines, and other Roman Catholic
orders continued their work on the Continent, though
often now under municipal or state supervision, and found
their way back eventually into the fabric of English and of
American life. Everywhere there were, as always, individuals who refused for private reasons to accept the popular
moral attitudes of the day and who continued quietly to care
for their fellow human beings, making *dilectio* a noun of
loving choice. As hospitals have learned better how to cure
people, many of these individuals have now turned their
attention to the care of those who are beyond the power of
science to mend, and whose time has come to make the final
journey.

Of all the threads that illuminate the substance and the
fabric of this time, one leads directly to St. Christopher's
Hospice in London, 1967. Following its path we can move
through four centuries of time, touching people who knew
and touched one another, and looked into one another's

eyes, over the span of some thirteen generations. First in this line was a French priest who was captured by pirates and sold as a slave shortly after the year 1600. After converting his third master to Christianity he returned to France and there founded a hospice for galley slaves, an orphanage, a number of missions to the sick poor, and a nursing order called Filles de la Charité. This man was Vincent de Paul. His Sisters of Charity were taught that their monasteries were the houses of the sick, and the streets of the city their cloisters. For three generations they went quietly about their work, bringing aid and solace to the rejected members of society. Early in the eighteenth century one Baron von Stein of Prussia visited the hospices they had established by this time throughout France. The baron was deeply impressed. Back in his own country, he wrote an eloquent public statement describing the "expressions of inward peace, repose, self-denial and innocent sprightliness of the Sisters, and their kind and benign treatment of the sick who were entrusted to their care."

Baron von Stein's influence opened the way for a young Protestant pastor named Fliedner to found Kaiserswerth, the first Protestant hospital to have an order of nursing sisters, or deaconesses. Kaiserswerth, like the hospices of the French Sisters of Charity, was dedicated to the aid of the destitute sick and the dying; and once again, three generations passed while the influence of Kaiserswerth and similar organizations grew and flourished on the Continent. In 1840 Elizabeth Fry, an English Quaker, visited these hospices, including Kaiserswerth, and was inspired to dedicate the rest of her life to prison and hospital reform in England.

Florence Nightingale was a contemporary of Elizabeth Fry. Rejecting the values of her proper Victorian family ("We are ducks," they said, "who have hatched a wild swan"), she fled the provincial and dilettante life they had planned for her, served some weeks with the Sisters of Charity in Paris, and went on to work for three months at Kaiserswerth. When she left for the Crimea, Florence Nightingale brought with her nurses trained by Elizabeth Fry, by Kaiserswerth, and by the Sisters of Charity; this was a group drawn from sources both ecumenical and international: English, German, and French, Protestant, Anglican, and Roman Catholic.

We remember the thousands of wounded young lives she saved, and we see her still, the Lady with the Lamp, walking the wards at Scutari late at night, while soldiers blessed her and kissed her shadow on the wall as it passed. She brought cleanliness, fresh air, decent food, and passionate concern for the welfare of each patient as an individual into a situation that had previously been a nightmare of filth and ignorance. She also established nursing as a profession worthy of respect, for the majority of nurses of seventeenth- and eighteenth-century England had been ignorant, incompetent, and all too often in need of medical attention themselves.

However, Florence Nightingale's concern did not extend only to those members of society who were curable. She herself suffered during most of her long life from painful attacks of an illness that may have been psychosomatic, the product of nervous exhaustion in a body weakened at an early age by strain, and a personality that was far from the norm. "How little the sufferings of illness are understood," she wrote, "how little does anyone in good health imagine himself into the life of a sick person! . . . 'What can't be cured must be endured' is the very worst and most dangerous maxim for a nurse that was ever made. Patience and resignation in her are but other words for carelessness or indifference." These are heartfelt words that might be taken as the motto of a modern hospice for today.

Florence Nightingale lived until 1910; and it was, in fact, one of the Sisters of Charity, her coworker and contemporary, who founded in Dublin in the late nineteenth century a place of shelter for the incurably ill, and called it, in English, a *hospice.* Sister Mary Aikenhead was her name, a remarkable woman, deeply devout, with a flair for leadership. The French still kept the name *hospice* for many of their shelters and orphanages; and it may have been that Mary had met this word during a period of training with the Filles de la Charité abroad. However, it is equally likely that, perceiving the dying patients she loved and honored as pilgrims departing on a longer journey, she chose for this reason to resurrect the gentle, medieval English name.

Around the turn of the century a number of other hospices appeared in Great Britain—and in 1892, a "Hostel of God" in London that still exists—but the direct line now leads from Dublin to St. Joseph's Hospice, established by English Sisters of Charity in London in 1906. After previous training at the Protestant Hospice of St. Luke's (also in London) it was at St. Joseph's during the 1950s and 1960s that Dr. Cicely Saunders further developed her work in pain control and, together with some of the patients who had inspired and enlightened her during this period, her plans for the founding of St. Christopher's. In 1967, Dr. Saunders opened St. Christopher's Hospice, where I will be going to work today.

Women, it seems, have been a significant force in the hospice movement since its reemergence in the seventeenth century. Women, and a slave and a priest, a powerful nobleman, a poor country pastor, a Quaker, and a brilliant child of the upper middle classes who dared to rebel—what had all of these in common? All, for one reason or another, were outside the system. None of them found it alluring to think of themselves as mere objects—even as rich, socially prominent, and therefore very important objects, setting a solemn example of respectability to their inferiors. Many of them probably knew the joy of forgetting to think about themselves at all. Not having any investment in the mercantile scheme of things, each was richly empowered to love God and do as he or she pleased.

And now I find that while I have been tracing the golden thread, the plane has already begun its long, slow, shuddering descent into Heathrow. Where has the night gone? Evidently I have been asleep at some time or another, although I don't remember it; but someone has done up my seat belt for me, and put a blanket over my knees. My white-haired companion has put his book away at last and is apparently giving his entire attention to a steaming cup of tea. Our journey is nearly over, and now it is too late for us to become acquainted. I feel some regret about that, wondering what his night thoughts have been, and what book it is, actually, that he has been reading.

The sky is very gray. Last night in London is already this morning—or rather, with nine hours missing, it is tomorrow afternoon. The plane thuds and lurches down now, on the ground again, and lumbers along the runway to an unsteady halt, groaning and complaining all the way about its electrical deficiencies, its internal disconnections, its unfortunate set of tires, its leaky valves. We are gods no longer. Wet snow is falling from the sky, melting and vanishing as it touches the ground.

Standing in line for customs, I look out of the dim, stained window in the wall of concrete block, and catch a glimpse of our marvelous flying machine. By daylight in starry snowfall, it looks like a cosmic reject, something that happened a long time ago, in the days of the dinosaurs, perhaps, by mistake. And yet what a sense of mastery, what a sense of power it has given us! A bird would laugh.

My elderly friend is standing beside me, and I am tempted to ask him whether or not birds laugh. He looks like the sort of man who would know the answer to that question. He stands with his hands thrust deep into the pockets of an old mackintosh, with a woolen muffler wrapped rather carelessly around his chin, and his lips pursed as if he might be about to whistle. Binoculars, I am certain, are somewhere in his luggage. He owns a small boat, I think, and putters around on it endlessly, splicing odds and ends of rope and making notes on the habits of sandpipers and terns. But he is not whistling, he is smiling. Our eyes meet directly for the first time, and I realize to my surprise that he is about to say something to me. His eyes, deep-set under coarse, white brows, are the curious color of sunlit amber.

He coughs gently, clears his throat, and remarks, "You know, of course, what Chesterton said about flying?"

"Chesterton flying? Heavens, what a thought."

"Quite."

"But what did he say? I would be much obliged—"

"It was in one of the later books, I believe. Flying. Yes. He said angels can do it very easily because—"

"Yes?"

"Because, you see, they take themselves so very lightly."

Delighted as a child discovering his first pun, he waits with beaming face to make sure I have got it—if I haven't, he will be more than happy to tell it again—and then, being an Englishman, turns with great delicacy away so as not to intrude upon my pleasure. Very soon afterward, rather suddenly in fact, he disappears.

6

A RARE COMBINATION

Not only is [the hospice idea] novel to the high-technology big-business system of medical care we have, but it embodies a rather rare combination of spirituality and hard medicine, a combination whose uniqueness may not be appreciated until one encounters it in such a person as Cicely Saunders.

Constance Holden

I haven't worked in an institution before, and had heard stories of places where you couldn't just get on with the job but had to be careful not to do another man's work; here it is not like that. We are just part of the team and we don't keep arguing about whose job is whose, but we just get on with it.

Stan Phillips, Maintenance Dept.
St. Christopher's Hospice

Surrounded by lawns and gardens in the residential district of Sydenham, some forty minutes by car south of central London and across the Thames, lies the cluster of brick and glass buildings known as St. Christopher's Hospice. Past a shared greenhouse space banked summer and winter with flowering plants, patients' rooms and wards in the central, four-story building look out upon trees and the rooftops of private houses nearby, and a busy neighborhood park with tennis courts. A play school for younger children of the staff (also frequented by older ones on holiday) is set just behind the main building and near a garden with footpaths, a reflecting pool, and flower beds: a protected place of meeting in mild weather for children, patients, visitors, elderly residents of the "Drapers' Wing," and for the people of all ages and many nationalities who train, study, and serve in various capacities at St. Christopher's.

The outpatient clinic and the chapel are on the ground floor of the main building. Across the lawn beyond a neighboring private home is the Study Center with its library, its bookshop, its seminar rooms, and a small auditorium for films, lectures, and special demonstrations. Here also is a functional model of a St. Christopher's patient-care unit where students are able to learn techniques of hospice care by acting out the part of the one who is ill, as well as the part of the one who is offering assistance. Students live on the grounds together with many of the permanent staff members and their families, some in a residence hall behind the Study Center and others in a recently refurbished block of apartments nearby. To the arriving volunteer, it is a puzzle of major proportions at first to understand which is doctor, which is nurse, which is social worker, seminarian, psychiatrist, administrative assistant, steward, or secretary; and even in the wards themselves it is not always easy to be certain at first glance who is sick and who is well. St. Christopher's is first and foremost a community; and it is very much a village community of individuals.

At Sydenham Hill the air is cooler and fresher than at Heathrow in the west, or in downtown London. A light, dry snow has fallen here in the night and has clung, so that the main building of the hospice in its shell of glass is luminous throughout with reflected white. Large oil pantings, vigorous and glowing with brilliant color, are everywhere: the work of Polish artist Marian Bohusz, friend of St. Christopher's. Pine trees stand in the hallways today, decked with

Christmas ornaments, many of which have been handmade by patients and other members of the hospice community. Outdoors the sky is darkly gray at noon, seeming to absorb its only light from below. The roads and footpaths throughout the area are slick with ice. It is a good day to be inside, looking out.

Indoors, the stamping of snowy boots, laughter, the clink and clatter of kitchen pots, the fragrance of beef broth and rice, warm bread, Hungarian goulash. In the main dining room, lined with glass doors opening out into the garden, a few blue-uniformed nurses are already finishing their midday meal; one sits alone, staring in silence out at the snow. Men and women from the Drapers' Wing are gathering at a table near the inner door, some in wheelchairs, some walking together chatting amiably, others on the arms of visitors or pink-uniformed volunteers. These elderly people, frail and without families of their own to assist them, live in a group of sixteen bed-sitting apartments donated by an organization, active since medieval days, known as the Drapers' Company (Guild). If they become ill or unable to look after themselves with minimum help, full hospice care is made available to them on a temporary or a permanent basis.

The children troop in now, staggering and giggling, with their hands over their bright, scrubbed faces. Someone asks them what the joke is, but they aren't telling. Matron darts by in her gray uniform with its silver, heraldic belt buckle: Miss Helen Willans, who in the United States would be known as superintendent of nursing. Then Dr. Cicely Saunders, tall and smiling, moves from table to table throughout the room, stopping to talk briefly with a young woman who is evidently a doctor, then with an older man in tweeds (resident? relative of a patient?), and next, leans over the kitchen counter holding her plate and conferring at some length with a cook's assistant who evidently has something special on her mind.

The joke is out. It is George's hair. Whenever the young man, age five, takes off his cap in this weather, his fine, white-blond headstuff flies out in all directions and causes mild hysteria among the other members of his age group. Scowling, George pauses beside the wheelchair of a lady who is only a little larger than he is, although she must be well over ninety. She murmurs consolation and reaches out a bent, arthritic hand to try and smooth him. A young administrative assistant arrives on the scene and produces a dampened comb, which does the trick; and it turns out that the staff member is, in fact, George's mother. For several years now, working at St. Christopher's, she has been able to have lunch with her young son every day, and he in turn is in charge of running errands for her and keeping the thumb tacks and safety pins sorted out in her desk drawer. This afternoon, residents of the Drapers' Wing will sing carols and have a tea party with members of the play school group while their parents continue to work, under the same roof.

In volunteer's uniform now, I am sitting at a long table near the garden with Dr. Saunders, Matron, and a mixed group of doctors, nurses, and other volunteers. Conversation is quick and light, full of cryptic little absurdities.

"Bird flew straight in at my window today."

"Left her card, I trust."

"Have you seen Sheila's new play?"

"Sat on my chair so I gave her a biscuit. Yes, marvelous. *Bed Before Yesterday,* wasn't it?"

"Bed before what?"

"Tot of rum in her tea as well, I trust. Sheila Hancock, she's a fabulous actress, and for you visitors, she's a member of our Council here at the hospice, too."

"Britain and America are two rather similar countries—who said it?—separated, unfortunately, by a common language."

"Mark Twain. Same chap said newspaper reports of his recent demise were vastly exaggerated."

Laughing, we turn to the question of British and American slang, trading stories about silly misunderstandings, and about the bureaucratic jargon that so often serves, on both sides of the Atlantic, as a substitute for thought; and now Dr. Saunders, like a master chef tossing crêpes, turns a delicious phrase, catches it in midair, turns it there into an even fresher bit of nonsense, and we all explode in merriment.

The conversation continues apace, but Dr. Saunders is suddenly quiet. She looks down at her plate for a moment in silence, puts her napkin aside, and abruptly excuses herself from the table. Returning a few moments later, she chats as agreeably as ever and does not explain to me until later, in her office, what has happened. "Mr. O'Hara has come in to us this morning," she says, working absently at a large, red and black question mark on her desk pad, "after having been looked after by our Domiciliary Care people at his home, until now." She reaches for another pen and begins to outline the question mark in bright blue. "Mr. O'Hara is very poorly—very poorly indeed, and in fact, I am afraid that he will not last the night. As we were all having such a good time in the dining room, I realized that his wife, Mrs. O'Hara, was just coming in and I could not bear to have her think we were insensitive to her situation. I went to her and apologized."

"I am sorry. I am afraid I always laugh much too loud."

"But of course. So do I. Have done, all my life. It got me into a lot of trouble at school." She puts the blue pen down, then picks it up again and begins to draw symmetrical blue loops outside the question mark. "Mrs. O'Hara is a remark-able woman," she says. "She has had a great deal of hard-ship to bear, and she has managed it all with absolutely tremendous courage. They are a Roman Catholic family." She speaks now of each member of the O'Hara family in loving detail: a story of grief and struggle, triumph and loss. "She was very kind when I spoke to her; she would be, of course. She simply said, *'But I understand, life must go on. . . .'*

"The pictures you are looking at there are of David Tasma, the one who looks so young—he died in 1948—and of Antoni, who was Polish as well, and there is my beloved Mrs. G., and Louie, too. Patients of mine, all of them, my loves, my support system. Patients are the founders of St. Christopher's. It was through David's eyes that I was given the vision of this hospice, in the beginning. As he was dying in a busy surgical ward, we talked for many hours of what his real needs were—not simply for medical care as such, but for someone to care for him as a person, to stand by and honor him for what he was—and it was he, a refugee from the Warsaw ghetto, who left the first five hundred pounds for St. Christopher's. 'I want what is in your mind and what is in your heart,' he told me. I saw then that what was needed was a place that was both a hospital and a home; and he said, 'I want to be a window in your home.' We have many windows here, as you see—look there, I think we will be having more snow this afternoon."

"You had trained as a nurse during the war?" I ask.

"Yes, but was invalided out with one of those hopeless backs—it still gives me trouble, now and then—and I've had to spend quite a time lying flat. Gave me a great deal of time, of course, for thinking. I then did social science at Oxford, a war degree, terribly fast—ridiculous, really—but after David, I finally knew that I must begin all over again, and do medicine. That took some time. Eventually, I had a research fellowship at St. Mary's with a grant from the Sir Halley Stewart Trust to work at St. Joseph's Hospice with the sisters and the patients there, particularly in pain control, and to develop what I had already learned at St. Luke's as a volunteer R.N. from 1948 to 1955. Nurses have to work directly with the patients who are dying, you see, and they have always tended to be the leaders in this field. I saw at St. Luke's that you could take the doctor's prescription for medicine 'as required' and if you interpreted that to mean 'as required for the control of pain' and not 'when the patient is already screaming'—and gave drugs on a regular basis—then the patient's life was transformed.

"It was while I was training as a medical student that I came to know and to love Mrs. G. She spent the last seven years of her life in hospital, finally lost her sight, and was almost totally paralyzed but completely alert, full of joy and fun and interest in everything. She loved everyone about her and we spent hours together over the years. She died in 1961. That was a bad year. My father—I adored him, we fought madly—and Mrs. G. and Antoni all died in one year. It was nearly too much for me. I got my bereavements so muddled up. But always at the worst, strength came—from God, through other people."

"I know that you are a Christian, and that St. Christopher's is very definitely a Christian foundation."

"Yes. We are not all Christians here, by any means, but our work is done in obedience to the Christian imperative. For me personally, it could not be done otherwise. At those times, in that bad year, when I would stop by the door of the ward where Antoni died, and think that it hurt too much, that I simply could not walk into that place again, I would look up at the crucifix and let it hold me. Then I was able to go on. I think there is a sense in which we help to complete the lives of those we love."

"Antoni?"

"Yes, above all, Antoni." She smiles in a way, with a radiance, that includes his living presence in the room. "I looked after him, of course, but he said to me once, near the end, 'You must go now—I am looking after you, too.' It's part of the story that is not finished yet. When he died, Antoni smiled—and looked amused. I believe he was seeing some of the answers to the questions he had been asking throughout his life, meeting the God he had always believed in so strongly. And I am sure he knew, too, that in the work I am doing now, I would be comforted. Life goes on, as you see, at St. Christopher's. In death's very midst it goes on, and I think so very often it is brought into sharper focus here because of the presence of death. There are important ways in which we heal our patients, and in which they heal us. Healing a person does not always mean curing a disease. Sometimes healing means learning to care for others, finding new wholeness as a family—being reconciled. Or it can mean easing the pain of dying or allowing someone to die when the time comes. There is a difference between prolonging life and prolonging the act of dying until the patient lives a travesty of life. At St. Christopher's, we try to offer people space in which to be themselves. We hold fast, but with open hands; because sometimes the most important part of loving can be knowing how and when to let go.

"For nurses and staff it means leading a true life, because they are helping others, of course. Yet it means more than that, too, because people nearing the end of their lives have so much to teach others, about the nature of relationships and about the meaning of life. They drop their masks and do not worry any more about inconsequentials. Most of us rush through our days, never stopping to wonder at anything; and yet, every now and then, if we can back off from it as the dying do, and see life as a whole, we begin to understand that marvelous things are happening.

"We learn, for example, that time has no fixed meaning as such. An hour at the dentist seems like forever, but an hour with someone you love flies past. And yet, wait a little and look back on it. The hour of discomfort and anxiety is totally forgotten. What is remembered forever is the hour of love."

There is a knock at the door and a television producer is ushered in. We are introduced, and it is explained that he is preparing a documentary film on St. Christopher's. At the same moment, the telephone rings and several staff members appear with papers, messages, and questions. When Cicely Saunders stands up in a small room, it is an event. It is not so much that she is larger than life in the physical sense, for she is not really so extraordinarily tall, and though obviously a member of the female sex, she is slender where it counts. The power of her presence depends partly upon its elements of contrast and surprise. Gray-haired, keen-eyed, she wears today a dress of brilliant emerald-green and a gold chain necklace, and over it a doctor's white coat with an ordinary nametag. As she muses on the past, recalling memories of great poignancy, she communicates at the same time a quiet and joyous confidence that is contagious; it seems for the moment that she has all the time in the world and has never been in a hurry. But when she is challenged by any present task, as now, we see immediately the warrior spirit, the ability to cut through nonsense and go straight to the point with tremendous dash and verve. Here is a woman who has learned the skill (or perhaps she was born with it?) of being resoundingly self-assertive without sacrifice of delicacy or femininity. She will go to great lengths to protect the sensitivities of others, but when her passion for St. Christopher's is touched, as it is when she deals with the media, I can see a flame here that may burn as well as warm the hands. After twenty minutes of discussion, the producer is sagging in his chair. "Well, if it isn't done right," she tells him firmly, with a dazzling smile, "it won't be done at all." He nods, exhausted. It will be done right.

The hallways are quiet, late in the afternoon, and the gray sky has gone dark. I had hoped to meet Mrs. O'Hara but have been corralled instead by the kitchen crew—a fierce gang, fast-moving, ruthless on the subject of absolute cleanliness, insisting that I must get food to the patients *now,* darling, while it is steaming hot and not next week, thank you very much. No, no, not there! Into the pig bin with that lot, darling!

"Pig bin?"

"Nothing goes back down to the main kitchen, touched or not, even a bottle of something that hasn't been opened. Never, never. Germs. Wouldn't be clean, you know."

"But, I mean, is there an actual pig somewhere?"

"Oh, yes, we have a contract with a farmer. He comes and gets it. And when you are done there, darling, scrub the bottoms of the pans as well. Not that way. Here, use this. Has to be done right, you know."

I scrub the bottoms of the pans.

Faces in the ward. An elderly woman in a soft blue dress and shawl, sitting in an armchair with her hands clasped in her lap. Mrs. O'Hara? A young girl sitting up in bed in a pretty nightgown, rolling up her dark hair in curlers while she watches ballet on television. A huge man in a raincoat, plodding along the hallway—father or brother of one of the patients, perhaps? But he leans over, presses the button for the lift with his forehead, and then stands whistling as he waits for it, tapping his foot while his arms dangle limply from his sides.

No telephone bells, no buzzers, no loudspeakers here, calling doctors' names. No smell of antiseptic, though everything is spotless and the floor under our feet shines with concentric circles of buffing and polishing. No smell of fear or sickness, no glittering banks of steel machinery, no I.V.s, no flashing lights. No one is moaning or crying out in pain. Statistics have it that there is one staff nurse per patient here, but, looking onto the ward, it seems there must be more than that, because people both in and out of uniform are sitting, visiting, and talking with patients, and no one seems to be pressed for time. The curtains around one cubicle are closed and I can see the feet of three nurses and doctors working simultaneously with one patient. A very thin old lady sits up in the armchair beside her bed while a white-coated woman doctor, stethoscope in pocket, leans an elbow on the bed, looking exhausted. They are chatting amiably, and after a few minutes, the doctor straightens up, gets to her feet, and helps the patient back under the covers. "This is the only place I know," Dr. Gillian Ford tells me later, "where patients continually ask you how *you* are feeling. I told her I felt rather poorly today, and she was very kind."

Azaleas, ferns, chrysanthemums, cyclamens, African violets. Two single rooms at the end of each hall, four beds in each large and airy bay, each with its own curtains that can be drawn shut, and each with its own furnishings around it—tables, chairs, armchairs, photographs, cards, books. Colored quilts, knitted coverlets, and plenty of down pillows on each bed. Fresh white linens, worn and soft. Letters, newspapers, cigarettes, lamps, baskets of fruit. A bottle of port and two glasses. A family of five walking by with a small, gray, and very nondescript dog padding agreeably along behind them on a leash. Beside the bed of an elderly woman in pink, a small girl is curled up in an armchair, sucking her thumb and reading a comic book.

"Haven't you got it all yet?" the old lady asks, amused. The little girl takes her thumb out of her mouth and says cheerfully, without looking up, "Go away, Granny." Granny grins at me. "Some is born sweeter than others," she tells me. "That's what I always say. Some has to work on those thumbs years and years, getting the honey off." She cackles with delight. Her head is like a skull, dark eyes blazing out of it from deep in the bone.

"What's in the book, darling?" she asks.

"Nothing."

Granny cackles again. "What did I tell you? Nothing in the book at all, see? It's the honey she's after."

In the bed across the way from them is a woman—young? old? fortyish, perhaps?—lying very still. Her pale blond hair is streaked with silver, and her skin is so pale and fine that it looks translucent, glows in the light of the lamp above her like milk glass, almost like mother-of-pearl. When I speak softly to her, she turns her head a little toward me and smiles with great, blue-violet eyes, welcoming my presence without question; says, yes, she is comfortable, thank you, feeling rather tired today, but she has been at home for several days and now she is resting so that she will be strong enough to go home again for Christmas. She sighs a little, smiling, whispers something I can't quite hear, then sleeps, as I sit beside her holding her hand that is so frail and light that it is like holding a flower, or a leaf, or the memory of a human hand.

In the half light of the hallway beyond the next ward

stands Dr. Thomas West, deputy medical director of the hospice. Having read his articles about death and dying, and about St. Christopher's, in the English medical journals, I recognize him immediately and am not surprised to find that his voice and presence express very directly the charm and compassion of the inner man. He is giving his full attention at the moment to a woman who appears to be in great distress; he speaks very little and listens with care to her halting words. Yes, this is Mrs. O'Hara. Her husband is lying in the nearest bed, just inside the ward. He is deeply unconscious, emaciated, curled on his side like a child asleep. His skin is a dull green-gray, and he takes a slow breath once or twice per minute. Two grown sons and a young woman sit with a blue-uniformed nurse at the bedside, quietly watching over him.

"You did the right thing, Mrs. O'Hara," says Dr. West very gently. "He belongs here with us now, my dear, and you with him, and the rest of the family as well."

Mrs. O'Hara's face is grief. No armor, no defense. Tears well in her eyes as she speaks slowly, dazed, groping for words.

"He was better for such a long time. I am sure that he was. I stayed home from work and saw that he ate his meals. He gained some weight, too."

"You did a fine job of it, Mrs. O'Hara, a wonderful job. No one in the world could have done better."

Seeing my uniform, she turns to me and takes my hand as if to reassure me. "They came from here, you know—and helped us so much. At the other hospital they told me he had only three months to live, but when he came home he did ever so much better."

"Nine months it has been, hasn't it?" says Dr. West.

"Yes. And he liked to go out so much. Last week I took him to Dorset where he was born, and he saw the old house

again, that he remembered. Only last week we had his
birthday, and he did enjoy it so. He never had any pain,
after the people came from here and he had his—you know,
the blue medicine, and he started walking around again in
the house. But yesterday morning it began again, and this
time, it was so bad, I knew it was time."

"And then you called us for more help, which was exactly
the right thing for you to do. You knew that we had a place
promised here for you, whenever you should need it."

"Yes, and it was such weight to bear, heavy like lead, but
I put it down at the door when we came. Now he is safe.
The Father has been to see him twice, but oh, I never did
get to mass today, myself."

"Tomorrow, then," says Dr. West quietly, putting his
arm around her shoulders, and they walk together to the
bedside. Mrs. O'Hara is an extraordinary woman and has
managed well, but Dr. West's concern extends itself equally
to those who prove far less able. "In fact," as he remarks
later, "the more inadequate the family appear to be, the
more marvelous it is that they have coped at all."

For more than two years now, Mr. O'Hara has been ill
with cancer of the stomach that has spread, despite radical
surgery and a course of chemotherapy, throughout his intestinal system. At home, visited by the Domiciliary Team
and by district nurses advised by St. Christopher's medical
staff, he has been active and comfortable with the help of
a round-the-clock, four-hourly prescription of the "blue
medicine" (an oral mix containing carefully adjusted portions of narcotics: see Clinical Appendix, pp. 341–363).
After a massive hemorrhage he has lapsed gradually into
unconsciousness, and death is now imminent. Since his arrival at the hospice he has been gently bathed, dressed in
a clean gown, and made comfortable; no medication has

been given except his regular narcotic by injection and intramuscular hyoscine 0.4mg to dry up the excessive secretions that tend to accumulate when a patient is dying. Thus, there will be no interludes of choking to disturb him, and no "death rattle" to distress those who are now watching and waiting with him.

The curtains around Mr. O'Hara's bed are not drawn; life in the ward continues and the nurses go by on quiet feet, but do not avert their faces. Dr. Saunders has been making her way through the wards visiting with patients and checking on details of their medical care for several hours now; she stops for a quiet moment with Mrs. O'Hara at the bedside here, says something to the nurse, and touches the arm of each of the O'Hara sons lightly and affectionately before moving on. Most of the other patients in this ward are now sleeping, including one elderly soul who evidently prefers, for some stubborn and private reason, to sleep sitting up in an armchair with a quilt over his knees. Time passes. Beyond the black windowpane, flakes of snow like feathers float, lift in the wind, and seem to spin out from the light, into space. Every now and then Mrs. O'Hara leans forward and strokes her husband's forehead, smoothing his hair back as he breathes. The time between his breaths is very long now, as if he were a man so preoccupied with the measure of his own stillness that the occasional breath has become an unwelcome interruption, a punctuation mark unnecessary in the flow of his private reverie.

Time. I lean my forehead against the cool window, and my breath mists the glass. Again, there is no way of knowing what time it is. A car passes, silent in the snow, its lights searching. When I look back, a nurse is taking Mr. O'Hara's pulse, and then Mrs. O'Hara suddenly reaches for the nurse, gathering her in a silent embrace. Heads close together, the two women sit for a long moment. Mr. O'Hara looks the same. The only difference is that he is no longer bothering to breathe.

The nurse kneels down at the bedside and they all kneel beside her. This is the moment when simple, traditional prayers are customarily used for each patient at St. Christopher's, for, says Dr. Saunders, "few families do not want to accept the offer of this commendation." Mrs. O'Hara holds her dead husband's hand in both of hers and rests her head against it as they pray. It is not like sleep, I think. It is something else. Pilgrim, fare well.

"That's the way I want to go," says Mr. Pippin to me in the morning. "Nice and peaceful. Not that I'm ready yet, mind you, for I've seen them come and go, and I am still here enjoying myself, which suits me fine. Do me up, will you, love? Yes, he had a fair and easy riding of it, he did."

Mr. Pippin is the tall, round man who whistles in the hallway "Believe Me If All Those Endearing Young Charms" like the true Irishman he is, on his mother's side. He cannot use his arms, so I fasten up his fly for him while he tells me about the musical comedy he is going to this afternoon in London. A volunteer will come and fetch him in her car. "Drives like blazes, she does," he says with anticipatory glee. "She'll have me there in less than thirty minutes."

Mr. Pippin is riddled with cancer throughout his spine; however, he tends to ignore the patient's role and has become instead inspector general, ombudsman, and purveyor of cheer to all in the community. If a patient needs a spit pan in a great hurry after breakfast, it is Mr. Pippin who tells the new volunteer exactly where to find one; he then takes it upon himself to make certain that the patient does not sit around feeling sorry for himself after having chucked up his morning toast and tea. When two nurses bicker over the morning change of linens, Mr. Pippin appears on the spot to tell them they are both looking prettier than ever today and he doesn't know how he will choose between them. "Mr. Pippin," asks Dr. Saunders, "what would you say to Matron that she should look for, when she hires a nurse for us? What is it that a nurse should have, first and foremost?" "Patience," he replies instantly. But there is a gleam in his eye and I wonder if I have heard him right. No use asking Mr. Pippin, however; he would only give us a wink and be off down the hallway again, whistling "Believe Me If All Those" and flourishing his grand red beard that came, so he says, from his mother's uncles before him. Hauls himself along now like a seal on a rock, Mr. Pippin does, yet in spirit he is light as a hummingbird, sipping a bit of fun here and there, poking his head into everyone's business, teasing, enjoying, tasting the mischief, the marvelous fragrance of life, and everywhere, pollinizing.

Day by day his ponderous body becomes more helpless and more useless to him, and therefore receives less of his notice. He likes it all right—admires his beard in the looking glass with a sort of absentminded, familial affection— and yet, the heavier his limbs become, the more Mr. Pippin himself is lighter, will not be bound down or pay homage to danger, embarrassment (only does up his trousers at all now, as the duchess said, so as not to frighten the horses), and one day the news will be, without doubt, that he has achieved transformation into something finer than ever, having slipped, with a grin and a wink at this world, from his cocoon.

The news in the nurses' lounge at all hours is fatigue. Also, the price of food in London (terrible), the difficulty of giving up smoking (worse), and the patient's husband (unspeakable) who prevents their twin daughters, age seven, from seeing their mother now that she is dying of cancer. The social worker has tried, the psychiatrist has tried, Dr. Saunders herself, it is rumored, has tried to help the man deal with his situation more sensibly, but he will not. He does not want his daughters to see "ugliness" and he firmly believes that they will "forget" the anguish of having their mother leave them for no understandable reason. The nurses are irate. They chip and peck away at the image of this villain who somehow grows larger and more menacing each time he is mentioned; and in their talk there appears to be a venting of general frustration, and of the anguish of caring so much, as these women obviously do, for patients who die. Is it exhausting work? I ask.

Of course it is draining, they reply. And yet, surprisingly, it is a tremendously satisfying job as well. We natter on about it because that's just the way we are. But we know we are relieving pain which is simply not coped with in other places where we've worked. We see them coming in to us in terrible shape, in agony, many of them, and some of them with bedsores neglected and other infections. We clean all that up. We get them comfortable, free of pain, get them to eating, feeding themselves again (many have been on I.V.s), and see them sit up in their beds, get up, and move around again when no one thought they ever would. Most of all, we see them part of their family again. Some go home and then come once a week to the Thursday clinic. Most of them can at least go out again on visits; and that part of it, of course, is marvelous. We are well paid here, too, salaries the same as National Health standard for work that is in many ways not as hard, because we have more time to do it in.

The frustrating part comes when sometimes there is a run of such terribly ill ones coming in all at once, and then dying before we have a chance to do very much for them. There was a time like that recently in fact, a "bad patch" in the summertime when it was unbearably hot. When they come in and die straightaway—as with Mr. O'Hara—it is mostly for the family what we do then, being with them so it is not such a frightening thing at the last. And we'll stay in touch with Mrs. O'Hara, of course, and the rest of the family, if they'll come to the Monday evening meetings we have. But the hardest thing of all is getting very much attached to one or another of the patients, particularly the young ones like that Mrs. Preston who was just confirmed and had her first communion here only last week.

We meet once a week with some of the other staff and once a month, you know, with Dr. Colin Murray Parkes (psychiatrist and author of a number of works on bereavement). Between them and ourselves we get things sorted out. Some of us go to the chapel and have a cry. And we do fume and fuss somewhat among ourselves as well, getting it out—taking it out, some might say. But the doctors know how we feel, and Matron, and they feel it too. We're all in it together and we are a team, that's the main thing.

"You wouldn't prefer to work somewhere else, then?"

"Not after what I've seen here, I wouldn't."

A network of meetings blueprints the inner workings of St. Christopher's. Staff meetings, ward meetings, doctors' rounds which in this case are more meetings; meetings of residents, council meetings, meetings of the bereaved, and meetings that cross the lines back and forth between various groups which in other institutions might coexist without intercommunication. There is even a Thursday meeting with a bar set up for patients and staff (including maintenance men) especially to share. After morning prayers for those who wish to participate, one of the most important meetings of the day is held regularly in the Admissions Office. Here, hospice principles are put daily to a test of definition and redefinition that is a constant, and at times anguishing, reminder of the delicacy and the difficulty of St. Christopher's chosen task.

In the small room crammed with desks, filing cabinets, and records, six people must sit almost knee to knee in the space remaining, while they struggle over the applications that have been submitted to the hospice. Matron is here, the admissions secretary, her assistant, the chief social worker, and a member of the Domiciliary Team. One by one, each individual is discussed on the basis of the report submitted by the attending physician, a report taking into account not only the medical situation, but geographical location, family relationships, life-style, present state of mind, and any personal problems that may have developed during the course of illness. Nearly all have cancer.

How are they chosen? Of six who may apply in a day, it appears that only half may be tentatively accepted. It matters, first of all, that there is pain—not temporary, not easy to manage, but chronic and overwhelming to the individual. Other symptoms persisting despite previous medical treatment are also studied with care. Second, the individual should have some reasonable hope of life expectancy beyond hours or days, and should have relations or friends within reach of transport to St. Christopher's. The question is often asked, can the Domiciliary Care people manage to take on the care of this one? However, this is a difficult question in itself, for home care brings with it the assumption of a bed at the hospice when needed, and this cannot *always* be so.

Mr. Jones, it seems, would probably do better at home just now. The real issue here seems to be that his daughter is anxious to return to her position at the bank, and does not know what to do with him in the meantime. St. Christopher's cannot address itself to this problem, but will participate, if wished, by advising. The admissions secretary agrees to talk it over at greater length today with Mr. Jones's social worker.

More information is needed on a number of cases before any decision or recommendation can be made. Referrals to other hospices or nursing homes are given in several cases of people at a distance, and arrangements are made for consultation with the attending physician if wished. The case of Mrs. Smith now arrives at the top of the pile. Already in a hospital under the care of a G.P., Mrs. Smith has suffered many months of devastating pain, dyspnea, and other complications of incurable cancer of the lung. She is deeply depressed and, when conscious, hysterical. Her prognosis: days, or perhaps hours. Her doctor, contacting St. Christopher's for the first time today, hopes for an immediate telephone call, and a transfer on the spot.

Members of the committee look at one another aghast. The social worker squirms in her chair, twisting her long hair between her fingers, the Domiciliary Team member sits white-faced and grim, biting her lips, and Matron, bolt upright as ever in her immaculate uniform with its gleaming silver buckle, looks ready to spit bullets. The agony of Mrs. Smith hovers in the room. "We cannot do it," says Matron. "No, we cannot." There are fifty-four beds in the hospice. Every one is now either occupied or promised to someone whose problem, in days and weeks past, has intentionally become St. Christopher's own. St. Christopher's is a house of life and of conscious, orderly transition for pilgrims on the longer journey; its integrity as a hospice depends upon its stability as a community. The time of transition requires medical and nursing expertise, love, intelligence, faith, cooperation, hard work. The physician in this case will be telephoned immediately and given information that, it is hoped, may be of service to him as well as to his patients, present and future.

The remaining applications are discussed. In each case, there will be a response offering some kind of consultation, aid, or advice, for each individual involved is a matter of concern for this group. At last, Matron jumps up from her chair saying, "*Yes.* Yes, this one sounds right for us. Indeed, I do think we can help her." She beams like a small girl who has just found the finest Easter egg of all. "You see, this one—Mrs. Green—she needs to be at home for Christmas, but then will be ready to come to us for a bit. Her family are quite close by, good transport, several more months, they expect, needs help with her appetite, partial paralysis, anxious and troubled, pain now increasing—oh, yes, we can help her. A sound, conscientious report from her G.P. and he understands what we are about at St. Christopher's. *Good. Mrs. Green.*"

Money is not mentioned during this part of the hospice proceedings. St. Christopher's was established in 1967 as a charitable foundation, and although at present some three quarters of daily patient-care service receives support from the National Health Service, other costs and working capital must come entirely from gifts. Public appeals for funds are not made, and it is through families and friends of the hospice that the majority of its financial obligations are met. There have been desolate moments when the budget (in 1976 nearly £600,000 annually) has seemed impossible to meet. Thus far, some donation or renegotiation of funds has always intervened; and no patient has been turned away from the doors of St. Christopher's for lack of money.

Had money been an issue, the woman who shall be called here Lillian Preston would have been turned away. Names, personal histories, and identifying characteristics of all patients here are, of course, thoroughly disguised. They speak, however, in their own words as I heard them, and as I believe they wanted to be heard.

Lillian Preston, age twenty-nine. She was the only child of aging parents, reclusive and impoverished gentlefolk. Married at twenty-two. A year later abandoned by her husband. Unable to find work, left with a baby daughter to care for, she returned in disgrace to the grudging parental home. Job finally found as a decorator's assistant in London, a two-year struggle ensuing to establish a home for herself and her daughter. Success at last; and then, on their first holiday together, a boating accident in which the child drowns. Six months later, Lillian Preston's doctor tells her that she has cancer, and that her uterus must be removed. Her uterus is removed, and after surgery she is told that her cancer has metastasized beyond hope of cure.

Mrs. Preston looks now like a woman in her late forties. She sits in a pale yellow quilted dressing gown, writing notes, in the armchair beside her bed, her abdomen swollen as if she were eight months pregnant. She has long, dark hair, thoroughbred bones, dark eyes and eyebrows, very white skin drawn taut over her cheeks, an aura about her that is not quite a trick of the light—a radiance. Prognosis: two weeks.

We talk of this and that. I clear her tray, help her into bed. Tomorrow the doctors are going to draw off some of the fluid, she tells me, and then she expects to be more comfortable. Now? Well, not too bad, really, only she is so heavy with it, and rather sleepy. Strange to feel so peaceful, so secure now, and almost to feel—well, happy, really, even though she knows—she tests my eyes—that she is not going to get well. It is such a relief, she says, not having to pretend anymore. It was so hard, more than she could bear for a very long time, being alone with the knowledge of it.

"Had you no one to turn to?"

"No one. After I was ill I had to stay with my parents again, you see, and my father wouldn't hear of it."

"But your mother?"

"He insisted on protecting her, you see."

"So you knew that he knew, and still—?"

"No one would let me talk about it. It was a horrible secret that everyone knew and no one would mention. And the worst of it was being so helpless, a burden on everyone. It was like having to be a child again, only worse, because they would say, *soon you will be getting stronger*—and this time, I could not. So I let them down, again and again, and I could see them actually hating me for it despite themselves. Then I started hating myself. Until I came here, I used to hope each night that I wouldn't wake up to live another day. Each hour seemed like a week, each day was like months. And when I was in the other hospital, I had to have morphine shots to knock me out for the pain, but that isn't living. When it is that way, you really can't call it being alive. The psychiatrist at the other hospital was very kind and he tried to help me, but he couldn't give me what I needed."

"Then it is very different here, for you?"

"Here I am treated as a person. I have a sense of my—dignity. Well, I don't mean that, it sounds so proud, but here I am simply myself, and no one minds. I am glad to live each day now, one at a time. I like to nap in the afternoons, but I am so busy here, it is actually hard for me to fit that in. So many people—friends I didn't know cared for me, people I used to work with—have written to me, come to visit me and so forth, now that I am here and it is all right to say what is happening."

"How long have you been here?"

"Nine, ten weeks, I think. Perhaps longer, I don't remember. It's strange, I hardly even remember the pain. I remember the fact that it was so bad, I could not bear it. . . . Yes, it was physical pain, and also the sense of being such a failure, having lost out on everything I tried to do. And the grief of losing the one child, the only thing that mattered. The pain was terrible, but I think it was grief that always made it past bearing. I was angry, too. At the world and at life, and most of all, at myself. And then I came here—have you seen how it is when we come? When we arrive? Matron comes straight into the ambulance, the moment it stops in front of the door. She does that for everyone. And she came in to me, and called me by name. I looked at her face and could see that she was glad to have me. It seemed as if she had been waiting, only for me. That is why I am always so near to tears here, it is such a relief. And all that time, I never believed in God. Can you imagine? Listen, a week ago something happened that was very strange. I felt in the night the Angel of Death, it seemed In my sleep. It was the presence of death just by my shoulder and I thought, this is my time to go. But it was not. It was the woman in the bed just there beside me, she who died that night. But I felt it, and I went up out of my body and floated above it. I knew I was in my spiritual body then, and I was not afraid, but I was glad to come back because I am still not ready. I have to work through things in my own mind that are not finished yet. Here at the hospice, you see, things are so different from all that I am used to. I have to go over my whole life again, it seems, sorting it out. Do you think that is strange?

"You don't," she continues. "Well, that is one reason why it is so good to be here, where no one thinks I have gone mad. Let me show you something—I hope you don't mind this—but I want to show you what it was like before." She pulls back the sleeves of her nightgown and holds her arms up to the light. The scars I have seen before, but never like this. Most people, when they cut their wrists, want only to bleed a little and frighten the people around them into being kinder. Lillian Preston has savaged herself, wanting to die.

"I did that," she says, shaking her head in wonder, putting her arms back under the coverlet again. "It never did heal right."

"When was it?"

"Before I came here. They had sent me to one hospital, then to another. Then, when I finally came to St. Christopher's, the young man—you know, the chaplain's assistant—he came to me and we talked about it all. He helped me."

She closes her eyes and lies very still, smiling slightly, pregnant with her own death, pondering her memories, biding her time.

7

NOW THERE'S TOMORROW

You matter because you are you. You matter to the last
moment of your life, and we will do all we can not only
to help you die peacefully, but also to live until you die.
Dame Cicely Saunders

*S*unday morning: a faint ray of sunlight gleaming in the
chapel. On the long wall, a spare and simple cross, two
branches of cherry wood from a nearby tree. The altar is
not, as might be expected, at the far end of the room but
at the side and center so that we can bring the beds into a
semicircle around it; and those who are too weak today to
sit upright can still see and participate.

Packed as the chapel is now with beds, wheelchairs, patients, residents, visitors, and members of the staff, the
scene is distinctly medieval. Once more we are able to
experience firsthand the time in history when the ward of
a hospice/hospital was in itself a holy place. In the monastic
way stations of the twelfth to the sixteenth centuries, the
ward with patients lying in it was shaped like the nave of
a church, and was in fact just that, arcaded beside the patients' beds and opening directly to the vaulted apse
beyond. The cross-shaped plans of later hospitals were not
originally designed for ventilation or for the convenience
of the medical attendant; their original purpose was to allow

as many patients as possible to witness the mass and to participate in communal worship even while desperately ill, or dying. The fact that the cross shape proved also to be useful in a practical way is one of those events, like Mr. Pippin's puns, perhaps designed to make us think.

By comparison with the fifteenth-century ward of the Knights Hospitallers at Rhodes, which had its altar at the side, presumably for the same reason, this room is small, modest, and austere. Compared to the lovely and gracious old monastic wards at Canterbury and Tonnerre, and even at Turmanin in Syria in the fifth century A.D., it is indeed very plain. Yet the same life goes on here, now as then. And in its obedience to the Christian imperative to heal and to come together for healing, it is a commanding room in the very power of its intimacy.

We sing a hymn; or rather Cicely Saunders sings a hymn, and the rest of us do the best we can with it. Actually, the sound of us all having a go at it together is not bad. People in bathrobes are singing, and people dressed, and people lying down in nightgowns and pajamas singing a capella. The human voice, even in such a situation as this, is a fine and hopeful thing. For indeed, it is strange, as Mrs. Preston might say—her favorite word, "strange"—to see people lying down dying, singing. But why is it strange? What is it that we have become used to instead? There she is now in her yellow dressing gown, lying back against her pillows, dying, singing.

Strange means alien, unrelated, foreign. Foreign to what? Strange means being a stranger, being away from home, coming across the fields at twilight, weary, needy— or coming across the Arctic Circle in a plane, frightened, in the night. Strange means needing to know what time it is, and not knowing. Not being able to find your way home. Where is home? To the stranger, the dogs at his heels in an unknown town are strange. He knows who he is, but they do not. Let them hurt him enough in the hour of his anxiety, and he may become a stranger to himself, unrelated, alienated—mad. But who in the world we live in today is mad? Is it madness to live with the sight of, and in the knowledge of, death and dying—or is it sanity?

I want what is in your mind and what is in your heart, said David Tasma. He wanted both a hospital and a home, bread, not a stone. What is home? Bread and wine and singing. Home is where the music is. Hospitality, like music, opens out a space where we can come together whole, heart and mind, and love, and be healed. And in this space there is not any here, nor there, nor boundary, nor judgment, nor distance set between us, nor any way of measuring who is a stranger; and in this space, because there is no measuring it anymore, there is no time.

World without end, amen. The brief Anglican service, built around the moment of Holy Communion, is concluded, made miniature so as not to tax the strength of those who are very frail; for Sunday at the hospice is a day of many visitors, excitement in the wards, children and pets, cousins and grandparents in the hallways, gifts and flowers arriving, and general celebration. The lifts are busy now, taking beds back to their usual places, the front door of the hospice is opening constantly, and the telephone at the reception desk is jingling.

The honored visitor in Dr. Saunders's office today is a cheerful and expansive lady by the name of Dame Albertine Winner, who is chairman of the Council of Management at St. Christopher's. A physician herself as well, and formerly Dr. Saunders's deputy medical director, she obviously cares very deeply about each challenge and problem within the hospice, though she claims it is all mere pleasure and holiday for her, coming on weekly visits to talk with anyone available, seeing an occasional patient in consultation—her particular joy—and working with other members of the Council. These she finds fascinating in themselves: representatives of the church, the theater, the law, business, banking, medicine, and social work as well as individuals with a special dedication to voluntary service. Matron attends these meetings also, as does the bursar of St. Christopher's and the architect; thus there are knowledgeable and experienced leaders in many fields, from the larger community as well as the hospice itself, available to inform and advise one another in all matters relating to the development of St. Christopher's. Dame Albertine's connection with the hospice began in 1961 when, as deputy chief medical officer in the Ministry of Health, she first saw what was being done for patients at St. Joseph's Hospice. At that time, she became a firm supporter of Dr. Saunders's plan for a place that would not only look after patients' needs, but be a center for teaching and research as well, and an ongoing community. A founding member of St. Christopher's Hospice, she has been its resourceful and determined advocate ever since.

The young doctors gathering today with Dame Albertine, Cicely Saunders, and Dr. Tom West must have been, some of them, in their cradles when the first vision of St. Christopher's Hospice emerged. Yet between them all, men and women, younger and older, there is an easy camaraderie and a sense of great mutual affection. In time for ritual libation before Sunday lunch, a bottle of sherry appears, and a set of stemmed glasses from the cabinet surrounded by books. Cicely Saunders pours. "Who will carve at Christmas this year, Dr. Saunders, in the wards?" asks one of the younger physicians. "Dame Albertine will, and Tom will, of course, and now that you mention it, you will too," she replies with a grin. "Cheers."

▲   ▲   ▲

"Do you never rest?" I ask her. We are driving toward London in the four o'clock afternoon darkness and I am acutely conscious of the fact that in San Francisco, this morning for most people has not yet begun. It is raining a little now, as we approach the Thames.

"Oh, yes," she replies. "I was so exhausted yesterday that I went home and slept eight hours straight. And I am on my way to a party now, with some of my Polish friends. Hospice work is very taxing, as you see. I believe it should not be embarked on at all unless one is the sort of person who really cannot help it. Someone, preferably a doctor, must be prepared to be a leader, have an over-powering desire to get it going, and be prepared to sweat and pray to do it. But we in this work, I think, are always somehow missing one layer of outer skin, and we must take care to renew ourselves. It must be done from within, by means of prayer above all, but celebration as well. The work of a hospice must be done right, and its spiritual dimension cannot be grafted on. *We must have ideas in order before it is possible to meet facts.* Yes, I do rest, and I celebrate, and I thoroughly enjoy myself in my small pri-vate life which is tucked away, around the corner from St. Christopher's."

She drives steadily, competently ("I find it restful to drive") at a fine clip straight down the wrong side of the road, which turns out, of course, to be the right side. The right side of the road, in the world we now inhabit, *is* the left side. *Looking-glass world,* as a visiting American doctor said today, speaking of hospice care, and comparing it to the treatment of the dying cancer patient in U.S. hospitals. And his question was, how is the decision made, when to move through to the other side, where automatic attempts are no longer made to conquer the disease, but instead, every effort is brought to bear in support of the person's physical comfort and spiritual well-being?

The reply was that these are in effect two complementary systems of treatment, and that there should be openness and interchange constantly between them. The attending physician, in consultation with the patient and the family, must take it upon himself or herself to make the decisions—and may, if there is doubt, call in consultants—but must always be on the alert to prevent patients from becoming locked into a system that is inappropriate to their needs.

"A patient should no more undergo aggressive treatment, which not only offers no hope of being effective but which may isolate him from all true contact with those around him, than he should merely be relieved of symptoms when the underlying cause is still treatable—or has once again become so," said Dr. Saunders. Patients suffer not only from inappropriate active tumor "cure" but also from inept terminal care, of course. The aim of a hospice must be to rescue the individual from both of these destructive alternatives. "The work of a hospice is to give patients the attention they need; it is a job equally demanding as that of a more conventional hospital but involving different skills, skills that are more personal. It's good, hard medicine all the same."

Personal, yes, I think the following morning, kneeling on the bathroom floor, powdering between the toes, one by one, of Miss Aurelia Robbins. Skills very personal and involving the most minute attention to detail at the same time that the mind is being stretched to its utmost limits in the opposite direction. Only in the life of the individual patient, in the body and soul of each person, seen one at a time very clearly, with great care, can these opposites meet. Hospice care, like life itself, is not a thing but a process. Terminal care is not really the right word for it, does not suggest at all the right kind of tension, the balance here between left-brain, right-brain matters. Miss Aurelia Robbins's left foot is rather different from her right foot, yet she needs both of them, to walk.

Walking, she sees herself, still (and likes to tell me about it) in a garden in Charleston, South Carolina, in the spring. There are lilies of the valley and violets under the trees, and she is a young girl, with her hair up for the first time, wearing a white dress. It is 1920, and the people in Charleston are very, very kind to her. She does not know how she could ever thank people, really, for being so kind. The air is warm and soft in Charleston in the spring, and she walks under the trees in her white dress, every day, never forgetting to tell me how kind these people are, because she knows that I am an American too. It is a great pleasure to dry Miss Robbins's feet, and to put powder on them.

"You have beautiful feet, Miss Robbins."

"Do I really, my dear? Why, how nice to think of that, because you know, of course, I haven't seen them in years." Miss Robbins is blind, and the skin of her face is crumpled like an old rose, but the skin of her body, which she has not seen for so long, is like a young woman's, innocent and smooth, wholly unconscious of itself. She sits in the deep, warm tub and says, "Ahhh . . ." when I squeeze the sponge over the lovely, blind skin of her back, and smiles a marvelous smile. Miss Robbins has been at St. Christopher's for seven years now, first as a resident in the Drapers' Wing and then, being unable to care for herself any further, within the wards of the hospice. "I never married," she says. "Wasn't that selfish of me?" She likes her lemon cologne after her bath, but she needs to be reminded that she likes it. Looking inside her mind is like looking into one of those glass baubles that you shake a little, and the snowflakes swarm, and then they settle down again, and grow still.

Sitting up today in her chair in her soft, peach-colored dress and her little shawl, with her hands clasped in her lap, she smiles and says, "I'm just an old fraud, you know. I'm not sick at all. I am just sitting here enjoying myself. Isn't that terrible?" Then she tells me again about the kind people in Charleston. "I don't quite understand it, really," she says. "Life is a great puzzle to me, but I think there must be a meaning to it all somehow, don't you?" Miss Robbins does not know it, but she is a challenge to the word *meaning,* as a rose is. She wants her cup of tea if it is there, and if it is not there, then she does not want it. Anything that might have happened to her in her life, and did not happen, was superfluous. She very simply enjoys being. Mornings, she says, "Oh, how nice of you to suggest a bath. I do love being bathed and I always forget, but you know, people here are so kind, they always remind me." Then we go into the bathroom again and I squeeze the sponge over her back, and she says, "Ahhh . . ." and tells me again about Charleston. Americans, she says, must be really the kindest people in all the world. She does not wonder whether the people in Charleston have forgotten about her, or whether, in fact, they may be dead. She does not want any more from them than they have already given her. She takes her pleasure now in offering her memory of them back as a gift, again and again, to me—the American—so that I, a stranger and far from home, will feel valued and cherished. Thus I, the care-giver, am cared for daily by Miss Robbins, am bathed and cleansed of my strangeness, my foreignness, and am welcomed, made at home. Thus she, who is unable to help herself, heals me.

▲   ▲   ▲

Miss Robbins is not known as "the senile glaucoma in 45-B" when hospice doctors meet for rounds. She is known, with great affection and appreciation, as a special person who has made for many years an important contribution to the stability of the community. Her condition will be carefully watched from day to day by skilled physicians and well-trained nurses, but it is the person and not the physical or mental disability that is of concern. Is she able to live her own life in her own way at the moment? Does she enjoy her meals? Is her radio working? Is there anything more we could possibly do for her? But then—and they smile—what could anyone do for Miss Robbins? Except, of course, to enjoy her, as they do.

This weekly "rounds" is held, not at the bedside, but privately, in an office. X-rays are discussed, chemotherapy, radiation treatment, and a certain kind of crutches that might be more useful to Mr. Jackson than the ones he has now. All patients, unless they specifically request to have it otherwise, are known by their family names with the appropriate title; in England, more than in the United States, this is felt as a mark of consideration and respect. Changes of medication are noted and discussed. Mrs. White has shown signs of discomfort and has been vomiting, thus she is now being given her analgesic by injection. Mr. Strauss has complained of cramps in his legs. Does he need hot packs, a different kind of orthopedic support, passive exercise, perhaps, some subtle shift in medication, or a combination of these? Has he been successful in finishing his project in occupational therapy? Does his family celebrate Hanukkah, and if so, has he been fully involved in the celebrations? Knowledge is pooled, and it is decided that Dr. West, who is particularly close to Mr. Strauss, will have a talk with him about the changes planned for his regime.

Mr. Pippin's latest X-rays are "a disaster." He has had

radiation treatments in other parts of his body, and has
appeared to be holding his own. Suddenly now, his upper
spine is in great danger, and it is a serious question whether
he should go to his dear old friends at Shepherd's Bush for
Christmas. A great day has been planned for him and all his
godchildren; he has been looking forward to it for months,
and it would be another sort of disaster if he were not
allowed to go. This may be Mr. Pippin's last Christmas. But
what would it do to the family, and to the godchildren
especially, if their merry, whistling, red-bearded god of a
godfather should suddenly collapse in agony, or even die
on that day in their midst? Could the family manage?
Would they feel forever after that they had been somehow
to blame? Would the children have a horror of Christmas
in the future if such a thing should happen?

After a lengthy discussion, a decision is made to provide
a particularly sturdy and extensive neckbrace for Mr. Pippin
immediately; then to have him transferred on the day itself
by ambulance, only for the celebration, and then to return.
"Oh, Mr. Pippin," says Dr. West to himself, looking sadly
at the X-rays. "Look at that, the entire structure disintegrat-
ing! Yes, my friend, you are an amazing man."

"What are you doing, writing a book?" A patient I have not
seen before has noticed me, standing beside the flower sink,
scribbling notes. I help her back from the lavatory and into
her bed and say yes.

"About the hospice, I suppose. Why, how absolutely
splendid, my dear. It's amazing how little people know
about this sort of thing. Do you have them in America? Not
that there's anything in all the world like St. Christopher's.
Be an absolute angel and hand me my wig while you're at
it. Cicely Saunders is a very dear friend of mine. Fabulous
woman. Sit down this minute and let me help you write

your book. . . . Oh, the wig is in that little box up there. Right, that one.

"Thank you. Not that I give a damn what I look like, but I'm going to a concert downstairs. Don't want to frighten people. Chemotherapy, you know. I've had cancer for ages, lots of secondaries and all that sort of thing. A frightful bore, really."

She is a large woman, Mrs. Kent, with the manner of a casual duchess rambling through her kitchen garden, philosophizing about aphids. She has a falcon's eyes, however, and probably rushes around Scotland—or used to—during the season, doing things with shotguns and stirrup cups. At home she undoubtedly has a closet full of floppy hats and floppy wigs, more or less indistinguishable from one another. Heavy silver on her table, and a great many large dogs under it, crunching bones during formal dinner parties.

"Have I got it on straight? Well, never mind. About this book of yours. Splendid. Everyone should be told. Hospices should be everywhere. All this talk about euthanasia is absolute nonsense. Well-meaning, of course, and I do sympathize, but the fact is, you don't have to kill people in order to make them comfortable. Look at me, for example. Not that I am anything unusual, though I am somewhat lopsided here and there, having bits and pieces chopped off of me hither and yon, but who cares about that? I am alive and enjoying myself. Every single person in the world should have a place like St. Christopher's to go to, when things get out of hand. I was absolutely howling with pain when I came in here, forty-eight hours ago. Hadn't been able to hold food down for nearly two weeks. This morning, I et like a horse. Feel quite fine, at the moment, and plan to go home again in about three days. All I needed was getting my medicines adjusted, and having a bit of rest. Tell them that. Personal experience, my dear, believe me, the only kind.

"They know what they are doing here, you see. They do miracles, I assure you, but not as a result of floating about in a sort of euphoric trance praying and all that sort of thing—not that I mind if they do, at this point—but it's all a result of absolutely tremendous discipline. And the moment you come in here you feel you are the only pebble on the beach. That in itself is the most incredible lift. Write your book and tell them everything about it, for I am perfectly certain as I sit here, that hospices are the coming thing. . . . How did I happen to know Cicely? Well, just as you do. I was once a volunteer."

Off in a wheelchair she goes now ("Don't need it, really, I'm just constitutionally lazy") to the concert of Renaissance carols in the Drapers' Wing; and I learn from Matron that an emergency situation has developed. An unexpected patient is arriving, a woman who until recently has been in a London welfare home that has been shut down. It had been hoped that Mrs. Doe could manage at home until after Christmas (in a filthy flat, which she fiercely refused to leave), but she has "had some trouble" in the meantime "needing to be sorted out." There is no space for her, but somehow space will have to be found. "We must put Mrs. Doe into a temporary situation, which is not at all the preferred way of doing it," says Matron cheerfully, "but it can't be helped. She is our patient, and she needs to come in."

The ambulance arrives, and backs up to the glass doors. The doors are opened wide. Mrs. Doe's bed is already waiting for her, just outside, with her name on it, fresh white sheets and coverlet turned back, and four down pillows. Two hot-water bottles in knitted covers have been warming the sheets for Mrs. Doe and are still there, where her shoulders and upper thighs will rest. Crisp and smiling, Matron hurries out—this is her moment of joy—climbs into the back of the ambulance, and bends eagerly over the cot. From the cot comes the sound of a small animal wailing, and I see her put out her hands to stroke it.

The drivers are tall and powerfully built, one male, one female, in similar uniforms, blue-gray, with caps. Very fast and smoothly now, some twenty feet from the back of the ambulance to the warmed bed, they bring the cot. The object lying on it, which does not appear to be a person, is wrapped in a red blanket. The drivers flex their arms, rub their hands, and then, very fast but very tenderly, begin the lift from cot to bed. The thing in the blanket screams. "There, there, dear," Matron whispers, bending close. "Everything is going to be all right."

Together we turn the blanket back. The smell is of un-washed flesh, sour incontinence, rags, vomit, and beer. In-side the blanket is a loose, gray mass of flesh and bone with matted hair. Objects such as this are seen sometimes at night, in alleyways of cities, propped beside the garbage cans. Hurrying feet of frightened and respectable citizens step past them, and in the darker shadows nearby, there are rats. It is hard to tell, really, whether these creatures are dead or alive. One hopes—but then, in such a situation, what is there to do?

Matron strokes the matted hair and says, "Mrs. Doe? Do you know where you are? You are at St. Christopher's Hospice now, and we are going to take care of you." We slide the blanket out, and pull up the top sheet and the coverlet. Another scream, and a babble of words, incompre-hensible.

"Well, good-bye now, Mrs. Doe," says one of the driv-ers. "Don't you worry anymore, sweetheart. No one is going to hurt you here." Calling to the drivers that they must stop for tea or coffee if they wish, Matron whisks the new patient's bed away; I help her slide it into the lift; the door closes, and they vanish upstairs.

Back in the kitchen again, scrubbing the pans, I see Matron darting past in the hall an hour later.

"Oh, my," she says, merry as a cricket. "They have put you to it, haven't they?"

"Oh, Matron, how is Mrs. Doe?"

"Settling in very nicely, thank you. Such a dear lady. She will be fine."

"But I thought—is she desperately ill?"

"Desperately ill? No, she is not." Matron is moving so fast that I must nearly run, alongside.

"She isn't? But I thought she looked—well, as you say here, rather poorly."

"Poorly, yes. Circumstances have not been favorable."

"I was concerned. Will she be better tomorrow?"

"We shall see." She stops so suddenly that I nearly collide with her. "Mrs. Preston wants her tea now, I think. It would be very nice indeed if you would take it to her."

"Why, how nice of you to suggest that, Matron. Mrs. Preston is a particular favorite of mine, you know."

"I know that," she says, glancing up at me with lips held perfectly firm and straight, but with the merriest eyes.

"It's such a strange thing," says Lillian Preston, lying back on her pillows in her yellow gown, sipping her tea. "I mean, how different it all is here, from what I am used to. I have so much to learn and have learned so much already, even in a little time. Today was a bad day for me, you know. I talked to Matron about it. They drew the fluid off yesterday and I thought that would give me strength somehow, but it did not. I am thinner but I am weaker even so. It made me cross. So I have been in a 'bad patch,' being tired of all these things my body does to disappoint me, feeling low and down, and taking it out on everyone around me. I was mean—well, I hope not mean, but really disagreeable—today at least six times before breakfast, and then, when I saw the same old mashed-up food I have to eat now, I was cross to the person who brought it. The chaplain says it is wrong to brood about the things you have done wrong; it is only a form of pride, thinking that you ought to have done better. Not really a way of loving God and being sorry. He says don't dwell on it, just tell Him that you are sorry, and try again. But when I think of it that way, then I know how proud I really am, and then I brood about that.

"Being confirmed, I suppose, was the dangerous thing. I mean as far as the devil is concerned, that is really the last straw. Oh, yes, I believe in the devil and I ought to know, for he has given me a very bad time. My being confirmed put him into a real fury, and now I am being tested, you see. The temptation for me, I am sure now, has been to believe that I would be perfect from now on, and that all the people around me, so kind as they are, would be perfect saints. They are only human beings, though. And they will do things that make me cross, and things that I do not like. They even make mistakes, sometimes. Love is the thing I have been learning. Love that accepts people the way they are. I have to do it now and it is a terrific struggle. But you know, I think it is the reason why I am still here. It is something I have to know about, or else my whole life has been wasted. And the only way I can really know it is to do it myself, no matter how weak my body is, just care for people and love them the way that they are. I never knew that kind of love before. I never had it given to me, so I never knew what it was like. Loving the baby, seeing her love me, was the closest I came to it. But we never really had a home.

"So now I try. And I go back over everything in my mind, and I think, sometimes, why couldn't people's homes be more like this? A hospice shouldn't be only a place you come to when you are very, very ill, do you think? I had a dream the other night. It was so strange. I dreamed about a place where I was not ill, I was well, and still I cared for people exactly in this way, and so did they for me. After that dream, I thought perhaps it was a kind of vision, perhaps that is what it is like on the other side of things. Thy Kingdom Come. I love sleeping now, I dream of dancing and swimming and all the things I am not strong enough to do anymore, all the things that I love. Do you dream in color? I never used to, but I do now. I never used to remember much of what I dreamed. I suppose I will be there soon, and then I will really know. More and more of me is on the other side now already. I am getting out of balance with it, and it is harder and harder to come back now, so uncomfortable here, with my body. Another week, perhaps. I will make up my mind, when I am ready. See how proud I am still? I am really very stubborn and proud. It is lucky I know God loves me in spite of that, isn't it? Oh, I am getting tired now."

I put away her tea things and help her to lie down comfortably. Leaning against the side of her bed, holding her hand, I am resting too. She holds my hand, and I hold hers. With her eyes closed, she says, "When I get there, I will ask them to make things ready for you."

In the morning, my last day at St. Christopher's, she is still sleeping. I scribble a note, and leave it beside her bed, glad that she is sleeping, and that we do not have to go through the ridiculous business of saying good-bye. Mr. Pippin is sporting a carnation in his buttonhole and a vast neckbrace that has caused some hasty renegotiation of his beard. Holding court in an armchair, he entertains a young, pretty volunteer. Miss Robbins has her bath, and tells me about Charleston. I powder very carefully between her toes. In the hairdressing room there is a new face under the dryer, small and pink, with very bright, blue eyes. Mrs. Doe is nowhere to be seen, but Mrs. White has stopped vomiting and is being a grouch, while the chaplain sits patiently beside her, nodding his head from time to time and sipping a cup of tea. Granny is having a nap, but I cannot find the pale, blond woman with skin so fragile, with skin like mother-of-pearl. Perhaps she has gone home for Christmas already, or perhaps—?

"Why, hello there, darling," says a cheery voice, as I wander by with a watering can, tending the plants.

"Good morning, how are you?" It is Blue-eyes, from under the hairdryer, silky white sausage curls not yet combed out, peering from behind the morning newspaper.

"Sit down here for a minute, I'll tell you," she says in the rich accents of East London, a village far from the purlieus of Oxford or Cambridge, Harvard or Yale. Shaking her newspaper, she says, "I'll tell you it's shocking, it is!"

"Shocking?"

"Murder and robbing, that's all they do nowadays. Look here! What's the world coming to, that's what I'd like to know. Where're you from, dear? America? California, that's part of Detroit, I know that, I've a nephew out there. You're a long way from home, then. Oh, well, times is hard now, dear, for all of us. I've seen some trouble myself, I can tell you. I've been so poorly, you wouldn't believe. I was bad with the pain, as God knows, though not being religious."

Her face is round and pink, and very clean. She wears a look slightly-puzzled, inquiring, but pleased; and a fresh, flowered nightgown with a touch of lace at the cuffs. Every now and then she pulls her upper lip down and touches it delicately with her forefinger, adjusting her teeth. "As God knows," she says, "it's only a matter of speaking, for you'll never see me in a church. Day to day's how I live, do the best that I can, but so poorly, these six months my legs wouldn't hold me. And now, here they tell me, tomorrow I'll get up and stand on my own feet. How is that? This is some kind of place. You work here? Yes, you will, wait and see, they says, that's what we're here for, to help you. Well, I never. Why do they bother with me, that's what I'd like to know? Now, you answer me that. Look at me, nothing left. Lost three stone, have a growth down in there, ready to do me in. Nothing for it. Do me in, doctor, I says, I see your white coat, I'm ready. You'll feel different tomorrow, he says, and him holding my hand. Oh, well, now there's tomorrow.

"So, what for, I says, I am nothing but trouble. And where does it hurt then, he says. Well, it don't hurt anymore today, but I'm tired of it, look at me, ready to quit. Why are they caring, I'm asking? Why are they kind? I've got nothing to give them. Sooner's better to end it and not be a bother to others, if anyone stopped to be asking me. Which they didn't. No, not them. Some kind of a place this is, I'll tell you. They know I am done for, so why give the likes of me—look, dear, you see my new hairdo? How is it? And get up tomorrow? Well, maybe I will, then, who knows. Maybe I'll fool every one of them, said I was nobody. They know my name here, look at that, put it right up on the bed. Had it waiting for me, when I was that poorly. But get up? I'm asking myself, how is that going to be, on these legs? Who would say such a thing? See here what I mean? These legs are no good. Well, come on now, just look at me, darling."

"Yes, Mrs. Doe."

8

THIS PASSIONATE CONCERN

The classical deathbed scene, with its loving partings
and solemn last words, is practically a thing of the past;
in its stead is a sedated, comatose, betubed object,
manipulated and subconscious, if not subhuman.

J. F. Fletcher

"General," murmured the tactful clergyman at Ulysses S.
Grant's bedside, "your time has come and the angels are
waiting for you." "Waiting, are they," roared the general, "waiting, are they? Well, goddamn 'em, let 'em
wait."

Apocryphal

*T*he elegant professor at the suburban dinner party is
astonished. "I simply cannot understand all this fuss
and bother about hospices," he says. "This incredibly pains-
taking method of care—though I understand it is far less
expensive than keeping vegetable personages alive on drips
and tubes—but why this passionate concern with the care
of the dying when it is so patently obvious that longevity
and surplus population are the real problems confronting
us? Do you realize that in 1900 only 4.1 percent of the
population in America was over sixty-five and it is now
something like ten percent and rapidly climbing? We are
going to be a nation of arthritics and drooling dodderers by
the year 2001. And look at the energy crisis. *Your* energies,
if I may say so, are being sadly misplaced. Look at India.

What the world needs is far more people dying every day no matter how they go about it. Not to mention far fewer of them being born in the first place. Look here, if we are to survive at all . . . and we wouldn't be in the catastrophic mess we are in today if only . . ." Thus he continues with great verve and eloquence for fifteen minutes or so to expound the theory that all this hospice talk is incredibly sentimental; and that another Noah's flood would be the best thing possible for the welfare of mankind and, with a bow to the prettiest of the ladies present (no chauvinist he), of womankind as well.

Professor N. is a sly man, sparkling with the sort of apocalyptic wit that makes people gasp a little before they burst into appreciative laughter. It is a pleasure to watch him as he expounds and expands, embroidering and elaborating the more he is applauded, enjoying his own eloquence, his own vigor as much as he enjoys the handsome company and the excellent Cabernet Sauvignon of his host. Waiting to hear (since we are suffering from a rather serious drought in California at the moment) what more practical solutions he may have for the population problem, I note, however, that the space around us somehow shrinks while he talks, and the darkness beyond looms larger, filled with shadows now and with shapes becoming stranger and more menacing by the moment. The world he conjures up is crammed to the brim with people not like us, people out there called "them" and called "they." These are individuals whom we do not know and will never meet face to face, it seems, if we can avoid it; but never mind, when the waters rise—we draw closer together in our little circle of candlelight—when the flood does come, we and people like us will be all right. Professor N., without quite saying it, implies in his charismatic way that it will be only the others, the nameless, faceless ones, who will die, while we here with him now, so bright and full of joie de vivre, rejoicing as we are in wine and quiche and candlelight, will survive; and that he will be our leader in the wilderness, his wit our Ark. The magic moment lingers on, for who could be so crass at a time like this and in such blessed company to suggest, even in an apologetic whisper, that our dear Professor N. does not know what he is talking about?

He does not, of course. He believes that he is talking about the population problem. "Look at India," he says, waving his arm vaguely toward the shadows in the corner of the room. But looking at India does not solve the population problem; and in any case, Professor N. is not looking at India. He is looking at the people across the table from him. He wants to know whether we like what he has been saying. I for one have a hard time concentrating on what he is saying, however, because I am trying instead to listen to him. When I listen to him, I hear something just under the surface interrupting the conscious message in a steady whine; I hear that he himself is now approaching the age of sixty-five, that he is bitter about his own life, and that there are a great many people in the world he is afraid of. I would like to ask him not to be so afraid, for I don't think serious, long-range plans are best made out of fear. Yet it is going to be very difficult to approach him in this respect. The people he is afraid of are all "out there" and there are a great many of them, all quite mysterious and invisible: invisible, just as Professor N. is at the moment, to himself. He can look down, I suppose, and see his hands, one wearing a thin, gold wedding ring and the other holding a glass of good red wine. But in order to find himself, charming, witty, and important as he really is, he must look again and again, searching, into our eyes.

Am I amusing? he asks us silently. Am I wise? Are you glad that I am alive? *Am* I alive? Am I worth it? We gather close and, laughing, enjoying him, say, Yes, the guest is worth his salt. Reassured, he himself laughs, embraces us with his eyes, and continues with his plan for the improvement of humanity that is really his system for personal avoidance—chivalrously including us, of course—of death. It is death who is his enemy, the death that he sees as personal obliteration, having dressed it in the foreign shapes called "them" and "they." But he does not know these people and therefore does not know what he is talking about because he does not know *who* he is talking about. I wonder whether Professor N. might have happened to see a *Pogo* comic strip a few years ago in which one of the characters reports from the front lines in some bewilderment, "We have met the enemy and they is us."

I make a firm resolution (knowing that it will crumble) to refrain from launching a counterattack in defense of the hospice concept. People who become deeply involved in hospice work, I know, tend to wear a kind of glow about them which at its best represents a healthy release of positive energy, but which can flare up all too easily into something resembling fanaticism. This is counterproductive, even though it is not difficult to see why it sometimes happens. Participation in this work is apt to produce exhilaration because of the changes we experience in our perception of such crucial matters as love and time, sickness and health, birth and death, and journeying, and the meaning of life itself. In receiving the dying as significant and fully conscious members of the hospice community, we are at the same time reincorporating the awareness of death into our own lives, and this is liberating.

A hospice does not address itself to many problems of politics and economics that are indeed very pressing today—but then, realistically, neither does Professor N. What the hospice concept does offer, I am thinking, is a sane position from which to approach these other problems, since it is a position soaked through with reality; and at the same time it is an affirmation of the value of human life that does not permit shadows in the wings, or self-deceptions about the comparative importance of "us" and "them" and "they." We are all going to die; death is in fact the great democratic leveler. The hospice acts out and embodies the provocative assumption that we are all one family responsible to one another in the meantime. Thus, though it does not preach politics, it is in itself a political as well as a philosophical statement.

"All philosophy," our host remarks, "is a preparation for death. Montaigne, wasn't it?"

"He stole it from Plato," said the professor. "Selective plagiarism, the modus operandi of the classical tradition."

"The modus of evolution as well," remarks the scientist, "if you want to have a look at the behavior of genes and chromosomes."

And (I am wondering) isn't it true as well that the awareness of death—one's own death—is the best possible preparation for living? Knowing that we are going to die, we refuse to fritter away our time on nonsense, we drop our masks, our little vanities and false ambitions and, like General Grant—to hell with politeness—we say exactly what we mean. General Grant was madly in love with his cross-eyed wife, and I always liked him for that. He didn't necessarily disbelieve in angels, he just didn't want anyone standing around his deathbed being smarmy about them. He was busy dying his own death, and didn't take kindly to being interrupted. To live fully, as warriors know, is to embrace life in all its transformations; and here, of course, is the hospice idea again. In its power to incorporate all forms of human life—young, old, healthy, sick, witty and dull, feeble and vigorous—into one working organism in which each part is useful and nourishing to the other, the fully-realized hospice community such as St. Christopher's is a paradigm of what a more highly conscious human life might be, and of what society might therefore become. This was the vision of the young woman who was called, in an earlier chapter, Lillian Preston—she is dead now—who learned only in the last weeks of her life, in a hospice community, to love and be loved. And yet she is not obliterated, in the sense that Professor N. imagines that he will be. "The communication of the dead," said T. S. Eliot, "is tongued with fire beyond the language of the living."

Remembering Lillian Preston, I decide that I must at least try to say something. With her letter in my pocket, written to me only a few hours before she died, the spoken word will come hard. And only this morning the other letter came to me from the chaplain's assistant: "She died very peacefully, quickly, on the Sunday and after the Blessing when she herself had determined that it would happen. She was herself to the last, and never faltered in her faith, or in her caring for everyone around her."

To hell with politeness. If sentimentality, I finally manage to say, is "unearned emotion," then sentimental the day-to-day care of the dying is not. Furthermore, anyone who imagines that he is being terribly kind and noble in doing it is almost certainly doing a rotten job. The dying give us so much more than we could ever possibly give to them. And part of the misunderstanding here is that many people think of a hospice as being only a rather specialized medical facility or a fancy nursing home, but it is not. How would I define it? Well, I have a letter in my pocket that says it ever so much better than I could do. My friend at St. Christopher's says it is a *caring community.*

Religious? Well, yes, if you believe that a caring community is necessarily religious. But in one very fine little English hospice I know of, two nursing sisters quit recently because they felt not enough religious ritual was being observed; and the director (who is both a physician and a deacon) asked them in astonishment, "But aren't you in the habit of praying with your fingertips?" So you see, it all depends really upon your own point of view.

Why are they necessary? Well, I suppose that a hospice is an expression of the fundamental urge to cherish what we value, and as far as I know, every culture worth the name has been built on the premise of valuing human life. Even the Neanderthals buried their dead with ceremony, and with flowers. But it is something else, too. It is also the embodiment of a recognition, deeply felt in almost every age and every culture since the Neanderthal, that life is a journey that will be continued in some other fashion, after death.

The word itself? Yes, I do think it is important. *Hospice, hospital, hostel* and *hôtel-Dieu* were at one time such similar concepts that the words were used quite interchangeably. Their later separation, in fact, is based upon the sort of performance that has worked continually to fragment society. The word *hospice* means a great deal to me because it is closest of all in our language to the ancient root, *hospes,* the mutual caring of people for one another.

With the growth of medical understanding, people who have contagious diseases have been separated more often from those merely in need of food and shelter, and this makes sense. However, the person who was dying, whether of wounds or disease or in the natural course of events (which we now see as unnatural!), was perceived through medieval eyes as a pilgrim, a traveler at a way station on the longer journey. As early as the twelfth century the hospital-chapel form, developed within the monasteries, began to be imitated beyond cloister walls. But here, too, the dying

were honored, and were tended with great care, whether
their hosts were friars or nuns, or guilds, or princely benefactors. Inns sprang up as a commercial venture meantime;
but for many centuries, kings and princes rubbed elbows in
the courtyards of monastic hospices with the humblest of
their subjects, and knew them by name; these were places
of meeting for all sorts and conditions of people, and places
of true *hospitality*.

If there has been a Dark Age (and if Professor N. will
bear with me another moment) during the past two thousand years in the history of hospitality, in fact it has been
ours. It was not until the religious and political upheavals
of the seventeenth and eighteenth centuries that such a
different view was officially taken of "incurables" and that
such an institution as the workhouse for the dying poor
could appear. The treatment of our own dying, both rich
and poor, in too many general hospitals today seems to me
to derive from a curious amalgam of this new, mechanistic,
and materialistic view of humanity, together with our neurotic, modern inability to face the facts of death. Our treatment of those who can be cured has grown a great deal
better in the twentieth century; but the way we cope with
our terminally ill has grown at the same time ever so much
worse.

"You are a Don Quixote," says Professor N. "You tilt
at progress, and at technology."

"Not at all. No, only at the ways in which we have
misused it. Having invented machines, we had no reason to
begin imitating them, to let them control our thoughts. And
having known better for thousands of years, we had no
business suddenly deciding that the true model of a man's
life is the machine which 'lives'—which is to say, *works*—
and then, when it runs out of energy or is broken beyond
repair, 'dies.' We know now that it is energy that is real, and

matter that is mere appearance. But the modern hospital deals with human life in terms of the material and the mechanical model. The modern hospice reaches back into the past and recovers a lost heritage that is extremely valuable."

"You make a serious mistake if you do not respect the mechanical model," replies the professor. "You bury your head in the superstitions of the Middle Ages and forget the stink of the Hôtel-Dieu in Paris, which kept its doors open to every stray and every disease, and ended by piling people six and seven to a bed. The filth of that place was one of the scandals exposed by the military during the French Revolution."

"It was filthy, you are right. But *you* make a mistake if you do not recognize the fact that industrialized nations, once they get any power at all, tend very quickly to solve their own problems of population control, so that your vision of Noah's flood is, if I may say so, rather more primeval than medieval. I didn't hear your recommendation of what to do with all the bodies after the water goes down. There was a delightful letter once, in some newspaper or other during the Vietnam War, in which the writer suggested that it is quite all right to kill people in a civilized society as long as you plan to eat them afterward. No, I do not at all condemn technology, and it is clear that it can help us in many ways. In fact the modern hospice can do a great deal better for its patients, on account of science and technology, than anyone could do at the Hôtel-Dieu in Paris in the eighteenth century. But let me choose another example in all fairness, because it was the condition of the sick and the poor at that time which after all caused the Revolution to begin with. The nurses who worked themselves to death there were trying to deal with a situation which was already, for reasons beyond their control, completely out of hand.

But compare St. Christopher's today with, for example, the really exquisite Hôtel-Dieu in the city of Beaune, a hospice built in the fifteenth century, generously endowed with income-producing lands by its patrons, designed by the finest architects of the day. Its long chapel-ward for the incurably ill and the dying is one of the loveliest rooms ever to be constructed; its courtyards, its tapestries, its galleries—"

"Oh, you are a dreamer! Who pays for all this?"

"Who's paying now?" says his wife. "You are paying, I am paying, we are all paying, not only doctors' bills but insurance this and insurance that and lab fees, and tests that are absolutely useless because the doctors are all afraid that somebody is going to sue them for malpractice if they don't do them. And now we are paying for all those malpractice suits with more insurance, and higher fees, and when we get through all that we have to pay for everybody else, too, when we pay our taxes. If I have to pay anyway, believe me, I'd rather go to some place I like, when my time comes."

"Pass the brandy," says Professor N. "Please. Where is Beaune? That's in the south, isn't it?"

"We never go anywhere," says Mrs. N. "I want to go to India."

"You would not like India, my dear. You imagine that India consists of the Taj Mahal by moonlight and a great many shops for you to buy beads and necklaces in. Like my adversary here, you romanticize; but if you were actually to walk the streets of Calcutta and smell the medieval odors there, you would be appalled, and I would have to prevent you physically from adopting two dozen grimy orphans who—"

"And I would do it, too."

"I know you would. And you would bring them back to

San Jose, California, and set up a hospice for them there, which they would hate—"

"How do you know they would?"

"—which they would thoroughly hate, and would hate you for it, although you would expect them to be very grateful to you. And in ten years' time they would all be on welfare and you, my dear, would be complaining about paying their medical bills. No, let others with stronger stomachs than yours and mine go to India—and in their spare time pore over the ground plans and plumbing systems of medieval hospices (for it is all the same sort of chaos, and smells the same). I meantime will stay in my study with my favorite pipe and reread *The Decline and Fall of the Roman Empire.*"

Applause, and the company moves away from the table, into the living room with its splendid, panoramic view of San Francisco. The hostess brings coffee, and we sink into deep, leather chairs and velvet-covered sofa cushions. Somewhat to my surprise, I find that Professor N. has chosen to sit beside me.

"We were interrupted," he says cheerfully, "by an expert. A very crafty flanking movement by the lady who has cherished me these forty years, though God knows why. She never misses an opportunity to remind me that we do not travel. She does not want to go to India at all, she wants to go to Paris. India was merely a threat, a bargaining point. She knows me well. Now, tell me about technology and the Hospice de Beaune."

"I will, thank you. But first, I want to say that I think you made a very important point about gratitude, which is the downfall again and again of the earnest liberal who, when disappointed, is apt to become the bitterest of all conservatives."

"She allows me to make a point now and then, in public. Of course, I don't give a damn what anyone thinks of me. But she will have her revenge, dear soul that she is, probably in the form of a pregnant cat she has rescued from the pound by late tomorrow, and installed at the foot of our bed. Marriage is a marvelous institution, isn't it? I've never understood why people needed anything else. Well, pray continue."

"My point really was that the care of the dying at a place such as St. Christopher's is a great deal better because of scientific advances than any that could be offered at Beaune in the fifteenth century. The hospice at Beaune offered great cleanliness, compassionate personal care, and spiritual guidance as well as aesthetic grace. But I see two vastly important developments in the modern concept, and one of them has to do with the relief of pain. We know that opium poppies grew in the medicinal herb gardens of St. Gall's in Switzerland as early as the seventh century A.D. and we know that something similar to heroin, morphine, and codeine—all derived from the poppy—was prescribed for severe pain, along with wine and alcohol, of course, in those days. And a sort of polypharmacy was in operation, even if some of its ingredients such as copper filings and the excrement of pigs (sorry!) were not altogether helpful in the long run. And yet we have learned so much better how to mix and combine and prescribe our medicines for pain relief, mainly because of the work done in the modern English hospices. And we are learning how to combine them with recently discovered mood-altering drugs as well as other specifics so as to get maximum comfort for the patient. We have learned various nerve-blocking techniques and we do not weary ourselves anymore—unless of course we are in an acute care hospital—with such things as bleeding and leeching. We have the development of modern technology to thank for this pain relief, and of course it should be used."

"Ah-hah!" says the professor. "Now I have got you. Now I see that this passionate concern of yours is really about pain. It is the neurotic, if I may say so—yes, definitely—the neurotic and totally unrealistic modern fear of pain that is your hidden agenda. You are tenderhearted and sentimental about pain, which is, after all, one of the truly important ingredients of human life. Have you read Illich? Well, then. You say yourself that you admire the warrior, the one who embraces life. Show me the warrior who has never known pain and I will show you a coward. You speak of mood-altering drugs, but how does that differ in any significant respect from submitting to being controlled by the machine? Tell me that and I will listen gladly to anything else you may have to say about hospices."

I look at him and we both burst out laughing. "No, no," he says quickly. "I take that back. We have a long drive ahead of us, and we go to bed early."

"You are making two separate arguments here, I believe. One is about the necessity for pain and the other has to do with being controlled by technology. Well, then—but first, look at that view!" We are on a mountaintop, and far beneath us the city flings its lights across the lower hills. A plane passes over winking its own lights, red and green, against the starry sky, and below, scarved in long, fragile skeins of fog, the place that has been called "The Cool Gray City of Love" lies moving and breathing like a woman asleep, perfumed and dressed in all her jewels.

"It will not rain tonight," says the professor.

"No, I am afraid we shall have to wait for your Flood awhile, and that in the meantime we shall have to do the best we can with human nature. Pain, I agree, is one of the important ingredients in our lives. But what is its importance, and what kind of pain are we talking about? Obviously, the pain of touching fire by mistake is useful in that it signals us to withdraw before we are badly hurt; and the lack of the pain reflex in a leper, for example, is one of the tragedies of the disease. But the pain of terminal cancer is not helpful in this way. Pain can be important spiritually, too. People who have not experienced any of that long-term, excruciating, and presumably hopeless pain—the kind that really annihilates us as human beings—do not know what they are talking about when they use the word *pain*. They are like a pilot in a plane looking down on the fire-bombing of Cologne and thinking it might be nice to toast marshmallows. I like the story about Einstein, who was approached by a philosopher who wanted to persuade him that pain was not real, that it was to be handled as a process of mind over matter. Einstein, without a word, struck him a tremendous blow, knocking him down, and then said, 'Now, tell me what you were saying.' So I agree that pain is in this way instructive. In fact, it might be a better world if all people who prescribed any sort of behavior for others had first experienced a good deal of it.

"However, the pain that too often comes with terminal illness is an utter waste. It does not serve to warn, or to instruct. Instead, it simply blots out, at one of the most important moments of our lives, all ability to perceive, to think sanely, or to be in any way master of the situation."

"Pain has an element of—what is it? Emily Dickinson, I believe," says the professor, and continues quoting:

> Pain—has an Element of Blank—
> It cannot recollect
> When it begun—or if there were
> A time—when it was not—
>
> It has no Future—but itself—
> Its Infinite contain

Its Past—enlightened to perceive
New Periods—of Pain.

"Thank you. Yes. And, of course, she could not have
written that in the midst of the sort of pain I am talking
about. She had to do it from memory. This is the kind of
pain that has no past but itself; it is all present, and no future.
The hospice cares for the future of the patient, and sees
itself as a way station. This is why knocking a person out
with morphine or heroin or whatever, in a hospice, simply
will not serve. The opium den is no place for a pilgrim. Are
you satisfied now that I am talking about the death as well
as the life, in a hospice, of a warrior—in other words, that
I am not being unrealistic, or even tenderhearted?"

"Indeed," he replies, "you are extraordinarily merciless.
My own death is something I would far prefer not to know
about. Give me some opium to put in my pipe when the
time comes, and I will happily smoke it."

"I see. On the other hand, you do not approve of mood-
altering drugs?"

"I approve of everything. It is you who are so particular.
What is the difference between taking these drugs and letting oneself be controlled by all the technology and the
machines you so deplore?"

"I did not make my point clear, then. Let me try again.
What I mean is that human beings should not behave like
machines, or think of themselves as a collection of machine
parts developing squeaks and rattles, and therefore becoming useless, with the onset of a disease or of old age. It is
the thought control of the machine that I deplore, the tendency we have to be brainwashed by them into believing
that we are like them when we are not. Mood-altering drugs
or mechanical procedures to provide relief from chronic,
long-term pain should be available. But they must be ad-

ministered by people who are wise as well as compassionate, so as to bring the consciousness of the suffering individual as nearly as possible to its normal, healthy state—not to produce false euphoria. I see no sense in attempts to seek spiritual enlightenment, for example, via drugs on the deathbed—or anywhere else, for that matter. Chemical euphoria is chemical, nothing more. And I do not think religious experience as an orgasm of the mind can be very authentic when artificially induced."

"A passionate concern," he says. "Yes, a passionate and an evangelical concern: *consciousness is all.* But you do not persuade me to go to a hospice myself or to support the concept, because I strongly suspect that you hospice people really want to tell me how I ought to go about dying, and that I won't have. No, I will die the way I want to die, thank you very much. Oh, I know what you are thinking. You are thinking, 'Good luck to you in the intensive care unit then, old boy'—but after all, perhaps it won't come to that. I may fool you. I may slip on a banana peel tomorrow morning and break my neck and there will be an end to it."

"He is always talking about this banana peel," explains his wife.

"Well, no," I reply, "that was not my thought. I was enjoying your determination to be independent, and thinking of General Grant. You rang very true just then, and you reminded me of a man I saw at St. Christopher's, sitting up sleeping in an armchair late at night with a bottle of port beside him, and a writing tablet on his knees. Which brings me, if you can bear it, to what I promise will be my final point about modern hospices and their improvement over the medieval model."

"Anything is bearable—as long as I don't have to go to Paris. I have been to Paris," he says.

"What I think of as the fully realized modern hospice,

since having experienced it at St. Christopher's, you see, is not merely a medical situation, but a real community. People there are living as well as dying, learning as well as teaching, growing as individuals and as members of a team which is not organized on military or even on purely intellectual principles, but which has all the richness of a loving, caring family life. Now this did not happen at such a place as Beaune—and does not happen at modern nursing homes—because they are specifically set up for the separate and reclusive care of the incurable patient, and the other members of a normal community are not present. To a certain extent, it was a feature of the monastic hospices, because the life in a medieval monastery tended to be quite rich and varied, and yet St. Christopher's has the advantage here of being ecumenical, open to all without respect to religious difference or indifference, and it is not cloistered or enclosed in the monastic sense."

"But you saw what happened at a place like the old Hôtel-Dieu in Paris!"

"This is why we need a great many more first-rate hospices. One place here and another there simply can't do it. Chaos would result if the admissions team at St. Christopher's did not grapple with it—sometimes very painfully—day by day. The integrity of the community is always at stake."

"Community," says the professor, looking down his nose, "is a word that irritates me rather extremely. You seem very fond of it. I had some dreams of my own once, for a sort of group—artists, poets, that sort of thing—and saw it fall apart because of what people are. Community to me means rubbing elbows with a great many individuals I happen to consider peculiarly unattractive."

"You enjoy your friends a great deal, though, I notice."

"Well, of course, they are foolish enough to enjoy me.

Not everyone would. But I myself am not like most people, and I dislike the communal approach to life that tends to put everyone into a mold."

"The sort of community I mean does exactly the opposite, however—that is, it lets each person do things in his or her own way. It is possible to be communal without being communist; in fact, to me, the communist idea is appalling, like trying to make up a human body using nothing but feet, or nothing but hands. A monster results."

"Still, I am a private man, you see, and if I have not been cured of that by my wife, I assure you that no one else will succeed in doing it. She will help you with your hospices, I am sure, and she would probably love to go and work in one or be ill in one, if it came to that. I would rather shoot myself like an old horse and get it over with."

"Well, I am afraid I am being very persistent, but in that case, you of all people I can think of, very definitely need a hospice. I haven't talked at all tonight about the home care programs that a hospice has, but one very important part of the hospice program is a plan to help anyone who wishes to, to stay at home. If you should become desperately ill and beyond cure, a hospice team could help you to stay quite comfortably in your own study with your pipe and your slippers, and you could enjoy once more the downfall of Rome while preparing yourself to die in your own way."

"Who's dying?" says his wife, taking him tenderly by the arm and leaning against his shoulder. "It's time to go home. Nobody's dying. Look at that view! Doesn't it make you just want to take off and fly, all over the whole world?"

"It does not," says Professor N.

"I feel like an astronaut whenever I come up here. What space! Isn't it gorgeous? Look how tiny the city is down there, and yet there are all those people, and what do you suppose they are doing?"

"Murdering one another as usual," he says, "and drinking bad wine."

"Your husband has been very patient with me, Mrs. N.," I tell her. "Professor, I have enjoyed talking with you and I appreciate the challenge of your point of view."

"I think it was very interesting," says his wife. "And I think these hospices sound like a very good idea. So you must tell us more about them sometime, and how to go about getting them started, and I hope we can have a whole lot of them in this country soon exactly like that St. Christopher's. And I will tell you one thing. No matter how long you live with a person and no matter how much you love them, one of you always has to die first and leave the other all alone, and that is terrible. I saw my own mother go through it and she was a wreck. She sat there for years afterward and wouldn't do anything. I can't stand to be alone, I can't even stand to think about it. So I have made up my mind what I am going to do, when one of us dies: I am going straight to Paris."

9

NEW HAVEN

I came up under such a dawn and with so tender a dying
crescent in the sky that I spent an hour in Paradise.
What are these days of glory? . . . I will hope that they
are premonitions, hints granted beforehand of a state to
be attained. At the worst, they are visions of a state lying
all about us, the home of the Blessed . . . the supports
of this life, and we creep from one to another like travellers from inn to inn.

Hilaire Belloc, *The Cruise of the Nona*

It's hard, traveling alone.

Jim Burnham
New Haven, Conn., 1977

*D*riving at high speeds on an unfamiliar highway, behind the wheel of a borrowed car, involves something that might have been identified by early New England
Puritans as religious experience. Consider, for example,
The Day of Trouble is Near, Increase Mather, 1674; *The
Bloody Tenent Yet More Bloody,* Roger Williams, 1651; and
Sinners in the Hands of an Angry God, Jonathan Edwards,
1741. Even so, as I make my way eastward through Connecticut in the early spring of 1977, it is pure joy to see a
rainbow springing from dark snow-clouds ahead, and swallows wheeling in pairs above the marshes that lie outside
the city, so gratefully named by English refugees three centuries ago, New Haven. At least one of the grim, procrus-

tean divines would have understood the deeper springs of this delight, for it was Edwards who wrote, "The beauty of the world consists wholly of sweet mutual consents, either within itself, or with the supreme being . . ." and, "Bodies being but the shadows of beings, they must be so much the more charming as they shadow forth spiritual beauties." Despite his reputation for extraordinary verbal savagery, it was not all gloom and doom with the young Rev. Mr. Edwards. He, too, loved rainbows and birds—and music, and mathematics, and spiderwebs; and it is said that his wife, Sarah Pierrepont, was extremely fond of him for one reason or another, as were their twelve children.

The offices of Hospice, Inc., in New Haven will not be hard to find today; they are temporarily lodged on the grounds of Albertus Magnus College, on Prospect Street. But the contemporary traveler plunging from the parkway into the city's gridlock, rush-hour traffic may feel a hint of the dismay experienced by the English pilgrims when they first landed on these shores. Coming as they did from a milder land, finding themselves suddenly in a place of brutal winters and tropical summer heat—with poisonous plants, snakes, and insects unknown to them, and natives who might or might not be friendly—they banded together in the archetypal pattern of self-defense, setting their backs against the wilderness, and facing one another across a providential and sustaining central green.

Early New Haven had a homogeneity of purpose and manners, was intellectually and architecturally spare, tense, uncompromising. A curator of American archetypes might wish it to be that way still, like the villages of childhood gilt-string bags, with their tiny block-houses and stiff little trees only capable of being rearranged in a limited number of patterns. But, of course, it is not. New Haven today is a far richer brew, less pretty but far more fascinating in its

bizarre juxtapositions. The slick high-rises of corporate industry loom downtown beside the graceful, neo-Gothic
spires of Yale; moldering red-brick mansions of the nineteenth-century urban rich now serve as pocket ghettos, or
display signs claiming them for art, research, commerce, or
social service. Prim, 250-year-old saltboxes perch beside
the most arrogant of Victorian fantasies, which in turn abut
newer structures of steel and colored glass. At the heart of
the ancient village where sheep and cows once grazed, the
Green lies empty now, shaken on all four sides by heavy
traffic, and bleakly regarded by a row of eighteenth-century
churches whose doors are locked, at most hours of day and
night, against twentieth-century crime. Waves of immigrants over the years have assaulted first the Indians' primeval ground, then the Puritan enclosure, bringing with them
the rhythms, fragrances, and social contracts of contrasting
cultures—Mediterranean, Irish, Scots, Eastern and Central
European, African—as well as the determination of each
succeeding group of refugees to take hold, and prosper, and
belong. The history of New Haven is to a remarkable degree the history in miniature of the United States itself; and
so it is appropriate that in this place of refuge for so many
over the years, scarred and marked as it is by human struggle and suffering, the first full-fledged hospice in the country should appear.

The gracious old building (once a private home) in
which New Haven's hospice offices are now located is a
hive of activity. Telephones are ringing, tea is brewing,
typewriters are tapping and jingling, it seems, in every
room. It is the sort of house, with unexpected stairways and
odd rooms hidden away at the back, that children love to
explore; and there are several of them here at the moment,
as well as a baby in a basket in the front lobby, mingling
with the nurses and volunteers who hurry in and out

dressed in jeans, business suits, slacks and sweaters, picking up their assignments for the day. Several young women, nurses and social workers from the Royal Victoria Hospital in Montreal, sit chatting in the lobby waiting for the arrival of Dr. Sylvia Lack, medical director of the hospice. I am taken in hand by Frank T. Kryza II, a tall, bearded young Yale graduate who spouts facts and figures as we race through the hallways, looking for a quiet place to sit down and talk.

The mood here today is one of jubilation. New Haven's Hospice, Inc., a nonprofit corporation as of six years ago, has been serving patients in their homes for the past four years. Now, a $1.5 million grant has been received from the state legislature; and the New Haven group will be able to build an especially designed forty-four-bed inpatient unit for homelike care of those whose needs cannot be met at home. Three million dollars, Frank Kryza tells me, is the fund-raising goal for the new facility. About $500,000 has been received in the form of private and corporate donations (they have had unusual success in reaching corporations). The rest of the funding must come from a combination of state, federal, and private sources. New Haven's hospice has operated for the past two and one half years as a demonstration center for the hospice program under a National Cancer Institute contract. In the next few months they must wean themselves from NCI and begin managing on a fee-for-service basis, trusting that public support will take care of the difference. Will they survive?

It appears likely that they will. Executive Director Dennis Rezendes, an energetic and experienced administrator, tells me a few hours later that insurance executives and legislators are now discussing the necessity for changes in health care reimbursement requirements so that the hospice concept can have more breathing space. Only 6.5 percent of hospice patients in Connecticut are expected to be self-paying; the rest will rely on insurance funds. But coverage regulations are a Catch-22 as they now stand; for example, the average hospice patient is now fifty-nine (and will be younger, when those under sixteen can be accepted) and thus too young to qualify for Medicare—but with an average income too high for Medicaid. Members of this group are eligible for agency home care, but only if it is arranged within two weeks after hospital discharge, and few admissions to hospice care are sought that soon. Rezendes is optimistic, however, about the changes in policy that may soon take place.

"Look, it's happening," he says. "We're doing it. Our people have been doing an incredible job, keeping up to sixty-eight percent of the patients at home. But they've also shown us that we have got to have a backup unit. When the patient needs twenty-four-hour care and constant supervision by physicians, it won't work otherwise. We thought at first we were going to need twenty-two more beds, but we're aiming now for some cottages on the grounds, instead—places where couples or families can stay together temporarily and have our kind of total care yet still have their privacy. There are special circumstances, and, also, some people need privacy at a time like this more than others. The wealthier people are, for example, the more they tend to be isolated even from members of their own families, and are used to depending on hired help for their needs.

"I wondered at first whether people from the old families in the East would go for the hospice concept at all. Have you read Stewart Alsop's book [*Stay of Execution,* 1973]? That was beautiful. He convinced me. Here was a guy from that kind of background, and he has a great passage in that book, telling how glad he was to have the companionship of an ordinary, working-class man, a person he wouldn't have had much contact with under other circumstances, but here he was lying in the next bed, and they were both dying. . . . That was very powerful, very moving. We find hospices answering a real need for all kinds of people when they are in trouble, bringing them together and offering a real sense of cohesiveness in the society. We want to have a teaching center, too, for people who are going to be doing this all over the country, and that will be connected with us, but separate, because teaching and research are not going to take over here. Our job is taking care of the patient's needs, and the family. Anything else we do, fine, but that always comes first."

Public consciousness is ready for hospices now, Rezendes says; and advocates find encouragement in the flavor of the present administration in Washington. In campaign speeches, the president [Carter] has called for "effective and low-cost treatment methods" in medicine, avoiding the "duplication of expensive and underutilized equipment and services." He has also urged insurance companies to "write coverage in such a way that it does not stimulate the use of expensive medical procedures and hospital care when less expensive care will be responsive to patients' needs." *By shifting the emphasis of care to the patient's needs,* a way through the mazes of the existing system can perhaps be found for hospices. Per diem cost of care at the new inpatient unit is expected to be economical, since it will not involve the elaborate machinery of diagnosis and aggressive, acute care treatment. Hospices in the United States will also offer a creative response to the demands of preventive medicine. Studies by Colin Murray Parkes and others have shown that the recently bereaved are at far higher than average risk of developing physical disease or behavioral difficulties, and of having accidents. The skilled counseling, and the spiritual and emotional support offered by a strong hospice community can help a great deal to avoid such outcomes as these.

Now well on the way to achieving the affirmation of government, Hospice, Inc., of New Haven has reached the fourth and final phase of a process described by George Rosen in his comprehensive study, *A History of Public Health.* The first move toward the solution of health care problems, says Rosen, is the recognition by an individual or a small, influential group that the need exists. Second, local experiments are undertaken in an attempt to develop practical solutions. Next, an attempt is made to enlighten public opinion and attract the attention of government; and finally, if the innovative model has proven itself at this level, government action with affirmative legislation will ensue.

The development of the hospice movement in the United States has closely followed this pattern, and the years 1975–77 have seen a sudden explosion of new teams, each now marked with a flag on the large map in New Haven's cheerful, sunlit lobby. As late as the 1960s, hospices were barely known outside the United Kingdom. By 1975 three U.S. teams were caring for patients on St. Christopher's demanding principles: New Haven, Hospice of Marin in California, and an interdisciplinary group within St. Luke's Hospital in New York City. By the spring of 1977 we find approximately six dozen flags on the map, showing hospice activity from Honolulu to Maine and down the East Coast to Florida; through the Midwest to Colorado, North Dakota, and Texas; and then, in clusters of California locations from San Diego all the way up the West Coast. There is also now a National Advisory Council, made up of 124 community leaders and concerned citizens from across the country. It is interesting to find so many hospice teams emerging in California and New York—

traditional sites of innovation and sweeping social changes—but significant also to find the program appearing in such widely differing communities across the map. The fact that New Haven was a jump ahead, a few years ago, may be partly due to the history and nature of the city itself, partly to the intellectual vigor of the university and medical center in its midst; but as usual with pioneering break-throughs, it is due in large measure to plain hard work by extraordinary individuals.

The Reverend Edward F. Dobihal, Jr., clinical professor of pastoral care at Yale Divinity School, and director of Religious Ministries at the Yale–New Haven Hospital, is one of these; Florence S. Wald, former dean of nursing at Yale, another. Ed Dobihal had been concerned for some time about the care of the terminally ill in his ministry and the tendency of modern medical practice to insist upon death-denying, dehumanizing procedures, long past hope of cure. Florence Wald, in the late 1960s, began collecting data on the thoughts and feelings of dying patients in an attempt to refine identification of their needs, and she dis-covered that one of their greatest needs was to be asked such questions, and listened to in return, by people who cared.

When Dr. Saunders came to Yale (as she did several times during the 1960s) to show slides of St. Christopher's, and to explain her methods of patient care, Dobihal, Wald, and a number of others with similar concerns began meet-ing at her forums and soon realized that they were all mov-ing in the same direction, toward a hospice that would be modeled upon St. Christopher's.

Early participants came from different backgrounds, dif-ferent faiths, and different disciplines: founding board mem-bers were Dr. Ira Goldenberg, professor of surgery at Yale; Dr. Morris Wessel, a New Haven pediatrician and author;

Katherine Klaus, R.N.; the Rev. Dobihal, and Dean Wald.
They were joined in early discussions by a psychiatrist, a
Roman Catholic priest, the director of a local nursing home,
other physicians, nurses, social workers, students, community leaders, and members of the clergy, Protestant and
Catholic, Christians and Jews. Socially fragmented as New
Haven now is, in so many significant ways, it has nevertheless managed to find in the hospice a place of "mutual
consents" and common endeavor, rather like the plot of
green that once served to nourish and refresh the original
pilgrims. Jonathan Edwards would be puzzled, no doubt—
but, I think, delighted as well. In a discourse on the Law of
Gravity, sounding much like an early Teilhard de Chardin,
he himself had written of "the mutual tendency of all bodies
to each other. One part of the universe is hereby made
beneficial to another; the beauty, harmony, and order, regular progress, life and motion, and in short all the well-being
of the whole frame depends on it. This is [an example] of
love or charity in the spiritual world."

The spiritual world is recognized as a reality by the
founders of New Haven's hospice. I ask Ed Dobihal to
comment, early the following day, on this aspect of hospice
work. "Our society is not really ecumenical even now," is
his response. "Religious groups exist here side by side, but
as separate groups. This has been an area of some tension
for the hospice from the beginning, but I see it as a creative
tension. Many of us—most, probably—have a religious mo-
tivation for what we are doing, but the way it is expressed
is, in general, very low-key.

"I myself see the hospice as a place of ministry, and as a
place for the consecration of death. But I can't have a satis-
factory conversation about that with a man who has a pain
in his gut and a wet bed at the time. We take care of the
physical, the medical needs first. We do what needs to be

done so a person can start feeling like a human being again. As a matter of fact my wife, Shirley, who is a hospice nurse, probably does more *ministering* in a sense to patients than I do. It was what I would call low-key at St. Christopher's, too. I went there daily when I was in London on sabbatical in 1969, observed, recorded opinions of some sixty to seventy percent of the staff, and filled in for their chaplain. You might expect a difference, with church and state bound up in that society which is so much more homogeneous than ours, in any case. But I startled some of them, when I spoke to their group before leaving, by telling them that they had at St. Christopher's many of the important aspects of a church—the corporateness, the congregational character, and the belonging, caring quality of their operation. Some of them really hadn't thought of it that way.

"Here in New Haven we have people from very different groups working together, and I think one of the reasons we have such esprit de corps even so, is that we haven't grown too large. We have those elements of caring among ourselves very much at hand and visible, though our expressions of it might not be the same down to every last detail. We give each other space, and we don't lean on patients for any kind of conversions, either. If they want to talk about it, fine; if they don't, that's their business. We let them know we are available any time, that's all."

Ed Dobihal sighs, throws his hands up, and makes a tragical-comical face as he reminisces about the long struggle during the 1970s to establish New Haven's hospice. At first, he says, it was committees and committees, meetings, research teams, and task forces of all kinds. St. Christopher's, they were convinced, had the finest model of hospice care available; their methods of operation had to be learned thoroughly, and ways had to be found for translation (pharmacological, psychological, financial) to the

American culture and idiom. Funding had to be found, community relations defined, and the need for a hospice clearly established with local hospitals, medical groups, and social service agencies as well as religious organizations. When they incorporated, Ed became president, and, later, chairman of the board. Grants were received for studies and for education of the public from several foundations. Forums and educational events were held, the media took notice, and volunteers turned up, many of them professionals in the health care fields; but it was not until 1973 when Dr. Cicely Saunders came again to New Haven, having received by now an honorary doctorate of science at Yale, that the group felt prepared to begin caring for patients in their homes.

What they needed now was a hospice-trained person to take on the tremendously demanding and challenging job of being their first medical director. Casting about, they consulted Dr. Saunders, then watched a film she had brought to New Haven, showing a young physician working with patients at St. Christopher's. "How would you like to have Dr. Lack?" she asked. The New Haven group was impressed and excited—so much so, that a telephone call was made on the spot to London, and Dr. Sylvia Lack was persuaded to consider the position.

"They called and asked me," continues Sylvia Lack, taking up the story, " 'how would you like to come out to the States for a year?' It was ten days before I was to take up the job in geriatrics I had always wanted; but I agreed, on Dr. Saunders's recommendation, to talk to them, at least. Then I accepted their offer, not realizing at the time that there would not be patients to work with immediately."

Another grant was necessary before the next step could be

taken; and when the proposal to NCI was written, Dr. Lack carried it down to Washington herself. It is interesting to speculate on the first reactions of people at the National Cancer Institute to the appearance of thirty-one-year-old Sylvia Lack, accompanied by stacks of grant proposals for Hospice, Inc. Blond, bright-eyed, and snub-nosed, she looks like somebody's nice kid sister who is president of the senior class and terribly good at lacrosse. But when she begins to speak, that image shifts, and the person who may have judged her on such a basis is likely to be left feeling more than a little abashed. Dr. Lack is a gentle person, not afraid (like so many British and Anglo-Americans) of emotion, but she delivers her message with unmistakably solid intellectual and professional clout.

"Sylvia Lack," several people have remarked by now, "is our secret weapon." Coming into the community as a fresh face, a foreigner, a woman, and a person accustomed to taking responsibility in a society where 22.5 percent of its physicians are female, she has been able to make herself heard. She has won over many people to the hospice point of view who might otherwise have been disinterested or even, perhaps, antagonistic. In a male-oriented power structure, her approach is comparatively unthreatening; and her crisp manner and her correct, British speech have undoubtedly been an advantage in Anglophile circles here. Sylvia Lack's public lectures often move people to tears, and to reaching for their checkbooks, or coming in to volunteer their services, although she has "rebelled," she tells me, from the chore of public speaking lately, since it interfered too much with her commitment to patient care, and to the support and development of the staff. Among staff, in the words of Dennis Rezendes, "she has promoted an environment for the development of team spirit, partly because in her case, the usual genuflection that goes on between nurse and doctor doesn't take place. She is young, young-looking, and very brainy. She thinks on her feet, and she is extremely articulate."

"How do you manage here, with our democratic habits, after coming from a society more used to the hierarchical ordering of things?" I ask Dr. Lack as we pitch into a pair of large, rather damp hero sandwiches at lunchtime in her office.

"Well, of course, we are a team," she replies with a grin. "But I am kidded a certain amount by staff here—was especially at first—when they sit around for hours muddling through some problem and then they turn to me, and they sigh, and say, 'Well, I guess it's time for one of Sylvia's *team decisions.*' I am in charge, I suppose, very much as Dr. Saunders is in charge at St. Christopher's, but we all work together and do what needs to be done."

"What kind of support system does your staff depend on? Psychiatric? Religious? Sense of community?" Not psychiatric, she replies. She has found the same thing true here that was demonstrated in a recent study at the Palliative Care Service in Montreal's Royal Victoria Hospital. The people who "stick" with hospice work are those (1) with some personal commitment to spiritual values, and (2) outgoing sorts who enjoy helping and caring for others. It is taxing work, and very definitely it isn't for everyone. At a recent meeting, she tells me, she was asked by a member of the general audience what provision was made at New Haven's hospice for psychiatric counseling of the dying, and she replied perfectly seriously, "But, of course, I don't consider dying a psychiatric disease," and, without any intention of doing so, brought the house down. Hospice, Inc., she adds, does have a regular psychiatric consultant who meets with staff and volunteers once a week with an open agenda, and who is available for private consultation if desired.

The culture shock for Dr. Lack has been primarily a matter of finding herself in a society that does not have an old, commonly agreed-upon sense of mutual responsibility among its citizens. She finds it odd that Americans, resenting and fearing government control as they do, are willing to put up with a system in which their vital medical needs are so thoroughly controlled by bureaucratic red tape. Compassionate physicians, she has noted, are apt to find themselves in the position of sending patients back to the hospital on somewhat invented grounds ("We'll just have to put an IV in her") simply because the insurance policy doesn't cover comparatively inexpensive home care of a far more appropriate kind. Hospice of New Haven has managed to keep the majority of its own patients comfortable at home with careful attention to pain and symptom control, and with the use of a variation of the English Hospice Mix.* "We try to maintain an atmosphere of open communication with our patients. We do not press them to talk with us about death and dying but make it clear by our attitude that it is okay to do so. Denial may be a useful and appropriate defense mechanism. If the patient wants to move to greater awareness, we try to give the necessary space and freedom."

"How is it that you are in hospice work, Dr. Lack? Where did it all begin, for you?"

"India," she says. "I grew up there. My father was in business in Calcutta. I remember when I was very small, Mother Teresa's nuns used to come to the kitchen door begging. It was always an event, when they came, and I was

---

* See Clinical Appendix pp. 341–363.

given to understand that this was something important. They really believe, you see, that a person has no right to eat until after the others who are starving have been fed. Then, as a young girl, I worked one summer in an orphanage in the Himalayas." (Here she speaks for a few moments very quietly, carefully, about a Christian "conversion experience" and continues.) "So I was convinced, you see, that I must go to medical school. I planned to study ophthalmology; so many, many people in India are blind, for reasons that are simple to cure. I saw a doctor there with people lined up on the ground, dozens and dozens of them with only a matter of inches between, waiting for him to come and remove their cataracts. His assistants prepared them and then he came along, zip, zip, from one to the next. Then another assistant came and bandaged them up, and soon after that, people who hadn't been able to see for years and years could see perfectly. I thought that was absolutely fabulous. Then in England, during my internship, I found myself looking after the dying patients as interns generally did (the consultants were no longer interested) and I saw them put into the beds at the very end of the long, long ward. And at Grand Rounds, the doctors would come along looking at everyone, but then they would stop just before they came to the last four beds, and turn back. I used to invent questions, anything to attract them to those patients who were dying, but they soon caught on to me. They would say, just before the end of the ward, 'Oh, Sylvia, would you mind . . .' and send me off to do this or that, so as to get me out of the way.

"One patient in great distress there for nine months particularly moved me. She had a great deal of pain, complicated by family problems. Inadequate medicines, not the right sort, and at the same time, the rest of her was not being taken care of. She loved gardening. I thought, after

she died, if only we could have responded to that, set up
a little garden right there for her, all around her bed, what
a difference it would have made. And that is the sort of
thing, of course, a hospice *can* do. During my residency in
ophthalmology, those were people who absorbed me—the
elderly, and those whose sight was deteriorating. I was
fascinated to see the strength in people adapting to stress or
to aging, the power in people whose lives had totally
changed, who had once been full of physical strength and
now were totally unable to help themselves. Still, in such
circumstances, they had such courage and grace. My basic
question, of course, was, *what is a human being?* When I was
at St. Bart's, they sent many of their dying people to St.
Joseph's Hospice, so I found out about that. Then, after the
year's residency, I worked part time at St. Joseph's, part at
St. Christopher's, still intending to go into geriatrics. Just as
I had the position I had wanted, they rang up from New
Haven. As you can see, I am still here."

Very much here she is, and closely in touch, obviously, with
all that goes on at the hospice. Having arrived unexpectedly, I find that my time is beautifully arranged for me by
some magnetic power or other that seems, very often, to
have emanated from the general direction of Dr. Lack's
office. I am given not only introductions and appointments
but photocopied directions for finding the homes of various
people who, as it turns out, were exactly the ones I wanted
to see (and who were, without exception, people who
wanted to tell me their stories). All this is done quite simply, and I am not given an opportunity until after it is all
over to realize what a nuisance I must have been. Stopping
for a moment in the lobby this afternoon to get my bear-
ings, I find myself chatting with a group of volunteers who
have come for "Family Lunch"—many of them bringing

their children with them—and after hearing an outside speaker, have settled down for a sociable hour together.

Sue Cox, coordinator of this program, tells me that she now has a core group of fifty trained people, men and women of all ages, although the hospice has never actively recruited them; most have turned up as the result of educational forums, news stories, or word of mouth. Nine are registered nurses and many more are L.P.N.'s, but all spend eight to ten hours of orientation with her, then do field work under the direction of hospice nurses before being given assignments. Nonskilled people serve in many essential capacities, freeing those who are skilled for more specialized work. All are treated equally with one another and with professional staff. "Volunteers are respected here more than at any other agency I know," Sue Cox tells me, "and this is an important part of our team program. We review our work daily, then meet in a team conference every Tuesday which includes the social worker, the physicians, and all nursing staff. We cooperate with other agencies in the area and they respect us because of the high level of our medical intervention and our nursing skills, but they do wonder, I think, at all our *listening* to patients! And this is why we allow a great deal of latitude in the hours and times our people work. Fifteen of our people may not be working at all during any calendar week (we have a waiting list of more than sixty, and we bring them in as necessary), but it is important for them to have time off, because in the case of the hospice volunteer the gift is so much greater—it is in a very real sense the gift of one's self."

By the front door, a distinguished-looking middle-aged man in tweeds stands talking with a young, very Yale-looking boy of about nineteen. Student and professor, perhaps? Member of the board having a lunchtime visit with his son? Not quite; both of these, it turns out, are volunteers. The older man tells me that he was in business, is now retired. Heard Sylvia Lack speak at Brewster's house [Kingman Brewster, then president of Yale] a while back, was fascinated. "Couldn't understand why they didn't pass the hat, then and there. Plenty of money in that room. Lots of people would have written sizable checks. Got to thinking about it, rather annoyed about it, in fact, so came round here to find the office and make a donation. Been here ever since, working as a volunteer. I do transportation, this and that. Talk to patients, mostly, listen to them. They like to have someone around who isn't in a hurry, and I quit being in a hurry the day I retired. I do this because I enjoy doing it."

"I've decided to go on to medical school now," chimes in the undergraduate. "We can't go on ignoring people who are dying just because we have become a death-denying society. That's got to change, and medicine has to change. I didn't know what I wanted to do with the rest of my life until I worked here, but now, that's no problem."

"What's happening in our medical schools and hospitals these days?" asks Dr. Morris Wessel, clinical professor of pediatrics at Yale University School of Medicine and a founding member of the New Haven hospice. "You walk in the door, you leave your humanity outside." We are seated in his living room, on a quiet street in New Haven, drinking tea. Dr. Wessel is a pediatrician of the sort who makes grown-ups wish they were small again and slightly sick with one of those ailments, like "growing pains," that kids don't get anymore. He would come to the house, put a cold cloth on your head, and you would know that you were loved. Actually, it is well known in New Haven that Dr. Wessel *does* make house calls, despite the fact that he is one of the busiest and most distinguished men in his field.

"Why did physicians stop paying attention to the human side of the patient?" he asks. "Doctors sitting around the place impressing each other, talking about diseases, not human beings. I am tired of it, it makes me sad. How did this kind of ethos get established? Of course I refer my children with leukemia to the specialists, but I help take care of them too. My colleagues often ask me, 'How can you stand being around the parents of a child who is dying, talking to them about the whole thing, and when the child is dead, having to take all the emotional outbursts?' They don't want to get involved. Why not? Of course it is painful, but how can you take care of a child without getting involved, without knowing and accepting the rest of the family the way they are? I take the flak, I *like* taking the flak, because I know it's helping and because that is what I am here for. That's what a doctor can offer at this tragic moment. He can accept the parents and other family members with their bitterness, and still convey the idea that he cares about them. Look, we need to have more G.P.'s in this country, people who deal with medicine as a whole, who deal with families as a whole. We need to stop separating our professional functions into little niches in the hospitals and in the medical schools, in the office or home. Doctors and nurses need to see the results of their work; and the young doctors today need to understand that human beings die. It happens; that's reality. They should be rotated through a hospice on a regular basis, let them see firsthand what it's all about."

"Doctors can't do everything," says his wife, bringing a plate of cookies. "Sometimes I think we expect too much of them."

"I'm not blaming doctors," he says. "I am blaming the system, the ethos of it, the way medical education is being presented these days to the students coming along. It is so clearly said, if not by words, by actions, 'Look, if you're going to be a doctor, you'd better stop being human here and now.' The students who really care about their patients are often looked down upon. That's just crazy.''

The telephone rings and the Wessels' teenage daughter, in bathrobe with hair newly washed, backs through the living room slowly, answering it, greeting the guest, continuing then to talk into the phone as she works her way toward the privacy of an adjoining room, with a cord of some seventy-five feet following her; then she disappears. This moment, somehow so much a part of the warmth of this home and of the welcome I have received from hospice people in New Haven, stays in my mind long after. You walk in the door and you bring your humanity with you when you work with hospice people; and this is true, whether you come as a physician, as a patient, as a volunteer, or as a nurse, or just as a visitor.

Gray trees, gray fields, gray sky, flurries of snow against the windshield; midstate Connecticut wan and dim now, as I drive north for an appointment at an address in what is now known as a "planned community" in the midst of many gray trees, gray hills. Patti Ruot, L.P.N., one of the nurses who has been with New Haven's hospice since its early beginnings, has just moved here with her young family. "What is a human being?" Sylvia Lack asked, tending the dying in London. In much the same frame of mind I now wonder, "Can a community be planned?" It is centered, I see, around a park, and spaces that will be green in the spring, and that can be shared. A good beginning, but can we come together in the geographical sense, for a grab bag of individual reasons, and then be transformed into a community? And if so, by what alchemy? The pressures of need and danger have been known to do it; many Americans, for example, discovered for the first time during the Depression, or during World War II, that they had neighbors. Must it be war or the equivalent of it in some crisis that brings us spiritually together? Or is it possible that peaceable ways can be found, simply in the natural course of things? "Sweet mutual consents" are certainly less likely than they might be, in a society that refuses to acknowledge the reality of death. Interdependency doesn't happen among people, each of whom believes that he is immortal in present form, so long as the medical factory keeps on supplying him with spare parts.

The dark side of the Puritan mind was perhaps a necessary adjunct to that extraordinary, luminous vision of life in all its beauty and richness that we also find in the best of the early New England writers. Edwards saw the lilies of the field and described the sounds of music with almost hallucinatory brilliance, filled with a sense of their fragile impermanence as matter, and their real, secret meanings as vibrations moving toward us from the world beyond death. In this, whatever we may think of his politics, he was as modern and as radical as our nuclear physicists, with their charmed quarks; and he would have no trouble understanding the radically spiritual dimensions of a modern hospice community.

"It is a spiritual thing," Patti says of hospice, "because it is a way of life, really. It isn't just a job. And I don't mean spiritual because of the clergy who are involved; I think there has been a lot of teaching *of* clergy here, as well as *by* them. But it is the feeling we have of absolute commitment to each other and to our patients in a different way from what you find in any other place. We are close to death all the time, and people ask me if that isn't depressing, but it really is not. Sad, but not depressing. The closer you are to it, the less you fear it. I feel like a daughter in the families where I've helped, or a sister. You know, when you are a nurse, you are supposed to be objective, do a job, not get involved, and look at your watch. We have to write down all the hours we work, the travel time, even the charting time, so the records can be kept straight, but it is very hard for us to remember to do that in hospice work. Time isn't important. You do what is needed, and if a person needs you then and there, you simply don't leave. People don't stop dying at five o'clock. I've seen some beautiful things happen within our families."

Patti's son, Brian, five, is dashing in and out as we talk, collecting mittens, reporting on the depth of the snow, and bouncing from time to time on the sofa beside his mother, while Melissa, eighteen months, gurgles in her playpen, gnawing rubber toys. I ask Patti to describe the nursing system at hospice, and she gives me facts, but this is not really what she wants to talk about. There are the equivalent of sixty-two nurses full time on staff; they work rotating shifts and are on call. Patients can be referred by anyone, but must have clearance from their private physician to be accepted on our program. A nurse visits the family to do an assessment visit, and if the family is admitted, he or she then becomes the family's primary care nurse, for continuity. Someone must be in the home, either family or friend, to help; and the patient must be geographically near enough to New Haven for close supervision.

"Let me tell you about some of the great people I've taken care of," says Patti. "There was a wonderful old lady who was so confused when we first went in, she thought she was in a nursing home. And she said, 'Look at this terrible, dirty place they have left me in,' but it was her own home. Well, we figured out what the matter was—mainly, just being lonely and having no one treat her like a human being—and we got her on the right medicines and got her resocialized to the point where she used to sit up and watch TV with me and argue politics. She was really sharp. I'll never forget her.

"Then there was one family, they were Italian, and they had the old grandpa right there in the kitchen with them while they were cooking, laughing, and singing, and he was part of the whole thing, while he was dying." Patti is nursing the baby now, and young Brian hurls himself onto her lap, thrashes around until he gets a hug, then settles on her knees. "Everything was going on all around him, and the last night I knew he wasn't going to make it, so I said I would stay. When we do that, it's called a 'bed-down visit.' It was time to wash him, and his daughters helped me turn him over, but I thought I had better tell them he was so weak that even a little motion might stop his breathing, because I didn't want them to feel guilty about it if they were doing something when he died. . . . Yes, Brian, he was dying, this very nice old man, and so I was taking care of him, that was the reason. Well, we did turn him, and he stopped for a minute, but then he started up again when we turned him back, very hard breathing (Cheyne-Stokesing is what they call that), so we knew the end was very close. I was so glad to see the daughters and the others weren't at all afraid. They were sorry, they were sad, of course, but they understood it was a perfectly natural thing. Having a chance when you are a family member to take care of the one who is dying is very important, I think. Then later in the night, he did stop breathing. His two daughters just lay right down next to him, and hugged his body as if they were keeping him warm, and they cried, but they weren't afraid of the body, or of knowing that he was dead. That's the way it ought to happen.

"I am technically retired, temporarily that is, because once you really get into hospice work, you never retire, but

I have to wait until the baby is a little older before I can go back, even to part-time work. It's ideal for me because I can do it part time and still be really involved. It is so reassuring, too, knowing that the next person from the hospice is going to give your patient exactly the same care, and you don't have to worry about them the way you do in ordinary nursing. I go down for meetings in New Haven all the time now, as it is. I can't stay away. And I go to see my patients and some of the families of my former patients. You might say it is 'bereavement work' when I go to see the family, but we go through so much together, those people are like my own family to me, and I couldn't *not* go.

"I find the physical care of the person who is dying is the thing that helps them to feel close to you and really trusting. It is when we are giving a bath or a backrub, so often, that the patients suddenly want to confide. They tell us about all kinds of things, like one young mother who was so angry about dying, she was so young, why did it have to happen to her? She was upset about her body image, kept worrying about how unattractive she must be to her husband, wanted so much to live until her daughter graduated from school. I was able to share that, and give her some help with it because I was right in there with her in the situation, in the physical reality of what was happening. I wasn't just talking at her from some other place. People ask me, 'What do you say to them, Patti?' and I don't know how to answer that. I don't have any formulas, and I don't have any solutions, really. It's just a matter of being as honest as I can and of really being there. One woman asked me, 'What's it like to die?' and she was crying and crying. I said, 'I can't honestly tell you because I haven't died,' and I just hugged her for a long time, and we both cried. I have cried many times with my patients, but it doesn't give me a sense of being pulled down, but of being lifted up. Just feeling so much and sharing so much with them, it makes you know you are incredibly lucky to be there, and to be able to help in any little way." As Patti says, you have to be a hospice person; it isn't just a job. . . .

"A hospice person" seems to be one who knows instinctively how to make others feel welcome in the universe. As Henri Nouwen says, it is a matter of giving space, really— space in which people can be themselves. "Dying with dignity" is rather an unfortunate phrase, for what if a person isn't dignified by nature, or does not wish to give a dignified performance at such a time? Are we not *dignified,* in the true sense, merely by being human: that is, *elevated* in some mysterious manner, not of our own doing, to the charmed condition of consciousness? (Must we be pompous about it and continent, and keep our teeth in straight at all times as well?) Contact with the living is, of itself, contact with life that is already in the process of dying; but contact with those who are about to make the final passage is a privilege not to be judged in ordinary terms. Against the dark, these lives blaze when given a little space, held tenderly; and the people fortunate enough to be truly present for the event are illumined by it.

It was a dying man, in fact, who in giving publicly the gift of self—though he had never until that moment been a public sort of person—may have done more than any stack of statistical arguments, or any of the perfectly healthy individuals involved, to tip the balance for New Haven's hospice when in 1976 they sought permission to build their inpatient unit in nearby Branford. The life and the death of Eugene Cote, U.S. Navy (retired), a quiet man, self-sufficient and independent by nature, will be remembered gratefully, as a result, by many who never knew him. Finding my way tonight over the parkway and down into the little town that is in so many ways still an eighteenth-century village, with crooked streets meandering and proudly floodlit, steepled churches, I see that I am, ten minutes away from New Haven's noise and bustle, suddenly in the heart of old New England, in a solid community very much aware of its past. Yet these are the people who led Connecticut into the fray when a computer in Washington denied funds for this new and innovative model of health care in America; they bombarded the Commerce Department with angry protests and pleas for reconsideration of the project. The people of Branford know what a hospice can do, and they want to have theirs, not tucked away behind a hospital in downtown New Haven, but here in their midst, on a residential street and across from a public grammar school.

Eugene Cote's widow, Barbara, and their two teenage sons, Michael and Robert, welcome me like an old friend into their home: I have come to hear the story of hospice care as they themselves, very directly, have experienced it. At 9:00 P.M., Barbara has come from a meeting of her choral group, tired, she says, but looking fresh and energetic, a sturdy and attractive woman, blond, expansive in her gestures, and obviously loving, not only to sing, but to talk. "I don't know what we would have done without the people from the hospice," she begins. "I don't know how to tell you what it was like before they came. You see, he had a heart attack, and his heart was bad, and then when they found his cancer—Michael, Robert, when was it Daddy went to the hospital and had the radiation treatment?—Yes, 1973, and because of his heart, they didn't dare operate. So he came home and he used to lie on that couch right there where you are sitting, and it was terrible. The pain was so bad, and he was a brave man, but if you touched him even very lightly or if he had to move, he would scream. The boys and their sister, Patty, were younger then, but they would take turns staying up with him all night, every night, trying to help him. He had chemotherapy, too, and it went on and on, and then the VA people finally recommended the hospice. We had heard of it, but we really didn't know what it meant. They came right in, Dr. Lack came, and Patti was our nurse. It was like the difference between night and day. It was a whole new life beginning then, for all of us. They never made any false claims. They said, we will help you all we can and we will kill this pain for you—and they did. Gene started taking the Hospice Mix every four hours at first and then he started feeling so much better, he only had to take it every six hours.* Finally it was down to eight. For about a year then, it was absolutely amazing. He was like his old self again. He was alert, he joked and took an interest in everything, and he went uptown every day to see all his pals. I saw a real change in him then, in his outlook on life. He had always kept to himself, but now he was being so much more out-going, looking at the other person's point of view, being so much more responsive to those outside the family circle. It was really wonderful to see him enjoying life that way, taking it day by day, because, of course, we knew the cancer was in him, all that time.

"Well, the time came when the people from the hospice were here in our town before the planning and zoning commission and they were asking for approval so they could put their inpatient building here. We went to that meeting, Gene and I. Some people didn't know what the hospice movement was about, and we heard some other people say it was gruesome, or sad, and they didn't want it around. We heard and saw one architect explaining his

---

* See Clinical Appendix, pp. 341–363.

plans, and it looked as if some people weren't really sure how they were going to vote on it. Then suddenly Gene stood up—I have never been so amazed in my life, because that wasn't like him, to push himself into the limelight—and he said, 'I am one of those terminally ill cancer patients the hospice is taking care of. . . .' He actually said those words, *terminally ill.* Well, you could have heard a pin—you could have heard a *feather* drop in that room. Then he went on and told what it had meant in his own life, having their care, and when he was through, then I got up.

"I don't even remember what I said. I guess I told what kind of a change this meant for the rest of us, knowing we could count on those people twenty-four hours a day. And you know one time, close to the end, I called them and said, I just can't handle it. I told the exchange I needed more help. They all wear those 'beepers' so you can reach them, and I hadn't turned around and walked up the stairs again before the telephone was ringing: 'What can we do for you?' It is the literal truth, there was an ambulance at our door fifteen minutes later. Well, knowing that, having that to count on, it changes your life. The people at the VA were wonderful and I love them, they helped us a lot. But what a hospice does is just entirely different. Well, you know how the vote went, and thank God, because if there had been a hospice inpatient unit for Gene right at the end, it would have been so much easier.

"But they didn't have it built yet, so we had to go back to the hospital. You know, in the hospital, they take your medicines away and then they do a workup, that's the way they have to do it there. He was in such terrible pain then, I couldn't stand it. He had told me, sitting right there, that he didn't want any 'artificial life' when the time should come, and he had time then to teach me all the things I needed to know about insurance, and where the papers were, taxes, all that—what he wanted done—and believe me, that is important. But it is one thing to hear that in your own home when you are feeling safe, and another thing to bring it up in the hospital. Then he had a stroke, couldn't talk at all, and how could I be sure? The hospice nurses came right in to the hospital and taught me how to communicate with him, asking him to squeeze my hand if he meant, 'Yes, I do want to go the way we have agreed.' I could see him trying so hard, so hard to squeeze my hand, and then he did. I knew it was right then, and the minister said I should respect his wishes; the doctors were good to us and didn't make him stay in the ICU anymore. I sat with him at the end thinking about the good times, hoping he was remembering them too, like the trip we took that last year down the Blue Ridge Mountains. He was getting much weaker by then, and without the hospice, we never could have made it. And our twenty-fifth wedding anniversary, too, that same year—what a celebration we had. We wouldn't have had that, either. I have a lot to be thankful for, twenty-five good years.

"I was very tired when it was all over, I had trouble sleeping—me, having trouble sleeping, I couldn't believe it! And I kept getting sick, little things, colds one right after another. That was when I found out how much it means, not being dumped by the people who have been all through it with you. If I don't call up the hospice office, they call me pretty soon, or come around to see how I am. Patti and the rest of them are all like a part of this family now, and I love them in a way that is really something special."

We talk about the larger community around the Cote family now, Barbara's church, her many close friends and neighbors; she is an exuberantly warm and outgoing person who loves her job teaching in grammar school, enjoys all of her contacts in the community and is obviously loved devotedly in return. Yet even under such circumstances, it has been all-important to her that the hospice offered support and companionship at the deepest of levels, during the time of struggle and bereavement.

"How do you feel about having the hospice unit just across the street from the school?" I ask her.

"I think it's wonderful," she replies with enthusiasm. "They will be able to look out the window and see the children playing, and hear them going by. And the kids should be encouraged to get involved, too. Dying is part of life, and they should know it isn't something secret and awful, or something that has to be hidden. Hospice patients are comfortable and they are alert to such a degree that I can't think of a better way for young children to be introduced to this whole subject than by seeing them and mixing right into the same neighborhood with them."

It is hard to leave this pleasant home, and the people in it. One does not merely "interview" individuals under such circumstances and then depart. Given such gifts of self, the inquirer becomes part of the process, and is bound into the hospice way of creating community.

The following day, in another part of the state, I am given the opportunity to speak privately with a hospice patient before beginning my long journey home. Jim's traveling days are over now; his journey takes place behind the closed door of a room in his mother's house in a quiet suburb where he has come to die. My world and his are entirely different today—or so it might seem—and yet I know that something significant will happen between us during the hour we spend together: a melding, an interchange of roles, a shared glimpse, perhaps, of what lies beyond. There is no way for this to be planned ahead of time, or forced, or even coaxed from the circumstances. The process called "hospice" is as mysterious as electricity. Like lightning you wait for it, and then you forget to wait for it. Then it happens.

The sign on the door says KNOCK LOUD, and so I do. An annoyed voice tells me to come in, and to shut the door behind me. I do that. Dark eyes, dark hair, a young, tanned body bare from the waist up, knees jackknifed on pillows, a thin cotton blanket over him. A hospital bed, although this is a private home in a modest, residential tract. Trapeze above the bed, at arm's reach; also at arm's reach around the bed, books, stereo, CB radio, filing cabinets, plants, a small refrigerator, pictures, trophies, musical instruments, shelves packed with papers, notebooks, mementos. He appears to be about twenty-five, angry. Very angry. Expecting me, of course, and now fully prepared to tell me a thing or two. We shake hands, I sit down, and we look at each other.

"The first thing you'd better know," he says, "is that I am not terminal. I am a very, very rare case, and I am an exception. I am not going to die. I have cancer, all right, but I am not licked and I have two different biopsies to prove they don't know what in hell is really the matter with me. What I need is for someone to pay attention to the fact that I am not like other people and do something about it, and I will talk to anyone and go anywhere and they can use me as a guinea pig if they want to, but I want them to see that I am not a typical case at all, I am something else. It started in my back. I went to a chiropractor because I had this pain in my back and he just shifted it down lower. Then my van and I, we went to California. I had a good little rock group going and I was the manager—I used to be the drummer but I got pushed out of that because I was a better manager than the rest of them and California was good to me, but it gave me cancer. I found out I had it at UCLA. I went to the hospital there, and they told me I had a choice of—Hey, I'm going to tell you the whole thing and I want this on tape, why aren't you using tapes?"

"I'm sorry, I never use tapes with a patient."

"Why not? I'm not ashamed of anything; I've got nothing to hide. Look, you can tell the whole world about me for all I care; maybe somebody will come up with a way to cure me then. Use my name. The guy from the newspaper already did a story on me, he used tapes."

"I guess I listen better without."

"Well, suit yourself, but get it straight that I am not a quitter and I have not given up on this thing. *I know how fast people lose interest in you in this world when you're not fighting.* They told me at UCLA I could have this operation where they would cut off my leg and cut a whole lot up around my hip, too, and if I didn't want to do that, then there was nothing else they had in mind. Well, I wasn't about to let them do that kind of shit on me, so I told them, look, I'm going somewhere else. You say even that won't definitely cure me, why should I go for that? So I went to this place in Chicago, then to New York at Sloane-Kettering; I was in there for two weeks . . ."

Fast and furiously he goes on, telling of his pilgrimage, back and forth across the country in his van, which is parked now in front of the house, which he cannot drive anymore. The disagreement of two doctors (he shows me the letters), the correspondence with the Mayo Clinic, the trips to Mexico, finally, smuggling Laetrile (no change that he noticed), then becoming weak, exhausted, having to come home.

"I'm independent," he says. "I'm a loner, always have been. Dad walked out on us when I was a little kid, and I was his oldest son. I changed my middle name that was the same as his, but it isn't anymore. I don't need him. I don't need anybody. I am the kind of person, I don't owe any-

body any money, they all owe me. Lying here like this—
I've been flat on my back now four and a half weeks—is
going to drive me nuts, and I am trying to control my diet
so I get plenty of protein and vitamins and good stuff, but
it costs, and that is really hard on the rest of the family." He
pauses, lights up a thin, small cigar, and takes a long look
at me in silence. Finally he says, "You want to see it?"

"Yes, if you don't mind."

"I don't mind. Have a look." He pulls the blanket down
toward his knees. It is a very large, rather pale swelling all
around the area of his left hip, firm and smooth to the touch.

"Are you in pain?" I ask.

"Not now, but I will be. Later. The pain now is in my
head, thinking how maybe there is a way to cure this, and
it's just nobody knows, and by the time they find out, it will
be too late. Some doctor in New York was going to do this
radiowave treatment on me and I thought a month ago that
was going to be it, they would just get that thing going and
melt it all down and then I would shit it out of me, if that's
the way you get rid of cancer. They carried me on a
stretcher down to New York, my friends did, but when I
got there this man just said they weren't going to try it on
me after all. He was really cold about it too, just said no.
Not that I blame him, somebody probably just put him up
to it and he had to be the one to say it, but that was a really
bad moment for me. I can't play drums anymore. I used to
be a really good drummer, we had a good little group. I
tried bongos, but I couldn't do that either. Then I thought,
maybe I could take up the guitar. I'm just too tired. No, I
don't mean tired now, and don't try to help me fix the
blanket because you don't know the right way to do it, and
I will just have to do it all over again. You know Dr. Lack?
I like her a lot. Yeah, these hospice people, they're all right,
they don't try and fake you out on anything and they don't

lay any trips on you, but that don't mean I'm giving up. That'll be the day, when I give up. My grandfather, he died of cancer and he never said a thing about it to my grandmother. She just found out at the very end when she saw, you know, the blood. I try to keep myself in shape.

"Look at my chart," he says, lying back, slowing down a little now, closing his eyes from time to time. "It's all there. Dr. Lack came over a couple of weeks ago and I got started with that stuff she gives. Before that I was popping methadone by the handfuls and it wasn't doing one damn bit of good. I give myself shots now, they taught me how, but I hate to stick myself with a needle and I hate any kind of drugs, I saw too much of that when I was in the rock scene, people on hard stuff, wrecking their lives, blowing their minds out; I smoke some in the afternoon—marijuana, I mean—because it helps me to keep up my appetite and I have got to keep that up. Look, you want to see the pipes I made? I carved them myself, I used to sell them. Over there is a picture of me, I'll bet you don't recognize me, that was two years ago. I was in pretty good shape then. Now I really think I am getting tired."

"I'm going in just a minute."

"Did you see that trophy? That was for being the CB operator that came from farthest away—no, up there, on top of the refrigerator, you're looking the wrong way, turn around—that was when we all got together and I was the one who came from the farthest. I always did like to win. I've traveled a lot. There was a girl—well, there were a lot of girls, but not too many. I traveled a lot, I kept moving. I guess I've been almost everywhere in the good old U.S.A. there is to go, now that I can't go anyplace any more. I see you notice that crucifix over my bed, well, that doesn't mean I am religious, that just means someone put it there. I went to catechism a few times, then I cut out and didn't

go, so the priest came and said if I just came for the last
lesson, they would let me be confirmed, and I thought, what
kind of a deal is that, it can't be worth much if it's that easy,
if they want you that bad to get into it, so I said no, thanks.
So I am not religious. I don't believe in all that hell and
punishment kind of stuff either." He is speaking very slowly
now, with eyes closed. The little room is very close, the air
is dense. He kicks at the end of his blanket, I try again to
help him with it, he looks at me and smiles. "When I die,"
he says, "I am going to be cremated. Or maybe I shouldn't
do that, maybe I should donate my body instead so they can
figure out what the diagnosis was. But then, even if they
find out, I will never know, will I?"

"Maybe you will."

"Maybe I'll be reincarnated and come back as a dog or
something, that would be funny, wouldn't it," he says, un-
smiling.

"No, not a dog. You're a drummer." We both laugh. I
am putting on my coat. His eyes are very tired now; he puts
one hand up to his forehead, touching himself as if asking
a question with his fingertips.

"You are going to California tonight?"

"Yes. I wish I didn't have to, but I must."

"Say hello to California for me," he says.

"I will."

We say a few more words, shaking hands, telling each
other that we will keep in touch. "Thanks so much," I tell
him. Then, standing by the door, having forgotten by now
long ago about rainbows and quarks, about charm and vibrations, lightning and lilies of the field, I suddenly hear him
speak to me in a voice so tender and gentle, it is like the voice
of a lover, or of a mother speaking in private to her child.

"Take care," he says. "You have a long way to go, and
it's hard, traveling alone."

10

APPLE ISLAND

The old order changeth, yielding place to new,
And God fulfills himself in many ways,
Lest one good custom should corrupt the
    world. . . .
But now farewell. I am going a long way . . .
To the island-valley of Avalon;
Where falls not hail, or rain, or any snow,
Nor ever wind blows loudly; but it lies
Deep-meadow'd, happy, fair with orchard lawns
And bowery hollows crown'd with summer sea,
Where I will heal me of my grievous wound.

                                    Alfred, Lord Tennyson

*I*n ancient Welsh mythology, Paradise was *Ynys yr Afallon,* which in translation is "The Isle of Apples," or *Avalon;* and it was to that magic island that the black-draped barge brought King Arthur, mortally wounded, after the last battle of the Knights of the Round Table. Avalon was the kingdom of the dead, and yet at the same time it was a healing place, happy and fair with orchard lawns, and if in those orchards apples grew, they were a symbol from times long before the beginnings of Arthurian legend, of fertility, natural renewal, and human love. Arthur had seen the end of his noble dream of a community pledged to the highest of chivalric ideals; destroyed from within, the old order failed after its brief flowering at Camelot. He himself

was near death—and the historical Arthur, a military chief-
tain and cavalryman, may have been buried at Glastonbury
in the west of England long ago. Yet in the minds of the
poets who sang his story, his ultimate destiny was one of
mystery, in which dying itself was seen as a journey toward
the island where he would be healed.

From Devon and Cornwall in the west, those starlit lands
soaked through with centuries of Arthurian legend, came
many of the tough, seafaring Yankees who first settled on
America's northeastern shores. Some of our early colonists
were chivalric, but many of them, unfortunately, had ideas
about the "New Jerusalem" they planned to found in the
wilderness that were anything but noble or kind. Survival
of the fittest, though not then a familiar phrase, was a
rule invested in early New England with all sorts of self-
righteousness and piety. The widow and the orphan were
not subjects for gallantry here; they were social misfits. If
they were ill as well as useless, then many of their neighbors
were ready to assume that it was their own fault. Good
health and material prosperity were, especially in the eyes
of second- and third-generation Puritan immigrants, a sure
sign of heaven's favor. Poverty, illness, and other forms of
social impotence were proofs of sin, and of punishment by
the wrathful Jehovah they invited to preside over their
narrow and obsessive, almost paranoid, readings of the Old
Testament. When plague and pestilence struck, "God's
Controversy With New England" by Michael Wigglesworth (1662) expressed the attitude of the time:

> One wave another followeth,
> And one disease begins
> Before another cease, because
> We turn not from our sins.

The idea of quarantine (literally, forty days of isolation)
for contagious diseases was by now a very old one and was

practiced, particularly in the seaports of the Western world, as a practical measure for the promotion of public health. "Foul vapors," "boggy places" and such were generally thought to cause disease, and germs were not yet understood, but it was common custom to separate victims of ailments like plague or smallpox, when possible, from the rest of society. To this separation and quarantine our early colonists could not help adding, because of their religious beliefs, a sense of moral rebuke. Foul sins, they thought, must have caused their neighbors to fall ill in this new land so pure and clean (as it was then), and the agony of disease and the shame of death were their punishment.

Under the circumstances, it is not hard to imagine the feelings of such a person as the Widow Paige of Boston when, on June 20, 1702, selectmen of the little town discovered that she and her family had smallpox. According to public health records of the day, a warrant was issued, soldiers came to her door—perhaps she had time and energy to gather up a few personal possessions or food and bandages to bring with her—and the family was loaded into a boat and banished forthwith. Had she tried to hide herself away, we wonder—kept the children behind curtained windows while she heard echoing in her ears the terrible sermons of the day? Had she bargained with God for the life of her youngest who, though "born in sin," had surely not yet learned to practice even the smallest cruelties? Was she a widow because her husband had already died of the disease, and if so, should she have nursed him in his loathsomeness or abandoned him to heaven's wrath? How strange it is, knowing what we do about the deeper meanings of the name, to find in the old public health records of Boston that the place of isolation chosen for Widow Paige was a nearby spot called Apple Island.

There, in the warm June sun with clear salt water to bathe

their ravaged bodies in; with fish to catch, clams to dig, wild fruits, and the air around them as yet unpolluted with cancer-producing chemicals, perhaps the widow and her family managed to recover, if not their moral credibility, at least some measure of physical health. But whether they lived or died on Apple Island, surely some inner healing must have resulted from their stay. It was sanctuary for such a group merely to be removed from the suspicion and contempt of their neighbors. And islands by their very nature, as all travelers know, have a way of luring the human mind out of old habits, sending it on farther, freer journeys.

Many sick people, of course, in the early colonies, were cared for at home by women who had learned from their mothers the ancient lore of herbal medicine, growing these "simples" in their kitchen gardens and adding to this heritage whatever could be learned from local Indians. The trick was to do it well enough to survive, and to help your family and your neighbors survive, without being taken for a witch. Until the mid-eighteenth century, American families were expected to care for their own minor ailments. If afflicted with something contagious, however, they were likely to be brought to a makeshift hospital or "lazar-house" that was actually a military fort with soldiers standing guard. The first general hospital for the care of ordinary citizens was founded in Philadelphia in 1751 under the auspices of Benjamin Franklin, who vastly enjoyed the political sleight-of-hand he employed in getting people to open their purses for it. Seeing that there was not enough money available, either in the public treasury or in donations from the rich, Franklin invented the device so often repeated since, and so peculiarly American, of "matching funds." Thus began the tradition of medical philanthropy that has continued to this day in the United States: one part practical benevolence and another consisting of a profound dislike for, and suspicion of, government control.

Incurable patients and those with contagious diseases were specifically excluded from this and other early "voluntary" hospitals in America, and a great deal of fuss was made over the distinction between the "deserving poor" who could not receive proper care at home and those judged "undeserving" of hospital care on moral grounds. It is interesting to find that the stated reason at the time for a public hospital to be built in Philadelphia was that, by now, too many strangers were wandering about with no one to look after them. The situation harks back to the opening of Fabiola's place of hospitality in the first century A.D., and to the tradition whereby pilgrims were welcomed, ill or well, in the medieval monasteries. Ben Franklin was himself a devout Christian, though he evidently bent the rules a bit whenever he had an opportunity to go to Paris; but he was also a wily politician and a supremely practical man. He chose exactly the right sprinkling of theological persuasion to sweeten his fund-raising appeals, reminding his fellow Yankees that these sick strangers "may possibly one Day make part of the blessed Company above, when a Cup of cold water given to them will not be unrewarded." If he had suggested bread and wine, fine linen, and silver goblets, after the fashion of the Knights Hospitallers, one wonders what might have happened. As it was, the image of Lazarus at the gates prevailed, well buttressed by a system of moral judgments and political-economic checks and balances. Franklin's campaign was a great success.

So it was with mixed motives and attitudes that our American system of hospital care for the sick came into being. Part fortress, part place of refuge for the "respectable" poor and potentially useful strangers, the American hospital has been, above all, a pragmatic response to the health care problems of society. During the nineteenth century, special hospitals for particular conditions appeared; and notions of hygiene improved to the degree that people with contagious diseases were now received into the general hospital for palliative care and, if possible, for cure. With the tremendous scientific advances of the past century, and the growth of research and teaching centers connected with our great, modern hospitals, the medical establishment has come to serve people at every level of society in ways undreamed of by early settlers. Medicine has become Big Business in the United States today, accounting for more than 10 percent of the Gross National Product, plus an ever increasing bureaucratic substructure, and a more and more phenomenal amount of sheer paper work.

Not to be put into the same ward as the Widow Paige, when we have come into the hospital for open-heart surgery or merely with a broken leg, is part of what we pay for when we deliver our bodies to the modern medical factory. We expect and demand hygienic conditions; and despite the continuing problem of infections lurking within the system, standards of protection in U.S. hospitals are probably the highest in the world today. So are the prices we pay.

And we pay a cost for hospital services in human terms, as well. Making our way—if we can—past the bloody battle-ground of the local emergency room, where exhausted interns and nurses try to stem the onslaughts of drug-related trauma and despair, we find ourselves held in a curiously prisonlike detention. The ancient Puritan attitude of moral rebuke is now unspoken, unrecognized, perhaps, but it is there in the way in which we are stripped, handled, numbered, and labeled, given isolation without privacy, and sterility without the sort of cleanliness that is refreshing to the soul. Our days in the hospital are numbered for us now by computer. We ourselves are not consulted; instead, decisions about our injuries and diseases are made via "DRGs" (diagnostic related groups) and "CBRs" (cost benefit ratios). And if we fail to be cured rather rapidly in this sort of environment, we are all too often treated as pariahs, exiles from grace, and banished to a world of misery and pain far, far less hospitable than Apple Island.

Very few individuals are now sent to hospitals for rest or convalescence, or, if they should be admitted for such a purpose, would find it a restful experience. And yet, too often we ship off our dying to the hospitals simply because they are dying, and we assume that this is what we ought to do. The reason for this is not so simple as the fact that we are afraid of death, and do not want to watch what happens when a person dies. The development of the medical establishment in the United States has woven a web of circumstance around us, leaving us feeling ill-equipped and unable to assume personal responsibility when the death of a loved one is near. In the "old days" the family doctor or general practitioner was available to come to the home daily to help the patient remain as comfortable as possible there with regular doses of powerful opiates. The family doctor participated in the events and processes of illness, death, and mourning both as a professional and as a neighbor and a friend. At present this sort of physician is so rare in our society as to be very nearly extinct, and this is not because American doctors have all become suddenly lazy or disinterested.

Aside from the demographic, financial, and epidemic problems facing the medical establishment today, there are unfortunate public attitudes about the role of medicine and of the physicians among us. "What's the matter with you

doctors nowadays?" an angry man remarked to his wife's
general practitioner. "I can fix any machine we own, but
when my wife gets sick I have to go to ten different doctors
downtown, and none of them can fix her." The G.P. had
been trying in the kindest way he knew, month after month,
to help this man understand that his wife had an advanced
cancer, that it was inoperable, and that she was dying. But
all this time, the man insisted upon viewing his wife as a
machine with a broken part in it somewhere, needing re-
placement or repair; and so, perhaps inevitably, he rushed
from specialist to specialist trying to find one who could
turn the trick. And the specialists in this case were all too
willing, unfortunately, to take his money.

The disappearance of the family doctor and his house
calls is also a response to the growing power of the corporate medical establishment. As early as 1899 in New York
City, citizens both rich and poor were beginning to turn to
the hospital, the clinic, and the dispensary for their medical
needs rather than to the individual professional. Sensational
new procedures multiplied so quickly in following years
that medical structures themselves became shrines of a sort
in the public mind, places where death itself might somehow be defeated. Life expectancy soared, largely because of
the disappearance of contagious diseases such as typhoid
fever and diphtheria, together with a sharp decline in infant
and maternal mortality rates. U.S. residents born at the turn
of the century could expect, on the average, to live only
forty-seven years. Ninety years later, that figure had increased to an average of seventy-five years overall, and
slightly more for women. Wishful thinking made it seem to
some that this curve might continue indefinitely.

Meanwhile, several generations of Americans, accustomed to using hospital and clinic staff as their physicians,
believing in the establishment's "fortress against death"

mystique, have grown to adulthood without ever having had the experience of caring for the dying in their homes, and without perceiving that older tradition as appropriate. Yet recent studies have shown that a large majority of individuals would prefer, if possible, to die in their own homes.

The situation itself is a sick one, and in an attempt to heal it, the modern hospice seeks to retrieve what has been most sensible and humane in past medical history. At the same time the hospice movement reaches toward the future in its continual development of better techniques for palliative care and in its enlightened concepts of personal value and the value of community.

Obviously, the modern hospice is a concept whose time has come in our culture. Here we are not dealing with a casual fad or fashion, but with a view of human life, and human death, that is based on sound moral principles. More yet is needed, however, if we are to have available for ourselves, our friends, and our families the kind of hospice care we can trust. Standards of care must be clearly stated, put into place, and carefully monitored. A U.S. government definition of hospice care is as follows:

> *Hospice:* A program which provides palliative and supportive care for terminally ill patients and their families, either directly or on a consulting basis with the patient's physician or another county agency such as a visiting nurse association. Originally a medieval name for a way station for pilgrims and travelers where they could be replenished, refreshed, and cared for; used here for an organized program of care for people going through life's last station. The whole family is considered the unit of care and care extends through the mourning process. Emphasis is placed on symptom control and preparation for and support before and after death, full-scope health services being provided by an organized interdisciplinary team available on a 24-hours-a-day, 7-days-a-week basis. . . .

This, during the mid-1970s, was a good beginning. Much more was soon devised by hospice professionals themselves, and learned on an experiential basis by the public, as hospice efforts began to bear fruit. Fortunately for us all, the early leaders of the hospice movement, both in England and in North America, tended to be thoroughly qualified individuals truly devoted to this work, and holding to the highest of ethical standards: most notably, Dr. Cicely Saunders (now Dame Cicely, with a dazzling string of honors after her name) in England; and in North America, Dr. Balfour Mount, professor of surgery at the Royal Victoria Hospital in Montreal.

During the 1980s, the Standards and Accreditation Committee of the recently formed National Hospice Organization also did yeoman service; various state and federal agencies joined in, and finally, the JCAH (Joint Committee on Accreditation of Hospitals) entered the arena with demanding specifications for hospices wishing to receive their approval. At base, however, the idea of hospice care can be fairly simply explained.

First and foremost, *hospice* is a caring community. This means that a group of well-intentioned people, wanting to be helpful in some vague way to others who are ill, will not measure up; nor will special-interest groups or individuals seeking financial advantage or political advancement. The true hospice consists of a group of people who have become a community by means of their shared dedication to a particular task: promoting the physical, emotional, and spiritual well-being of the dying and their families. The diagram of a community is a circle with a center. At the vital center of hospice is a person who is dying, surrounded and supported by the belief of this community that human beings are more than mere flesh.

To the Christian, the suffering patient is, quite literally, a representation of Christ. To the Jew, the patient may be seen as the angelic messenger who, in the form of a wandering stranger, must always be treated with great courtesy. Muslims, Hindus, Buddhists, and members of other faiths have similar beliefs; and so does the compassionate humanist. While it is not necessary for a person to belong to any religious group or congregation in order to become a valuable member of the hospice team, a sense of the spiritual dimension of life does appear to be necessary. True caring and true community do not happen among people who think of one another as functional units in a system designed for efficiency. Thus, hospice will not work if it is conceived as a business, even though efficiency and common sense are necessary. For the same reasons, a hospice cannot be constructed by systems analysts, and then have money poured into it, and survive. Such entities may or may not live on as something quite different, but they are not hospices. People who come into hospice work without being suited to it, or fail to understand its basic premises, generally tire of it rather quickly, and drop out. In this way, the hospice community is quite efficient as a self-pruning organism with its own destiny.

Second, a hospice is a community of persons highly trained in their various skills, particularly in the art and craft of medicine. The medical and nursing staffs must be expert not only in conventional disciplines, but in the methods of pain and symptom management pioneered at St. Christopher's. They must be available twenty-four hours a day, seven days a week to any patient and family accepted into the program. A group of "caring people," no matter how well-intentioned, cannot do hospice work without the practice of hard medicine of this sort, and the staff to provide it as needed. Thus, faith-healing groups and prayer groups, whatever their accomplishments, are not hospices. Groups or individuals promising to provide "an easy death" by removing the patient from medical professionals and performing hocus-pocus of some sort (or by providing convenient means for suicide or euthanasia) are the very antithesis of hospices and should be guarded against by all means. People who are receiving proper care, and the love and support of a good hospice team, simply do not want to end their own lives.

Third, the hospice offers its services and its fellowship not only to the patient but to the entire family. These services are practical in every possible way, from transportation to aid with finances or making a will; they are also psychologically effective in that trained counselors and therapists are on the job to notice difficulties and to offer guidance as wished. Close attention to the spiritual well-being of patient and family is an integral part of hospice care, with clergy and lay persons of various denominations available to provide companionship at the spiritual level and to perform whatever rites may be appropriate. The hospice community embraces and supports patient, family, and close friends, not only during the final days and weeks of the patient's life, but long after death, offering comfort and consolation to the bereaved.

Fourth, the hospice cares for as many patient-family units as staff and volunteer support will allow, without discrimination on the basis of race, color, creed, sexual orientation, nature of illness, or ability to pay. Most hospices have several different sources of funds. Direct payment for services is acceptable from the family that can afford it; and many will be able to offer appropriate reimbursement from public and/or private insurance sources. However, empire building is not an acceptable motive or modus operandi for a hospice. This is a work that is meant to be done in *caritas*.

Finally, the hospice team of whatever size and strength

must find a way of offering inpatient care, as needed, of the same quality and degree of excellence as the care offered in the patient's home. The hospice inpatient unit in a hospital or other health care facility needs to be autonomous and must function not as a fortress removed from the rest of society but as a house of life, a place where dying is seen as a natural part of the human pilgrimage. Death must receive appropriate consecration in such a place. It must offer true welcome not only to the patient but to his or her family and friends, to young children, pets, personal possessions, and whatever amenities are usual to this individual, whether this be food of a certain ethnic variety, or wine and music, or silence and privacy. Provision should be made for visitors who may wish to stay overnight; and couples should have the opportunity to share physical intimacy even during the final hours if they wish.

Growing plants and garden areas are an important part of hospice inpatient care, reminders as they are (like music and the other arts) of the forces of renewal in nature and in the human spirit. The patient's physical and emotional comfort must be the highest of all priorities here, and while medical staff must remain alert to any sign that a more aggressive treatment of the illness might be appropriate in different surroundings, the mechanisms for heroic resuscitation and maintenance of artificial life do not belong here. In the hospice inpatient unit, nurse-patient ratios must be far higher than those found in most hospitals and nursing homes. Members of clergy need to be visibly present, available, and part of the team. Trained volunteers are also an important part of the inpatient unit, for they can take on many of the simpler tasks that become so important in such a situation, freeing those with different, more highly developed skills. However, what the janitor says to a patient one morning may very well be a valuable form of ministry.

What a visiting child does to amuse and enlighten the same patient may be the best thing that happens all day; thus, the life of the larger world needs to flow in and out quite naturally. With great care and vigilance this can happen (as it does at St. Christopher's) in an atmosphere of healthful and refreshing cleanliness, without the life-denying sterility of the general hospital, and also without the rank unpleasantness found in all too many of our "nursing" and "convalescent" homes.

It is true that the hospice way of caring is unusually demanding—unusually *conscious,* as caring goes—and unusually kind. The benign influence of hospice care made visible in our general hospitals cannot be underestimated. Indeed we in the United States have come a long way in a short time from the day when the widow and her children were hauled away in disgrace to Apple Island. A grass-roots phenomenon such as the hospice movement tells us now, I think—at the end of the twentieth century—quite a good deal about the nation we want to become. In a fine book on hospice architecture, Deborah Allen Carey wrote recently: "Hospice is a reaction to the anonymity of mass culture . . . concurrent with other movements to promote . . . common interests and community." I agree. We hate anonymity and today we battle it constantly: think of the credits at the end of every film; they go on until everyone has been mentioned, down to the person in charge of making the coffee and walking the dog. This is rather bizarre, but it is also wonderful; it says something, I think, about a thrust toward new social health. The body of society as a whole is injured when we do not look at one another, when we do not care. The vast quilt in memory of AIDS patients is another cry against the loss of personhood; so, of course, is the Vietnam Veterans Memorial in Washington, D.C. When we give infinitely patient, skilled, and loving care to one dying patient, and then another, we are saying in a visible and powerful way that each person matters, every single one. We are saying, among other things, that we are all travelers here, all strangers who have come briefly to stay together, sharing as equals this small and so very beautiful, so very fragile, island home.

11

GREATEST OF FEASTS

Love reveals more than hope can, for love is a mystical possessing *now* of all that hope looks for in the future.
George Congreve, S.S.J.E.

*A*gain and again throughout these pages, the image of journeying recurs; and the writing of them has been in itself a kind of journey, a search not only for facts, but for meanings: the shapes and forms that invisible energies take in our lives. To journey is to move, to grow, to be in process, transforming what we see and hear and touch along the way, and experiencing the mystery of our own transformation. Material things and events are devoured by our senses, becoming the stuff of the mind, energetic and magnetic, that is the means, the fuel—and the map, as well—of our constant thrusting and voyaging into the unknown. Often, the traveler does not know what he is seeking until he has found it; and the pilgrim's goal in the end, whatever its symbolic form may be, is never really a location or an object, but the achievement of a new state of being. *Pilgrim's Progress* is one way of telling the story; the epic *Gilgamesh* from ancient Babylon is another. Dante's *Inferno* is a journey and a pilgrimage of transformation; so is the tale of St. George in Spenser's *Faërie Queene*. Princes and paupers made such journeys throughout the early folk tales and legends of our culture, seeking to find the secrets of their true being in the winning of new wisdom and the capture of a new level of consciousness. Arthurian knights sought wholeness in the vision of the Grail that could be achieved only by the pure in heart; and in Greek mythology, Jason and his Argonauts risked their earthly lives to gain powers of renewal in the form of the Golden Fleece. In China, Tao has been for centuries the Way of Enlightenment: the pilgrim's path and, at the same time, his ultimate goal. "I am the light of the world," said Jesus. "He that followeth me shall not walk in darkness, but shall have the light of life."

The great events of life, as we observe them, are still clearly recognizable as journeys: conception and birth, the various places of passage such as puberty, entrance into adulthood, work and creation, marriage and generativity, maturity, old age. The invention of a new device or concept is the result of a voyage of the mind and a return to port, ships laden. To learn a new skill is to dare a movement toward growth, and in the very process of daring it, to grow. Prayer and meditation are journeys; so is the making of a poem or the composition of a symphony. To fall in love, as we all know, is to experience a stunning process of movement and change; and to explore that love over a period of many years is both a journey and a transformation.

It is not surprising, given the persistence of such realizations by people in so many lands and ages, to find that dying has also been seen throughout human history as a process of journeying. The understanding of death as one in a series of quite natural, though ultimately mysterious, personal transformations is so common among members of the human race that it could almost be called a definitive trait of our species. There are exceptions to this rule, of course. Entire societies get trapped from time to time in a sort of

gray, empty space of confusion about the facts of death; and
this happens most often when the current state of scientific
knowledge appears to contradict the larger body of experience on which we base our sense of what is true. Western
attitudes toward death and dying have obviously suffered in
the past century or so from a period of such confusion. And
at almost any time, a group or a tribe can be found tucked
away in the hills of some primitive land, where death is seen
as an assault on human dignity and a cosmic outrage. To the
Juiraros, for example, a tribe dwelling in recent years on the
eastern slopes of the Andes:

> . . . there is no such thing as a natural death. While they
> may realize that death is a separation of body and spirit,
> they cannot seem to understand the general relation of
> natural causes to it. Each death to them is unintelligible,
> unnatural and accidental. . . . Since every death is pre-
> sumably a murder, great excitement results. This is evi-
> denced by the beating of the signal drums. . . .

In civilized Western society, sirens and telephones serve as
our signal drums. Frightened and outraged, feeling defeated by death, we forget the ancient wisdom that is our
heritage and that is, even today, being returned to us by a
new set of observations.

The Navajos, curiously enough, are one of the few cultural groups in the world ever to have taken the position
that there is no life whatever after death. Individuals, of
course, have always appeared with intellectual systems designed along such lines; but societies as a whole have believed otherwise, and have passed down to succeeding
generations the observation that something leaves the body
at the moment of death and seems to enter another form or
level of existence. The Navajo groups who denied this
found it very difficult to deal with the consequences of their
denial; and their management of death and dying in such

circumstances is interesting in comparison with our own, in conventional medical situations today.

The seriously ill Navajo was carried away from his or her hogan and isolated from all but one or two members of the tribe who stayed, waiting in dread for death to come. Silence was the rule; no mourning or mention of the event was considered appropriate. Quickly then, the body and all personal possessions of the deceased, including the hogan, were burned, and the ashes were buried out of sight. So powerful was the need to deny the reality of death in these groups, that the person who had stayed with the dying, and performed these final rites, was shunned afterward as taboo. Death was the end, it was consciously believed, and thus was too terrible an event to be admitted into the process of tribal existence. Yet in such a situation, death is obviously not the end after all; for death itself in such a society has to be dealt blow after blow in a ritualized attempt to kill it. It is life that dies, under such circumstances, while death lives on.

Our own defense mechanisms on the subject represent just such a ritualistic defeat of conscious purpose. Yet we do have a choice. We can dare a new point of view, and in daring it, we can change. In the presence of death we can make the decision to stay open, not to draw back in dismay from the person who is dying, not to shun (on the excuse of embarrassment, but really in dread) the bereaved; and not to defend ourselves foolishly against the demanding realities of the mourning process. And if we care to place any trust in the vast accumulation of humanity's knowledge of the subject, and informed belief about it, we can stay open to the experience of our own dying with the sense that it will be in some way a familiar journey, not unlike the journey of being born.

"My bags are packed," said Pope John in 1965, "I am

ready to go." This has been the attitude, not only of the wise, the elderly, and the religious throughout human history; not only of the mystics, poets, and prophets of every age; but of countless millions of simple, practical people who have "watched and waked" at the deathbeds of friends and parents, spouses and children, who have held these dying people in their arms, looking straight into their eyes, hearing their last words and noticing closely what was happening to them. "The old folk . . . Russians, Tartars, Votyaks . . . didn't puff themselves up or fight against it . . . they prepared themselves quietly and in good time . . . and they departed easily, as if they were just moving into a new house," writes Alexander Solzhenitsyn. "But 'tis the way, lad Kerry," says the ancient wise woman of the village in Donn Byrne's *Destiny Bay.* "Dying is like a boy's voice breaking and his putting on trews, or like a young girl and she letting down the hem of her skirt and putting up her soft hair. . . . We are like childer on the floor, and the dead are grown up."

Out of centuries of experience has come the repeated observation that death appears to be a process rather than an event, a form of passage for human life that in some way continues to exist, journeying on. Rituals designed to respond appropriately to this view are in themselves life-enhancing, and among simple people are often as realistic and practical as their care of the dying has been. In the villages of Eastern Europe, for example, all doors and windows of the house have traditionally been thrown open immediately upon the death of an occupant so that the spirit could move without hindrance into the life beyond. For the same purpose, holes were made in the rooftops of houses in rural Mexico. Ashanti tribes in Ghana have an ancient tradition of giving water at the very last to the dying, so that the thirsting spirit may climb more easily up the steep hill to eternity; a handkerchief is placed in the hands of the dead to wipe the sweat of this struggle into the world beyond. Buddhists in Japanese country villages sew a white pilgrim's garment for the body and put a bag of coins at its belt so that the departing spirit can pay the ferryman for its passage into eternity. Villagers in Muslim Turkey leave a light burning forty days and nights after a death, in the belief that the newly released soul may need its help in the process of learning to live without a physical body.

Death as a form of liberation is a motif familiar throughout the cultures of the world. In India the *shraddha* ceremony is performed by Hindus to help the spiritual body to its celestial abode; death is perceived as the moment of freedom when this final journey can begin. The *Cho-Hon* ceremony in Korea represents an "invitation to the soul" in this stage of its pilgrimage; and *sajas* (like the spiritual companions seen at the last by contemporary patients of Kübler-Ross) are the messengers who come to guide it on its way. Viking chieftains who died were sent out to sea in their ships with all their possessions on board for the journey to the afterlife, and the ships were then set ablaze to help the spirit free itself from the last of its material bonds.

These are universal responses to a mystery, a process in human life that has been observed over the ages by people in wholly contrasting cultures as essentially the same: a journey toward the liberation that exists beyond time and space. The following words might have been written by a poet or a prophet from any one of these ancient cultures; actually, they are the utterance of German theologian Dietrich Bonhoeffer, who was imprisoned at the time, and later executed, by Adolf Hitler:

Come now, thou greatest of feasts on the journey to
   freedom eternal;
death, cast aside all the burdensome chains, and
   demolish
the walls of our temporal body, the walls of our souls
   that are blinded,
so that at last we may see that which here remains
   hidden.
Freedom, how long have we sought thee in
   discipline, action, and suffering;
dying, we now may behold thee revealed in the
   Lord.

Fed on this part of our journey by our five senses and by
all the beauties and gratifications of this world, we are aware
still of being imprisoned by the limitations of self, and we
hunger for something beyond. Mystics have taught us for
centuries that spirit takes only a temporal, restricted form
in us while we dwell on earth; and that our five senses
continually blunder, misinforming us and distracting our
gaze from the essence of life, which is holy and eternal.
Time and space, they have insisted, should not be taken in
the way we perceive them here and now, as practical measures of truth. Mystics are unpopular, however, in a world
full of technological marvels and material riches. As consumers of such goods they are strangely lax and disinterested; the signs and symbols of worldly power habitually fail
to impress them; and so "mystical" has gradually come to
mean foggy and foolish, unrealistic, a little daft, maybe; and
we have turned to the engineers, the technicians, and the
scientists when we wanted firm truth.

Now, though, faced with a new set of scientific facts, it is
we who sometimes must admit that we feel foggy and foolish. Einstein teaches us that for modern physicists, "this
separation between past, present, and future has the value
of mere illusion, however tenacious." Space, we are now

told, somehow starts out more or less as we thought, then turns around and folds back into itself. What a poetic scientist has called "the gentle pressure of starlight" insists to our waking eyes that it is proceeding from a living, burning source; yet we know now that many of the stars we see above us went dark and died thousands upon thousands of years ago. Trying to deal with reality now, our scientists themselves are becoming poets, and physicists are working in the metaphysical realm that once belonged to mystics and prophets from Dante Alighieri to Gerard Manley Hopkins, from Mechthild of Magdeburg and Julian of Norwich to Vaughan, Herbert, and Traherne.

To Christian poets such as these, dying is a process of transformation and transcendence continually happening during the measure of our earthly life. The journey of the soul toward God is a pilgrimage demanding that we strip away falsehood, pride, and the greedy demands of the ego so that we may move at last unencumbered, spiritually naked, into the process of union with the divine. Glimpses of the goal are received along the way in a series of small deaths, moments of self-forgetfulness, worship, and sacrifice that seem to stand beyond time, intersected by the flow of pure energy that is God's love. In this mode of perception, biological death can be understood as the annihilation of the final set of barriers between man and God, and as the supreme achievement of transcendence. Time does not matter here: "Before Abraham was," said Jesus, "I Am."

Images of blazing light appear very often in the attempts of seekers and religious mystics to describe these moments of dying to self and thus moving beyond space and time. An oceanic sense of joy, peace, and wholeness accompanies the unearthly radiance of this white light, which has been seen at such times and reported similarly, not only by poets such as Eliot and Blake, Wordsworth and Henry Vaughan ("I saw Eternity the other night / Like a great Ring of pure and endless light, / All calm as it was bright . . ."), but also by ordinary people of various cultures and backgrounds studied in psychology texts, such as William James's *The Varieties of Religious Experience.* Moses saw such a light in the burning bush; and Saul was temporarily blinded by it on the road to Damascus. The disciplines of the Oriental sages are often built on an attempt to slip from the bondages of daily life and achieve this same sort of vision; and in fact, our way of expressing any sudden attainment of superior knowledge and wisdom is based on it, for we speak, not only in esoteric circles of "achieving enlightenment" but in plain language, of "seeing the light."

It is not so remarkable, perhaps, to find a matching set of experiences among seeking and journeying people in a number of different cultures as it is to discover that these very same experiences are now being described by individuals who have clinically "died" and then, on account of modern resuscitation techniques, have recovered. Research by Elisabeth Kübler-Ross reports them, and more are documented by Raymond A. Moody, Jr., in the cases of individuals who have been very close to death or who, having been pronounced biologically dead, later "have come back to life." All report the experience of dying as something like a journey, a movement out of space and time in an indescribable spiritual body "like an energy, maybe" or as one person put it, "something I can best describe as an energy pattern." Like Kübler-Ross's patients, Moody's subjects very often reported the presence of spiritual companions during this part of the dying process, and they also told of going through dark, tunnellike spaces on their way toward the brilliance of the light. Then came emergence into tremendous radiance and joy, in the presence of a "being of light" whose love for them was overwhelming and indescribable:

> I floated . . . up into this pure crystal-clear light, an illuminating white light. It was beautiful and so bright, so radiant, but it didn't hurt my eyes. It's not any kind of light you can describe on earth. I didn't actually see a person in this light, and yet it has a special identity, it definitely does. . . .

said one subject. And another:

> I was out of my body, there's no doubt about it, because I could see my own body there on the operating room table. My soul was out! All this made me feel very bad at first, but then, this really bright light came. . . . It was tremendously bright; I just can't describe it. . . . Yet from the moment the light spoke to me, I felt really good—secure and loved. The love which came from it is just unimaginable, indescribable. It was a fun person to be with! And it had a sense of humor, too—definitely!

Religious people tended to describe this "being of light" as an angel, Jesus, or God; and even firm atheists, Dr. Moody reports, perceived it as some sort of religious figure. On returning from these journeys, as all his subjects obviously did, they felt powerfully changed by them, lifted to new levels of consciousness and committed to a set of values in which things of the mind and spirit took new precedence over the merely material. Many felt commanded by the experience to work toward a personal transformation that would allow them to love others on earth as they in their "time out of time" had felt loved. Though Moody himself makes no judgment of these cases and merely reports them as they occurred, it seems reasonable to state here that these were experiences of personal transformation, conversion, and spiritual growth.

One patient of Dr. Kübler-Ross was a thirty-nine-year-old man near death after a massive coronary:

"He experienced himself floating out of his body toward a beckoning light. He said later that he felt that if he had gone much closer to the light he would not have returned to his body . . ."

"And what is the light?" [the interviewer asked].

"That light is God [Dr. Kübler-Ross replied]. God is the light and love these people experience. They are entering His presence. That, for me, is beyond the shadow of a doubt."

This patient then heard the voices of his young children (who were not present at the time) crying for him and realized that he must return to life to take care of them; and many of Kübler-Ross's and Moody's subjects have experienced similar "recalls," sensing that they must go back, or that they were being sent back to fulfill their responsibilities, by the "being of light." In the experiences of most, the matter of responsibility did not end with "dying," in fact. There followed, in the presence of the light, a miraculously rapid review of the actions and events of the person's entire life. This resembled the Judgment in ancient Egyptian and in medieval Christian traditions except that it was done in a wholly loving and accepting way, demonstrating mistakes with the sense that one should learn from them to comprehend more and do better. The individual then returned to ordinary existence feeling in some way reborn.

Symbolically, we perform rites of this sort, or rites allowing for this sort of experience to take place, when we undergo religious disciplines of fasting or meditation and when we baptize, recognizing that new birth and transformation cannot take place without a letting-go of self, which is a sort of death. The Judgment appears in various dramatic forms in such ancient works as the Egyptian *Book of the Dead,* the Tibetan *Bardo Thödol,* and the medieval Christian work, *The*

Craft of Dying (Ars Moriendi); and all agree that the state of mind of the dying person is of great importance to his ultimate destiny. Many of the experiences reported by subjects of modern research appear in very similar form in the works of two thousand years ago; differences seem to be mainly cultural and, interestingly enough, connected with differing ideas about the purpose of human life in its relation to space and time. All see death as a form of journey. The description of the process in the "secret" Tibetan book, which until recent years was unavailable except to the initiate, is very complicated, and its imagery is unfamiliar to the Western reader. But, of course, this is the reason why it is so fascinating to see the same perceptions turning up in parallel forms in the experiences of our contemporaries.

Tibetans teach that the dying person will see almost immediately, at the moment when life ceases, a brilliant light. A series of struggles will follow, which represent various levels of spiritual development coming under attack from negative forces of worldly temptation. Escape from the almost certain fate of reincarnation (perhaps in some lower form) can be achieved only by resisting all of these illusions and entering, at last, in the ecstatic state known as *samadhi,* into the Clear Light of the Void. The esoteric *Bardo Thödol* is a sort of instruction book for the newly dead, and is supposed to be recited by the person's spiritual guide for a period of many days so that, in all the confusion of the passage, its wisdom will not be forgotten. Medieval Christians in *Ars Moriendi,* not believing in the possibility of reincarnation, felt that such spiritual counseling must take place as the person was dying, and emphasized the necessity for confession of sins and death of egoistic desires before the individual should come into the immediate presence of God. Both agreed, however, that "to know how to die is to know how to live," and that these spiritual teachings should be a part of the daily life of all who sought enlightenment.

Both agreed, too, along with most other major religious groups in the world, that the manner of death is deeply significant (suicide, for example, is seen as destructive, if not fatal to the soul) and that the care of the dying was a delicate matter to be handled by the yogi, the priest, or the elder with great powers of spiritual authority. As the delightfully forthright little volume *Ars Moriendi* puts it,

> When any of likelihood shall die, then it is most neces-
> sary to have a special friend, the which will heartily help
> and pray for him and therewith counsel the sick for the
> weal of his soul; and moreover to see that all others do
> so about him or else quickly for to make them depart.

Right dying, Tibetan sages say, is an initiation. Therefore this is a process that should happen consciously. *Ars Moriendi* agrees, and gives the example of Isaiah the prophet:

> For when the King Ezechiel lay sick and upon the point
> of death, he glosed him not, nor used no dissimulation
> unto him, but plainly and wholesomely aghasted him,
> saying that he should die.

The idea of "wholesomely aghasting" someone on his deathbed was to make certain that he got ready for his journey "up Godward" at this time of passage. But the wise person lived continuously in a Godward direction and was not distracted by the illusory successes or failures, pleasures or terrors of this world any more than was the obedient Tibetan by the demons and the visions of the world below. The ultimate goal of union with God is the same in both traditions, and the fact that East and West have tended to disagree on how long this takes and where it happens becomes relatively insignificant in view of the fact that both disciplines aim to help the individual out of space and time, into eternity.

"Is There an Answer to Death?" inquires the title of one book on the subject, suddenly so popular, of death and dying. To this perhaps we had best reply, as Gertrude Stein is said to have done on her own deathbed, "What was the question?" Bumbling around as we are in a universe so complex that we may glimpse only once or twice in a lifetime, at best, any really intelligent question to ask about it, we are not very likely to seize upon a system here and now that will answer all of our questions about death and dying. Our present attempts have got to be modest and ought to contain—like the "being of light" many have perceived—a very definite sense of humor; for we should keep in mind the sort of equipment we are using when we try to grapple with these ultimate issues. As geneticist François Jacob reminds us:

> This evolutionary procedure—the formation of a dominating neocortex coupled with the persistence of a nervous and hormonal system partially, but not totally under the rule of the neocortex . . . is somewhat like adding a jet engine to an old horse cart.

It is a tinkerer's universe, Jacob says, made of structures put together with odd bits and pieces of whatever was lying around. If so, then it is a poet's and a prophet's universe as well, where metaphor is a handy tool for the geneticist describing it. The jet engine causes the old horse cart no end of trouble, heaving it hither and yon until it splits its seams at last, casting cargo over the landscape and ending up abandoned by the side of the road. Perhaps this is why there is so often a sense of terror associated with the highest functions of this new energy ("Go, go, go, said the bird: human kind/Cannot bear very much reality"), and perhaps this is why we, the living, think of dying as such a frightening catastrophe. Something in us wants to be pure energy, without even the casings of a jet. Throughout our lives we

grope toward a goal that feels to some like personal liberation and to others like union with the divine. Religious
people of many cultures would say that it is both, and that
the agent of all our transformations along the way is that
"being of light" which is called by so many of us, God.

To those of us who are concerned today to find better ways
of caring for the dying, both Eastern and Western traditions
have much to teach us; and those who have worked with
patients in the modern hospice situation can confirm the
view of both that the process of dying offers tremendous
potential for personal growth. In the caring community of
a hospice, the individual is provided with the kind of time
and space that does not concern itself with worldly status or
the winning of any advantage, but only with the process of
pure being as it unfolds itself in the giving and receiving of
love. Those who do hospice work, whatever the structure
of their religious or philosophical beliefs, tend to feel for
this reason that there is a sort of centeredness and holiness
about it. Whether they are offering massage or medicine for
pain, clean linens, or a hand to hold and a listening heart,
they sense that these are gestures of obedience to Love of
higher order. And the dying who are cared for in this way
are offered, without any preaching or intellectualizing
about it, a clear representation of that "time out of time"
that is celebrated by our poets and our prophets, and in our
liturgies.

What are the strange journeys of the Egyptians and the
Tibetans in their underworlds, and the voyages of the dead
or dying people studied in modern times? I am not sure that
it matters very much whether people are clinically dead or
clinically alive when they have these experiences, though
the borderlines of our judgments about clinical death may
shift somewhat as a result of such observations. This is not

what proves to me that there is something eternal in life, and something holy. What seems to me important about these journeys is the sense of bliss, of sudden understanding, and of arrival in the blazing presence of Love, which is the same experienced in the "small deaths" of ritual, prophecy, and poetry. To be at home in the universe is to be a pilgrim, and yet not a stranger. A kind of space is required for this, in which we can change and grow while being welcomed in all our transformations. The hospice offers this kind of space to the dying. Time is insignificant in this setting except as it serves the patient's awareness. Space is ordered here in such a way that bodily discomforts do not distract, and the mind and the soul can roam at their ease, unconfined. Heaven indeed is open (as they believed in sixteenth-century Spain) to the dying who are received and welcomed in the hospice community; and here they are offered, by the disintegration of the material body, a richer matrix than ever for spirit to grow in.

To those of us who are witness to such events, the phrase "life after death" tends to become inadequate to the experience, if not altogether irrelevant. Lillian Preston did not begin to live until she reached the time and the place where she lay dying. In a garden in Charleston in the spring, Miss Aurelia Robbins still walks under the curving glass of time, sheltered among her lilies and her snowflakes, blind and smiling and so very, very grateful in her soft, white dress. To have known these people—and Mr. Pippin, and Mrs. Doe, and Jim Burnham, the young musician—is to have experienced in the here and now a kind of immutable wholeness, and holiness.

"Let me tell you, Doctor," said an eighty-three-year-old Hospice of Marin patient, "dying is the experience of a lifetime." What she meant by these splendid words remains, like the fabric of life itself, a mystery. "I think I was meant to come here," says Lillian Preston's final letter from St. Christopher's Hospice, "so that at last, I could experience joy." Caring and being cared for in such an environment, she was transformed. To have lived in the hospice community, to have watched and waked with the dying throughout these pages has been for me, as well, a journey of personal transformation. The people I have come to know here are part of me now; and those who have left on the longer journey before me have brought, in their caring for me, a great part of me with them. Together, living and dead, we now dwell in a place of eternal hospitality where there is no before and no after—there is only love.

12

REMEMBERING ANNE

*F*emale, single, Caucasian, age forty-seven—and in a general hospital because there was no hospice unit available yet to receive her—on Midsummer's Eve of 1977, my friend Anne died. It had been a long struggle: cancer of the esophagus; then, after the skilled surgical intervention, a sudden, explosive spread of malignancy throughout her body.

Anne was private as a cat, fastidious, aloof, and quixotic to the point of eccentricity. I loved her. Many people did not. She was proud, quick-tempered, wrote odd poems, painted watercolors no one wanted to buy. She quarreled regularly with her neighbors over such matters as disappearing trash-bin tops and dogs that barked in the night. Anne was "difficult"—a determined loner—and though few people knew it, by the end of her long illness she was literally destitute.

Yet despite all this, and despite the lack of a hospice facility in her community, Anne did not die in despair, a surgical-chemical cripple automatically overtreated, then abandoned as a medical "failure" at the last. She did not die screaming, calling out for help. The final days of her life were filled with loving-kindness given and received, with moments of wonder and of humor, a new sort of openness, trust, and tenderness about her; and at the end, the huge, dark eyes that seemed by then almost all that was left of her gazed quite clearly, with fierce curiosity, into the unknown.

Under the circumstances, it was a makeshift sort of miracle that happened. Nevertheless it did occur, and it served to remind those of us who witnessed it that *hospice,* at base, is not a new form of magic, but an ancient and sensible, decent form of human behavior. Anne's death was proof that hospitality can be brought to bear in the most difficult of situations if only people understand what it is, and are willing to work for it.

It would have been better, of course, if Anne could have died in the quiet simplicity of a hospice community. As it was, she died owing—and being owed—debts both financial and emotional that can never be repaid. She should have died, if not in a hospice bed, then in her own little garden, watching her hummingbirds at their feeder—they were her greatest joy. She should have died hearing her favorite Mozart and Vivaldi instead of the loudspeakers in the hospital repeating their litanies of panic, day and night, down echoing corridors. Anne loved fresh air, polished pebbles, feathers, the smell of the herbs she grew in other people's cast-off, broken pots, the slant of the morning light in the little studio apartment where she painted, almost to the end, intensely shy and cautious renderings of leaves, buds, birds, and shells. Her ward in the hospital smelled of disinfectant, pus, and fear. No sun came in. Toward the end I thought more than once of carrying her away from there, bundling her out under a cloak or in a laundry bag. She was so small and frail by then, I could have done it. Her suitcase, when I carried it away for her later, was far heavier. But where . . . ? And who would help with the kind of care she needed? There was no hospice building waiting to welcome her.

There was, however, a hospice team forming in the neighborhood just then; and part of the miracle was that several of its members had already become acquainted with Anne, over the years. As her illness progressed, we discovered that she was willing to share a part of her life with us that she badly needed to conceal from the rest of the world. Anne had been taught young to despise weakness. Seeing that we did not, she did not feel ashamed to show herself, as she was, to us. Day by day growing more needy and more helpless, she drew a circle—a very small one—of "hospice people" around her, and in doing so, brought us closer to one another. Dying, she helped to create community.

Anne's physician, though not formally a member of the hospice group, was aware and sympathetic, a sensitive human being as well as a fine medical man. When he had done all that was possible to combat the malignancy, he did not turn away. He focused his attention not upon cancer, the disease, but upon Anne, the person. Pain was not a major problem in her case. Discomforts there were, however, and these her physician noted and negotiated constantly, directing her nursing care so that Anne could have every possible relief. Feeding, which she emphatically rejected toward the end, was never forced. Oxygen was available as she needed it, but machinery was not applied to coerce her lungs; and in her final hours, Anne was not isolated from the presence of those she had chosen to draw together in the intimacy of a family circle. Visiting rules, as far as we were concerned, were quietly eliminated. We came to her when she wanted us—or when we sensed that she did—separately and together, feeling our way, learning as best we could from her day by day, moment by moment toward the end, how we might help.

Nurses and aides meantime came and went on their various shifts—how seldom we ever saw the same one twice!

Some of these were disinterested, perfunctory; but others, both young and old, male and female, were tender and sensitive, noticing our presence with grateful eyes, asking us questions about hospice work, and slipping in quietly from time to time during their busy rounds to join our circle at Anne's bedside.

At the very end, a telephone call came across the country for Anne, from a man she loved. The hospice team had located him that day, and had let him know that the end was near; but in the meantime the central switchboard had been told, no more calls for her, it was too late. Technically, of course, it was. Anne was by now far too weak to lift a telephone, even to speak. But in the temporary absence of the hospice group, it was one of the noticing, questioning nurses who intervened. Understanding what must be done for Anne, she fought the switchboard and rerouted the call. Then, holding Anne in her arms and the telephone close to her ear, she stood by until the last words were spoken, so that Anne was able to hear at the very moment of her death, in the beloved voice, "Anne, I love you."

A small miracle, but a real one. And an important one because, unlike cancer, the hospice point of view is definitely contagious. Wherever it goes, if its intent is clearly stated, it will tend to work its gentle, stubborn, persuasive way. Within the hospital its presence brings subtle changes that will help to alter our entire society's attitudes about death, and thus about those who are dying. With hospice home care groups proliferating, and freestanding hospices appearing here and there as communities within community, its healing transformations are now coming about even more rapidly. In time, perhaps people like Anne will not feel such a desperate need to hide themselves away, and those of us who are newly enabled to receive the dying into our midst will be helped to accept from them their very real, very great gifts.

Freestanding, purpose-designed hospice units are not always possible. But it should be clear by now that mere architecture, however pleasing, cannot make a hospice, and that true hospice care cannot be artificially programed. Care is care. It is not a building, a grant, a law, or a committee. *Remember Anne,* I think, when I hear of would-be hospices designing themselves around the latest wrinkle in reimbursement policies; renting or buying elaborate space and equipment before making their work known in the community; or calling in "outside planners"—presumably to make elaborate and expensive plans about all that has not been happening inside. This is not hospice work; this is mere fiddling and politics. Hospice does not begin with flowcharts of administrative function, or lists of potential sites, or willing benefactors. Hospice work begins with the question, *What does this patient need?*

Anne needed a great deal that we were unable to give her. The place she died in was wrong for her, the pace of it was cruel, the confusion of constantly shifting personnel hurt her, the sounds she heard and the very air she breathed were debilitating and distracting to one in her condition. Yet even in Anne's situation, a kind of healing was possible. Seeing day by day that she was acceptable to our small group, that we honored her no matter how she looked or felt or behaved at the moment, Anne, who had always been so withdrawn, began to reveal a hidden side of her character. All this time, we discovered, she had wanted very much to care for other people and, like many who are equally shy and aloof, had a secret, passionate need to be needed.

Our reaction to this, we realized in talking together later, had been—at the time of her great physical and emotional weakness—to let her see that we quite honestly depended on her, valued her advice, needed her support as individuals, and, as a developing group, were nourished by her encouragement. Some of us told her now, for the first time, our personal troubles, somewhat as travelers tend to confide sudden intimacies to the stranger who will be leaving the train or the ship at its next stopping place. Illness had aged Anne's face, stripped it bare of all but wisdom and nobility, so that huddled in her little chair in the garden, and later, in her hospital bed, she seemed at times like the ancient crone in the forests of mythology who gives the seeker a password or a magic token that will help him find his way. As her body withered, her spirit blazed more fiercely, her wit grew sharper, and her words—measured out now by the claims of physical weakness—were more profound and simple, wise and direct.

Four nights before she died, Anne achieved a major personal triumph. Private in her ways as she had always been, she felt deeply the trespass and insult of lying side by side with other patients, having her bodily functions casually placed on view, and being forced to witness the intimacies of others. On this night in June, a large, black, middle-aged woman, sobbing and wailing, was placed in the bed next to Anne's "for observation" after an automobile accident. Anne learned from the nurses' talk that the woman's only child had been burned to death in the crash that afternoon, and that the woman's condition in all probability was "just emotional." The woman was given sedation, told to go to sleep, and hastily left to lie alone in the dark with her grief. Anne was furious. Although she had been too weak for several days to take any nourishment, or even to sit up in bed, she somehow managed to clamber down to the floor, crawled on bare knees across the intervening space, and pulled herself up to embrace her sobbing neighbor. In the hour that followed, the dying tended the living in a way that no professional person present had thought to do. Six months earlier, I doubt that Anne could have done it herself. Shyness and scorn for her own grief, as well as the grief of others, would have held her back. As it was, Anne transformed herself into a hospice worker before she died.

"Not dying," she informed John, our hospice chaplain, in no uncertain terms when he arrived for his usual afternoon visit, on the last day. She knew perfectly well what was happening to her. But by now John and Anne had established a relationship filled with mischief and bantering—that was their mode. John took her hand and held it. "Anne, my dear, you are very, very sick and you know it," he said to her sternly, with a twinkle in his eye.

"So?" she replied with a wicked grin, and closed her eyes, content. As far as she was concerned, she had won that round. Three of us stood around her bed then, looking at one another, caught between laughter and tears. Anne had been moved to a sort of utility space, windowless, curtained off, out of sight. In a moment she took up her conversation with John again in a perfectly normal tone but in words, suddenly, that none of us could understand. Her hands were like shells to hold, so fragile, cool, and dry. There was so much she wanted to tell us. She talked and talked, mystery.

"What can we do for you, Anne?" asked the chaplain and then, seeing her moving away from us so quickly, called after her louder, "Anne, what can we do?"

"Stay," she whispered. We did. She was quiet for a time, then opened her eyes, looked from one to the other of us, and firmly commanded us, "Pray."

Loudspeakers blared, calling for doctors, as John anointed her forehead with the holy oil. She smiled up at

him, whispering . . . something. A joke? Gurneys rattled by.
"That's how Joshua smelled at the Battle of Jericho, Anne,"
said John. She smiled again, words tumbling out endlessly;
she was trying with the last of her strength, it seemed, to
tell us what it was like for her now, where she was going,
what she was seeing, wanting to bring us with her, letting
us know it was curious—bewildering—amazing—but yes,
all right. "For I am persuaded," John was saying, "that
neither death nor life, nor angels, nor principalities nor
powers, nor things present, nor things to come, nor height,
nor depth nor anything created can separate us from the
love of God . . ." and to these radiant words of Paul's
Epistle, Anne responded instantly with words of her own,
incomprehensible, passionate, magnificent. She saw something then that the rest of us may have glimpsed at moments, opened her eyes, started to speak—and then did not,
assuming, obviously, that we could see it too. In her garden
one morning early, with almost the same strange smile she
had said to me, "Look!" and made a puzzle out of it, a
treasure hunt. At last I understood that day, it was the
hummingbirds. She had just put up their feeder, and they
had found it. "Their wings," she said. "Look, look, their
wings move so fast, you can't really see them. Yet they are
there."

When I think of her now, I sometimes see her in the
garden as she was that day, but even more clearly as she lay
looking up at us in the hospital, utterly certain that we too
had found the treasure and were rejoicing with her in the
glory of it. Happiness is not the word to describe the look
on her face at that moment, nor is peace. Joy is not strong
enough. There was humor in it, and rapture—and something even beyond. Perhaps Anne gave up speaking to us
after this, even in her own private language, for such rea-

sons. There was nothing more to say. We thought a few moments later that she had fallen asleep, but she had not. She was waiting for her telephone call.

Remember Anne.

13

MAKING CIRCLES: 1970–1990

There is a tendency for living things to join up, establish linkages, live inside each other, return to earlier arrangements, get along, whenever possible. This is a way of the world.

Lewis Thomas,
The Lives of a Cell

[Care] is something much more than techniques, skills or training. It is something that involves the PERSON of the caregiver in a creative relationship with the PERSON being cared for. It is characterized by its freshness, originality and it is easily recognized by its attractiveness.

Fr. Tom O'Conner, OSCam
Chaplain, St. Joseph's Hospice

*I*t was treading thin ice, or rather more like walking on eggs, when I wrote the original edition of *The Hospice Movement* thirteen years ago. Very few people in the United States had heard the word *hospice,* and if they had, even fewer wanted to know a great deal more about it. And so it was somewhat strange for me to be insisting at the time that hospice was a lovely old word with an important history, and that the care of dying people could be a desirable thing to know about, that it could be something filled with beauty and value, joy as well as sorrow, and reverence for life, side by side with the awe that we feel as vulnerable human beings when death is in our midst.

Thus I need to begin the chapter called Making Circles anew, and with it, the wholly new part of the book, by asking my readers to notice with me how much our attitudes have changed in little more than a decade. Death is no longer a wholly taboo subject, banished from ordinary discourse, served up only as a bland and neutered event on TV crime shows and in brutal films about war. Death, in fact, has very nearly stopped being pornographic. We talk now about dying and grieving, loss and bereavement, much more freely than before, accepting all these as parts of our own reality. Speaking as one who does not intend to *pass away*—speaking personally, that is—I am still waiting for people to stop saying that a friend or relative has "passed" when the good Old Norse word *died* seems to me so much more real and solid, and therefore so much healthier. We all have our own ideas about what happens afterward. I myself feel that if we have loved life, then death, which is obviously a part of it, is something to be trusted. Yet I still hear people occasionally saying that they have "lost" a husband, a wife, or a baby, as if they had somehow left this person with their car keys on the post office counter and walked away without thinking. The truth is, of course, that we never lose anyone we have loved, because love knows nothing of time: the tense of love is always present perfect.

Still, things have been changing very rapidly. We not only read today of death and dying, "near-death" or "beyond-death" experiences, grief and bereavement, but are now able to find books on hospice management, hospice nursing and medicine, pastoral care in hospice, even hospice architecture, along with the constantly developing protocols of palliative care. Those reading about death or the care of the dying no longer feel as if they must carry the latest volume around in a plain brown wrapper, and these days I am quite comfortable telling strangers what I am writing about, which wasn't always so. The presence of some two thousand hospices in the United States today has been a powerful force in this transformation. All of those working on or helping with the hospice effort—all who have read or heard or thought about it, or have experienced hospice care for a loved one and shared that news—each and every one has participated in an extraordinary sea change in the emotional condition of this country. It is particularly interesting to me that the healing presence of hospice is more evident in small towns and villages across the nation than it is in the larger cities. Here in America the hospice concept seems to have wrapped itself into an embrace with old notions of simple neighborliness, the intimacy and connectedness of small-town living. In crossing the Atlantic, hospice has been met and matched by attitudes and concerns that are very deeply American, and the linking process here has been filled with passion, energy, and freshness.

There is another side to the story, of course, and we must keep that in mind: the witless "packaging" of hospice services here and there in the United States today; the inroads of wholly antithetical bureaucratic, political, and business interests; the ever destructive financial squeeze. However, the way of the world as noted above by Lewis Thomas suggests rather strongly that the hospice process is going to be around for a very long time in our culture, one way or another, as it has been already for centuries, though often invisibly; the modern hospice is not the dream of a mere decade or two, nor an innocent fad, destroyed once its surface charm is co-opted by cynics or used as camouflage for corporate greed. Perhaps what we need to do now is to think of hospice as an organism, a living and growing creature that has surfaced once again in our culture, and study its processes. This may help us to understand where it is going, and how, and what we ought to do about it. It may be that we have not taken up hospice during the late twentieth century so much as hospice has taken us up, including us once again within the many and variously linked circumferences of its own existence. Perhaps hospice is now recalling us to "earlier arrangements" while teaching us new clues and responses to the enigma of human suffering, and offering us, at the same time, new insights into the great, twin mysteries of death and love.

"I never knew how to live until I came here to die," said an elderly, blind gentleman of St. Joseph's Hospice in London. St. Joseph's will be a hundred years old in the year 2005, and in its history we can trace, in miniature, the development of the modern English hospice, from which our own hospice movement has come. Founded in 1905 as a haven for the sick and destitute by those remarkable women, the Irish Sisters of Charity, St. Joseph's has come to represent a blend of spirituality and hard medicine like that noticed by *Science* writer Constance Holden in the person of St. Christopher's medical director. The Our Lady Wing at St. Joseph's, added in 1957, was set aside especially for patients dying of cancer, and it was here that Dame Cicely Saunders did some of her most important, pioneering work in pain control during the 1950s and '60s. The relief of pain is seen in such a setting as a moral and medical imperative (in religious terms, a "most marvelous act of mercy"). Feeding into the blend, offering it constant enrichment, is the energy that creates a certain atmosphere, that of a lively and affectionate family whose members are attentive to one another's needs for understanding and respect. A special effort is made, in the Our Lady Wing, to include those who have little or no family assistance, 19 percent of the present patient population. Some individuals with motor neuron disease are also accepted, and persons with AIDS were welcomed until a fine facility designed and funded by the Department of Health for this specific purpose was opened nearby.

A true community, a matrix for human nurturance, is in existence at St. Joseph's and in the past few years it has been expanding, cell by cell. In 1977 a residential rehabilitation center (Heenan House) was added for the physically handicapped. Here, short-term, respite residence is also offered for some cancer patients otherwise being cared for in their homes. A more recent addition is the Norfolk Wing, serving in part as a day care and recreation facility for the ill and disabled, and in part as a residential teaching center for doctors, nurses, social workers, and senior medical students. Patients, care-givers, and all others involved in the St. Joseph's family experienced a day of rejoicing when Queen Elizabeth came on May 17, 1984, to officiate at the opening of the Norfolk Wing.

Thirteen years ago I stumbled across icy, snow-covered streets to Sir Michael Sobell House at Oxford, hoping to meet Dr. Robert Twycross, and in a typical gesture of kindness, he left a family gathering that day to welcome a weary and somewhat disoriented traveler. This was the afternoon he shared with me (hoping they "did not sound too pious") what he calls the Ten Commandments for physicians coping with the pain of terminal cancer:

1. Thou Shalt not Assume that the Patient's Pain is due to the Malignant Process.
2. Thou Shalt try Simple Analgesics in the First Instance.
3. Thou Shalt not be Afraid of Narcotic Drugs.
4. Thou Shalt not Prescribe Inadequate Amounts of any Analgesic.

5. Thou Shalt not Use the Abbreviation PRN [as needed].

6. Thou Shalt Take into Consideration the Patient's Feelings.

7. Thou Shalt Provide Support for the Whole Family.

8. Thou Shalt not limit thy Approach Simply to the use of Drugs.

9. Thou Shalt not be Afraid to ask a Colleague's Advice.

10. Thou Shalt have an air of Quiet Confidence and Cautious Optimism.

These commandments may as well be carved into stone now, for they are not likely to become outdated.*

This small hospice on the grounds of Oxford's Churchill Hospital has its home in a charming stone and timber building rather like a modern country dwelling, with patients' rooms airy and pleasant, and much use of natural wood throughout the interior. It is connected to the hospital by a covered corridor, but Sobell House manages to retain its own ambience of life and growth, freedom and intimacy, with a great variety of activities and therapies being offered: arts and crafts, music, flower arrangement, hairdressing, massage, and even aromatherapy. Partly on account of budgetary restrictions, fewer inpatients are to be found here than in the 1970s (a reduction from twenty to fourteen beds). However, a great many more people are now receiving skilled care in their homes and in Sobell's new (1983) day care center, and still more are being served in a larger geographical area by means of networking with other agencies. A Bereavement Support Service is now in place, largely staffed by carefully trained and supervised volun-

---

* However, see note 226.

teers, and further outreach is constantly in progress through teaching, research, and publication of new materials on palliative care. The Sobell Study Center was added in 1987. Educational activities cover all aspects of palliative care, and a "working party" is currently in progress there, exploring the interface between science and religion, healers and hospices, in a series of discussions between nurses, physicians, theologians, and members of clergy. Recently designated by the World Health Organization as a Collaborating Center for Palliative Cancer Care, Sobell House received professional visitors during 1989–90 from many countries, including Norway, Switzerland, Hungary, Tasmania, Poland, Japan, Argentina, Australia, and the USSR.

On December 7, 1971, the mayor of Worthing in West Sussex broke ground for a new project, now known as St. Barnabus' Hospice, by driving a bulldozer onto the site. Unlike St. Joseph's and Sobell House, which receive funds from the National Health Service as well as charitable donations, this hospice was to be independent, the culmination of a long community effort, and connected to no other agency. In part the building was a tribute to a beloved local doctor, F. R. Gusterson, who for some time had been giving enlightened care to the terminally ill in their homes.

The building itself is modest, inexpensively built of prefabricated units set in the shape of a cross, at the end of a long, curving drive. There are gardens and large areas of glass-faced patio, and a favorite daily ritual of patients and care-givers is the feeding of visiting birds. "Dr. Gus" was a devoutly religious man with a twinkle in his eye who believed that hospice work itself was a form of worship. He said, however, "that the religious side of our work must be played very low-key. Our main concern is to give patients love and care; where we get the strength to do this is our own affair." In September 1981 Dr. Gusterson died, very peacefully, in his sleep. His successor, Dr. Alan Kingsbury, says, "If anyone had prepared well for death, it was ["Dr. Gus"]. He taught me an enormous amount about *caritas* and I shall always be grateful to him."

Deeply rooted in the life of its community, this little hospice has been remarkably well supported financially, and also by the work of volunteers. Nevertheless we find familiar changes here during recent years: the shift of emphasis from inpatient to home care; the reduction of the number of beds from thirty to twenty-six; the training of a home care team that networks with other nurses and physicians; and the addition of a day care center. "Patients prefer to remain at home if they possibly can for as long as they can," says Dr. Kingsbury, "and this has been increasingly possible." St. Barnabus' in the meantime, also reaching out, now employs a full-time social worker who has developed a more extensive bereavement program, and this hospice has also become a teaching center, offering nationally recognized courses in the care of the dying patient, with resident tutors in nursing and medicine.

In having a look at these three rather different English hospices, we can see a definite pattern emerging. All have their basis in the paired disciplines of medicine and religion, and all are involved one way or another today in outreach, from a simple journey to the patient's home to air links with like-minded people as far away as Tasmania and the Soviet Union. Their circles of care and nurture are being enlarged, both in content (centers for day care, studies of family psychology, bereavement support, new kinds of therapies) and in influence, via teaching, publication, and liaison with various other agencies. At St. Christopher's, by now the internationally recognized leader among all modern hospices, we find the same sort of process going on: a new Home and Day Care Center; more emphasis being placed upon family psychology, including more extensive bereavement support; and visits by nursing staff now reaching a much wider area. The Study Center at St. Christopher's is a constant hum of activity. The Fifth International Conference (1989) attracted four hundred representatives of thirty-seven nations, including Uganda, Turkey, Iceland, and China, all hoping to bring hospice philosophy and skills back to their own countries. Nearly every imaginable award has been given to Dame Cicely, not only the British Medical Association's Gold Medal for clinical expertise and the Anglican Church's rarely bestowed Lambeth Award for outstanding humanitarian service, but the OBE (Order of the British Empire), the DBE (equivalent to a knighthood), and the Order of Merit, a personal tribute from the Monarch. There are only twenty-four holders of the Order of Merit at any one time, and before Dame Cicely, Florence Nightingale was one of only five women ever to receive it.

But what is all this about psychology? Massage? Aromatherapy? I wonder what Mr. Pippin would have had to say? If I'd suggested any such thing to Mrs. K. or Mrs. D. at St. Christopher's in 1976, I'm sure they would have put it down—kind as they were—to my having lived too many years in California. I do recall trying to give a cautious massage of the hands one day to an old dear at St. C's who was causing the chaplain, and a dozen others on the floor, no end of trouble. She snatched one hand back immediately and sat on it. When I continued working on the other she began looking at me so oddly that I quit rather suddenly, with the definite impression that she was about to lean over and bite off my nose.

The interplay of English and American thought on appropriate and acceptable hospice therapies became a sort of dance in the years that followed. The "human potential movement" of the 1970s had found its best weather, and its most enthusiastic apostles, in California; and a number of would-be hospices, particularly on the West Coast, began with hand-holding and fine thoughts, while sorely lacking the necessary medical expertise. The heart was in the right place, but the head needed training. Gradually, however, over the years this situation has improved itself. Some of the finest medical hospice work is now being done in the West, and more than a dozen West Coast hospices are now directly associated with major university medical schools. In the meantime, England has taken on a slightly more American point of view, it seems, paying more attention to family dynamics, psychiatry in general, and the potential benefits of some of the newer, more experimental physical therapies.

The beginnings of the modern hospice movement in England were placed on a very firm foundation: a national health service; a long, commonly recognized, and state-approved religious tradition; and the innovative brilliance of British pharmacology. Above all there was the towering genius of Dame Cicely Saunders, and the loyalty of her many gifted colleagues, such as Dr. Thomas West who serves today as St. Christopher's medical director. In *A Personal View*, Dr. West wrote recently, "Twenty-one years ago a one-woman multi-disciplinary team opened St. Christopher's and began the world-wide hospice movement. Dame Cicely brought her nursing, social work, and medical skills with her and, it should be added, her Christian convictions." This affectionate tribute rings with truth and at the same time suggests a problematic challenge to those in other countries who in very different settings have since set out to do hospice work.

▲ ▲ ▲

There were many in the United States and Canada during the 1960s and '70s more than ready to hear the hospice message, and the leaders of all three of the earliest modern hospices in North America had close connections with St. Christopher's. Three variations on the St. Christopher's theme appeared in 1974 and 1975 in New Haven, Montreal, and New York City. Dr. Sylvia Lack, who had worked both at St. Joseph's and at St. Christopher's, began with a home care team in New Haven. A separate unit for hospice care was opened in the Royal Victoria Hospital in Montreal under the direction of Dr. Balfour Mount, a physician and professor of surgery who had spent a sabbatical year at St. Christopher's. And a "scatterbed" approach to hospice care within St. Luke's Hospital in New York was inaugurated in consultation with Dame Cicely by her friend and colleague the Rev. Carleton Sweetser. All of these early hospice efforts have survived and developed, each in a rather different manner. Hospice, Inc., of New Haven has now become Connecticut Hospice, with a very large budget and staff, a notable teaching center, and its own, purpose-built inpatient facility. St. Luke's Hospice in New York, known for its excellent inpatient and home care of a primarily low-income and minority population, is now the Palliative Care Service at St. Luke's/Roosevelt Hospital.

In French Canada the word *hospice* in the mid-1970s was taken to mean an almshouse for the elderly, and thus Dr. Mount chose to describe his work as a palliative care service. Some years ago, when I questioned the ability of a PCS within hospital walls to provide true hospice spirit, Dr. Mount corrected me in a delightful letter:

> Not only has there been a christening [here], and visits from bridal parties, complete with flowing gowns and confetti, but the regular celebration of birthdays, the

visiting of children and pets (including, on one occasion, a part timber wolf) but the regular celebration of life and its small details, the playing of poker for penny chips with volunteers while sipping a good scotch, singsongs with patients and staff.

What could be better? This celebration of life, of course, is the soul of hospice; and here we find it coupled, *as it must always be,* with meticulous attention to pain and symptom control via the interdisciplinary team approach. All three of the earliest hospices on this continent, in fact, placed their initial focus upon teamwork and excellence in medicine rather than upon the need for a separate building, thus avoiding, for the time being, at least, what an irreverent friend calls the "edifice complex." And although the handsome building and grounds of Connecticut Hospice have surely added much pleasure and convenience to their situation, architect Lo-Yi Chan made a point when he told an interviewer in 1976, with great modesty, that "with the right staff it could work in a motel."

The setting of the Royal Victoria's PCS was not unattractive, and in atmosphere it was actually much like St. Christopher's. The year 1976 in Canada saw the publication of a 516-page *Report of the Palliative Care Service (Rapport de la Service des Soins Palliatifs)* in two languages side by side at this hospital, and this admirable document suggested quite early on some of the problems that would be involved in "translating" England's hospice methods to other countries. Both staff and patients in Montreal came from widely varying backgrounds, urban and rural, rich and poor, Catholic and Protestant, atheist and agnostic, French and English, Greek and Chinese. There was no generally agreed-upon tradition, point of view, or set of religious or philosophical beliefs. There was not even a common language. Members of the group who had not worked out their own belief systems found it difficult to cope with others who had, and vice versa. In a landmark keynote address at the First Annual American Conference of Palliative Care (Boston, 1984), Dr. Mount tackled these and other difficult hospice questions. Pastoral care in a secular age has been one of his continuing concerns, and his 1984 address tells of an interesting experiment in this connection. A weekly gathering called Partage was being held for patients, family members, and staff, in which a specific theme was examined each time, such as Community, or Fear, or Hope. "Through readings, music, shared quiet, symbols, and actions, we learn something of both our shared vulnerability and our potential strength," said Dr. Mount. One almost hesitates to mention it, but this is, in fact, a sort of church—a secular church—and the people who gather together regularly in such a mode of humility and shared vulnerability will almost inevitably find themselves emerging as a linked group, a human community. Church or not, it is in such settings as this that love finds its ultimate grounding, and peace its methodology. In the words of Scott Peck, "It is only among the overtly imperfect that we can find community. . . . Our imperfections are among the few things we human beings all have in common." Peck also points out (in *The Different Drum: Community Making and Peace* [1987]) that communities of whatever sort tend to move toward drama, regularity, liturgy. It may be that, in so doing, we have a particularly deep, human need to imitate our Creator.

Among serious people, and those under serious stress, it seems that the move away from faith in a pluralistic society really cannot be tolerated without a complementary move toward some form of spiritual discipline. Self-knowledge and "centering" are all the more necessary for those in the front lines, where there is no commonly recognized social contract, no commonly acceptable language of belief.

As to power channels within the hospice structure, they are bound to be different in different societies. However democratic the English hospice's team concept, there is still a deeply assumed, deeply accepted sense of hierarchy on that side of the Atlantic. Matron is boss; and above Matron there is probably going to be an adored and/or exalted director. Let a duchess come to visit—let the queen herself come to open a new wing—and the entire system goes into meltdown. I go into meltdown right along with them if I am there. And everyone is mad with joy in a way that simply does not happen in America when a movie star—even a movie star who happens to be president—arrives on the scene. One must be frank enough, I think, to admit that.

Consequently, there has been a good deal more work to be done, on this side of the Atlantic, on the whole matter of the hospice interdisciplinary team system. Who is really in charge? Is it possible for people in different disciplines fully to support and respect one another? Hospice process is a powerful challenge to the old-world, hierarchical structures we have tended to maintain here, for one reason or another, within the medical establishment. Dr. Mount asks:

> What in the world happened to our traditional roles when we mixed them into hospice? . . . The holistic orientation of hospice care forces the physician to adopt a more egalitarian role. . . . The administrator is called upon to respond to the demands of the whole team rather than those of a hierarchy. . . . Too often team members see decision making in hospice as being autocratic or dictatorial, while the director may feel that there has to be a referendum on every topic to keep the team happy.

This is not a comfortable position for the care-givers, and yet it is a position providing for excellent care of hospice patients! It also calls for, and provides an opportunity for, considerable personal growth on the part of staff members as well as families of patients and the patients themselves. Roles are being reversed and upset in all directions, for in the hospice situation it is ultimately the patients who are running the show. Here they are not expected to defer to and flatter the care-giver; they are expected to be the doctor's mentors, the nurse's teachers. Again and again as we study it closely we find the hospice process forcing people into the sort of doubt and discomfort that can bring to birth truly creative responses. Even the act of standing by a dying person, and being present for the bereaved, will challenge most care-givers' fundamental belief systems. But the hospice process as a whole is a good deal more demanding than that.

In a typical hospice paradox, Dr. Mount himself is now seen as somewhat larger than life, and is probably the most generally admired figure in the North American hospice world today. Others in the larger community of hospice people are grateful for his identification and acknowledgment of difficulties such as these, and for the courage and creativity with which he has met them.

While the immediate heirs of St. Christopher's settled down on the East Coast, something closely related to that adventure was beginning to happen, apparently quite independently, in the West. During 1973 and 1974 in the San Francisco Bay Area, an Episcopal parish priest and his friend, a physician and psychiatrist, were meeting regularly for a series of conversations. Often they met under a tree in a neighborhood park so that they could be away from their telephones and other office distractions. The subject they returned to most frequently was their mutual concern for people in the neighborhood who were dying, usually of cancer, slowly and in great pain, without proper help or support for themselves or their families. This, as it happened, was the beginning of Hospice of Marin, which we have visited at a slightly later stage in chapter 4.

It is safe to assume, by now, that similar conversations were taking place at that very time all over the United States. From the time when our first half-dozen hospices appeared, it has been clear that this was a groundswell, a tremendously powerful grass-roots movement. There were many contributing reasons for this, one being demographic: an older population in the 1970s and '80s, and more of them dying with medical problems capable of being well managed in the home. There was also the financial reason: high-tech hospitals were already less and less financially *hospitable* in those days. There was the medical reason, a response to the inappropriate treatment so often given to patients in the acute care setting, and the truly appalling ignorance of most American physicians about pain control. However, even this does not explain the passionate, wildfire quality of the movement, and the eagerness of so many members of the general public to participate. I am convinced that so-called "health care delivery"—a hideous misdescription, by the way—is not at all what the hospice phenomenon is about, even if the phrase is understood in its broadest sense as pertaining to public health and involving the people's moral as well as physical well-being. The truth, I believe, lies somewhat deeper.

One useful way of looking at it may be to ask what hospice is doing—and in some cases has already done—to change the lives of individuals and of certain particularly sensitive small groups of people within the country today. There may be truth in Lewis Thomas's statement that "we haven't yet learned how to stay human when assembled in masses." If so, perhaps it will be up to the few to teach the many, during the coming century.

One of the striking things I have noticed in talking with hospice people recently, and visiting a good many hospices, is the recurrent motif of personal transformation. Hospice doctors have said such things as, "I have enjoyed the practice of medicine in an entirely new way since my embracing the hospice concept," and, "I knew—or thought I knew— all that there was to know about bones, muscles, and trauma before [hospice], but I realize now that I never knew one-two-three about people." A retired physician who had come back into part-time service with a hospice in Virginia said, "This is wonderful! At last I have time to get to know the people I am working with, and time to spend with the patients. It's what I've been waiting for all my life." A happy though rather exhausted hospice physician in Colorado said it eloquently: "It is a life-changing experience for a physician to become involved in hospice. My patients can see now that I understand their pain, that I have something to offer them. I stay with them, and we talk. In the past, I never gave out my private telephone number to patients and their families; now I always do. I want them to know that they can call me, that I really care for them. And I feel loved in turn, now, by my patients. All my relationships have changed on account of this—my marriage, my family, my entire life has opened up and taken on new meaning. It doesn't matter to me that some of the things I am doing now really amount to nursing. It doesn't matter at all, because I feel at last now like a whole person."

The hospice nurse has been tagged, in the usual jargon, as "superior to others in self-actualization," and so forth. I myself much prefer the description by a hospice administrator, business-trained and new to the field: "Independent, opinionated, and stubborn—a real management problem." Evidently, our hospice nurses don't intend to be managed. They intend to be treated as independent equals, and hospice theory allows, in fact *invites* them to take this role. Despite a nationwide shortage of R.N.'s at present, this may be one reason why we still find them working, often for modest salaries, in hospices. *(Question: "Why is there a shortage of nurses all over the country?" Reply, from the Midwest: "There are many more options open to women now, and they are tired of being bossed around and treated badly by the doctors, who get all the credit and all of the money.")* It appears that the many personal satisfactions of hospice make it particularly attractive to those who are willing or able to work part time, or for something less than top salary. Yet there are some receiving standard nursing wages for full-time hospice work, and preferring hospice because it reflects and supports their own belief systems. From a nurse at Hospice of Marin (by now a large, stable, and well-funded organization): "It gives me the incredible luxury of truly practicing nursing skills. I see hospice as "female": it's about caring and nurturing. It says, I am the handmaiden of the people I am serving. And you know, we really have changed mainstream medicine!" A nurse in a small town in the Northwest says, "I've gone back—temporarily, I hope—into public health, and it's amazing how different that feels. Now I just feel like *a nurse,* any old nurse, but before, I felt that I was doing something special. And the way people reacted when they heard that I was doing hospice work—they were so fascinated and full of admiration. It was as if they thought it takes a special kind of person to do hospice, and, I guess, maybe that is true. By comparison, when I walk down the street now, I feel sort of invisible."

▲　▲　▲

The sense of wholeness experienced by professionals in hospice work brings a kind of healing to them, a way of being that directly contravenes the tendency of the industrial society to objectify and dehumanize its workers, and inasmuch as medicine has become an industry in America today, this is the sort of healing its practitioners badly need. There is a recovery, too, in hospice, of the feminine power that enables us all—men and women alike—to nurture one another and to cherish life itself in all its forms. The reach toward greater integrity of person in the hospice process allows the male physician to enjoy the tenderness of a nursing role, while the female nurse is encouraged to explore her own independent power and autonomy.

The high rate of volunteerism in hospice work is also telling us something significant. At times we forget that the word "professional" once referred, by definition, not to the attainment of superior technical skills, but to the profession of a faith. In the hospice movement the ancient meaning of the word is recovered. The offer of healing where cure is impossible, the donation of time and energy without any promise of material reward, and the launching of new modes of caring into the chaos of a nervous and fragmented society, all are acts of profession, of faith that there is meaning and value in human life. In the service of this belief, hospice people bring to bear the skills that have been traditionally considered professional: medicine, nursing, architectural design, psychiatric and pastoral counseling, art, social work, administration and communication, fund raising and engineering, teaching and research. For that matter, the cook who brings a delicious, hot meal to a patient, or the blue-collar worker who comes in and washes the floor, is as much a professional as the oncologist or the pharmacologist here. The same, central faith is being expressed by all, and in the close interdependence of the hospice community, each individual must depend upon the commitment of every other.

The tradition of faith, and the ancient religious belief that dying persons should be honored, has been rather inconspicuously present in the American scene for many years. It was found in the work of such groups as the Sisters of the House of Calvary in New York, and in the leadership of dedicated individuals like Rose Hawthorne Lathrop (Nathaniel Hawthorne's daughter) who have established "homes" in the past, with decent standards of care for the terminally ill. What we have not seen until recently, however, has been the tremendous outpouring of care and effort in this field by the general public. Perhaps the statement being made now is that this work belongs to all of us, that we are now mature enough to value one another not for our material productiveness or for our contributions to the convenience and wealth of society, but rather for the qualities of soul and spirit that lie within.

The nature of the hospice process is revealed in the teams we build, the way those teams are organized, and the way we must treat one another as well as our patients, day by day if the program is going to work. In its authentic form, hospice is *an intimate transaction between human beings in community.* The conventional hierarchies of the military-industrial establishment function so as to separate people from one another, and control them by making them relatively powerless, anonymous, and interchangeable. Hospice process, however, demands an altogether different style, and a different world view. This work simply cannot be done right unless people come together in ways that are mutually trustful, nurturing, and supportive, with the personhood as well as the skill of each care-giver fully recognized. Only when the care-giver's *person* is honored by the group will that individual be ready and able to enter into a creative relationship with the *person* being cared for, that human process which, in Father Tom O'Connor's words, is so easily recognized by its "freshness, originality . . . and attractiveness."

There are so many fine hospice groups in the United States today that one might choose almost at random to find models worth closer study. Some are now based in our larger hospitals and medical centers; others work in alliance with other agencies for health care, such as the Visiting Nurses Association; still others are independent and community-based. There is even a large, for-profit chain of "hospices" now in this country, and there are group homes for AIDS patients in several of the larger cities, without hospice medical care or management but, unfortunately, sometimes referred to as "hospices." These are the hazards of inventiveness, and this sort of exploitation is the bane of the creative minority in any society. The more stubborn, outspoken, and persistent hospice people are in the next few years about defining their own principles, standards, and priorities, the sooner the public will be likely to reject such misnomers and abuses.

"Hospice is a medically directed, multidisciplinary program of care providing physical, psychological, pastoral, social service, and bereavement support to the terminally ill," reads the bulletin of a small, authentic hospice group in Bozeman, Montana—a random choice among its kind on my part, since I went there recently on another errand. But I had friends in the town, and wondered what Iain and Madeline would find should they ever have need of hospice. "Hospice is a community-based, non-profit organization," the bulletin continues, "free to patients and family members through volunteer efforts of professional and lay people. Hospice will seek third-party reimbursement for some services. Fund-raising, private donations, and memorials are essential . . ."

This hardworking group, in a town of twenty thousand set among vast mountain ranges near Yellowstone National Park, has become an important and respected part of the life of the community during the past seven years. They cared for twenty-two patients last year (91 percent cancer) with the help of one paid staff member and no less than 116 volunteers, five of them registered nurses. Their core team includes nurses, pastors, a nutritionist, and a consulting physician. They work closely with the local university (Montana State), offering an accredited program in Community Education and Training twice a year. They also have a speaker's bureau, and an excellent program in bereavement counseling and support that has been made available to the entire community. The Loss Support Group is an extremely important offering to the public in this relatively isolated spot with its rugged winter weather and no mental health organization within many miles.

The State of Montana has licensed Gallatin Hospice, and good relations have been established with several private insurance companies, but this hospice has elected thus far not to apply for the federal Medicare benefits available since 1984, feeling that the bureaucratic struggles involved would not be worth it. Instead, members of the group have worked with great enthusiasm and persistence to make themselves visible, to explain hospice principles to their neighbors, and to enlist direct financial support from foundations, and by means of homespun strategies such as a fund-raising "Hospice Tree of Memories" at Christmastime in a downtown bank. The Lutheran church has given them rent-free office space, and business people have contributed a great deal of time, labor, and equipment. Like barn raising and quilting bees during pioneer days, this sort of effort touches a deep place in the heart of America, helping to strengthen community while lending greater strength and autonomy to individuals.

People are tough and independent in Montana. They don't like going to hospitals, and the hospice nurses have to persuade them, at times, to take their pain medication. But they also understand the meaning of *caritas*. Pat Newby, R.N., and I visited a patient who summed it all up for me one day. The proud father of a young family, he was dying of Lou Gehrig's disease, but he sat bolt upright in his chair, fully dressed in an outdoorsman's checked shirt and trim, khaki trousers, to welcome us as his guests. We drank coffee together, and when I asked him what he thought of hospice, he said, "I like this hospice—yes, I do. It's a kind of a neighbor to neighbor thing."

It was not by random choice that I visited Appleton Community Hospice in Appleton, Wisconsin. Both the National Hospice Organization and the Hospice Education Institute had told me that this was a fine group, and I was interested to hear that the State of Wisconsin's Controlled Substance Board had inaugurated, in 1986, an Initiative for Improving Cancer Pain Management with the support of the World Health Organization. The Initiative was a result of studies showing that there was serious underuse of narcotics by physicians in Wisconsin when treating cancer pain, and the pilot program calling them to account for this is now serving as a model for many other American communities.

Appleton is a pleasant and prosperous town of sixty-two thousand in the lush, green Fox River valley in the eastern part of the state. A series of paper mills along the river has provided steady employment for decades; this was known as "Happy Valley" during the Depression, for its relative lack of poverty. Its inhabitants tend to be outgoing, forward-looking, and energetic people, interested in the arts (there is a small liberal arts college in town), outdoor sports (hunting and fishing), religion (Catholic and Lutheran, each about 40 percent, plus a smaller Jewish community), and good health care. Mary Runge, R.N., director of the hospice, is a former teacher of acute care nursing with considerable experience in the home health field as well. As a student nurse at the University of Wisconsin hospital some years ago, she became aware of the plight of dying patients and felt moved to help them, although she did not know yet of the existence of modern hospices in England. Later, a personal experience of extreme pain, untreated for days because disbelieved and discounted in a traditional medical setting, helped Mary to determine her future direction. A videotape about hospice theory was brought to her attention in 1977, and a series of meetings with like-minded people followed: nurses, physicians, social workers, teachers, spiritual counselors, administrators and lay persons, a good representation of the community at large. It was determined by a committee of this group that 90 percent of Appleton's people were dying alone in institutions, and that families trying to care for a loved one at home often became exhausted. On the basis of these findings, the group sought funding from the two community hospitals and the Visiting Nurse Association of Appleton, and Mary Runge was hired as coordinator to begin forming and training a hospice team. Appleton Community Hospice celebrated its tenth birthday on October 18, 1990.

This hospice now operates in collaboration with the local Visiting Nurse Association, with Mary serving as president and executive director of both organizations, and with the full support of both the Catholic and the Lutheran hospitals, even though those two institutions have had their differences in the past. Mary Runge is a sensitive and good-natured diplomat as well as a rousing public speaker who has successfully lobbied community leaders and the general public in support of this hospice program. Their current $500,000 annual budget for hospice comes from Medicare, Medicaid, private insurance, donations, and grants. The Medicare benefit, Mary says, is "acceptable as long as you don't let it run your program." And she adds, "In general, if I were to talk about a concern I have for hospice, it would be that many hospices in our country are becoming mirror images of the [restrictive] Medicare hospice benefit."

One of the first things I noticed in the colorful and attractive offices of the VNA/Community Hospice was a chart showing a series of intersecting circles, with patient and family in the large, central circle, where they belong. Smaller circles on the outside overlapped, representing the various care-givers. It was a nice relief from the rows of little insulated coffins we see on the organizational charts of industry and business. Something rather different is happening here: people are actually communicating, touching, caring for one another, in a network of relatedness, linked together by common concerns. In comparison with Gallatin Hospice this is a very large organization (forty-five patients per day, a paid staff of 172), but because hospice principles are understood here, and have been carefully guarded during a period of rapid growth, very high standards of care have been maintained. A central, or core, hospice interdisciplinary team is in charge of all hospice activities within the organization. In another series of intersecting and overlapping circles, three subteam groupings have appeared, with each team serving a different geographical area. Mary Runge says, "Hospice was not . . . seen as a place in this program, but a *concept* of care . . . that would surround the dying patient and family throughout the dying process whether the patient was at home, in a hospital or extended-care facility. . . . *It is our philosophy that we should always plan the care for others based on how we want to be cared for when we are dying.*"

Charlie Lingelbach, a retired business executive, is one of Appleton Hospice's many faithful volunteers. Arriving with his toolbox under his arm one afternoon, he told me of his pleasure in fixing things around the office and doing frontline work with patients. "I was in the Air Force during the war, in Italy, Africa—that taught me not to be afraid of death. A little blood and gore doesn't bother me either, I was used to it. What I like about this work is that hospice people are good people. I enjoy helping them out, and I'm always interested in being with the patients and their families. It's just a matter of being a good neighbor, really. There was one place I used to visit where the wife couldn't stand housework, but, oh, how she loved farming. What a character. It was her husband who was dying, and he said to me, 'Good thing I married the biggest, strongest woman I could find.' As soon as I'd get there, she would ask me to hang the wash on the line or something like that, so she could get out there on the tractor and bale hay. Well, I was happy to do things like that for her—why not? In her situation that was the least a person could do. Hospice work is great, but it's a thing that can get you down at times, you get to feeling really blue. When that happens, I have a little place in the country, and I just go on up there by myself for a day or two, and chop some wood."

A man brought to the hospital with a badly broken leg was lying there in traction, groaning, agonized and forlorn, when he noticed another patient on the ward receiving plenty of pain relief, a gentle backrub, a glass of wine with dinner, and various other comforts, including the presence of a friend who sat there long past visiting hours, quietly holding his hand. The one with the broken bones protested, and when it was explained to him that the other was a hospice patient, he exclaimed, "My God, do you have to be dying to get that kind of care around here?"

The renowned University of California at Davis Medical Center in Sacramento, I learned, had a rather special little hospice tucked away somewhere on its grounds. Without any clear idea of what to expect, I found my way one August afternoon to Camellia Cottage, a modest bungalow on a lawn adjacent to the imposing, modern buildings of the UC Davis Medical Center itself. I found smiling faces, the fragrance of coffee, office cubicles brightly furnished, attractive pictures, photographs, much-used bulletin boards, and a small meeting room into which more than a dozen of us soon gathered. Who was the leader? They were all leaders, it seemed. It was Hospice Program Director Mary E. Kennedy, R.N., O.C.N., M.S., who brought me a cup of coffee. Everyone else was evidently a "coordinator" of one thing or another—patient care, bereavement support, social services, and so forth. We sat around quite at ease, amid a good deal of laughter and mutual enjoyment, and with all sorts of information flying about, in a comfortably casual circle that included two physicians. Frederick J. Meyers, professor in the division of hematology and oncology, was the hospice's medical program director. UCDMC psychiatrist Saul Levin, it turned out, had previously founded a hospice program in his native Johannesburg. When I asked how the group managed to teach hospice medicine in a traditional setting, the answer, with a grin, was *"Insidiously . . ."* and a great roar of laughter went up.

Members of this group were obviously well cared for. This was not merely a collection of people with useful skills; it was a community. How had this come about? "One of the unique things about UC Davis," says Dr. Levin, "is the fact that while the hospice team is taking care of patients and patient families, counselors are dealing with the hospice team. There are very few programs in which health care professionals take care of other health care professionals." The staff, including volunteers, attends weekly meetings of a support group to talk, not only about patients, but about their own thoughts and feelings. Trust has been carefully built here, and consciously maintained, so that spiritual and emotional as well as practical concerns can be freely expressed. An important device has been the annual "retreat" during which group members are helped to become "better facilitators and cooperators" with one another, learning about each other through games as well as discussions, and studying their own group processes. The following contract, prominently displayed in the hospice office, was drawn up by members of the first Annual Retreat:

TEAM COMMITMENT

We recognize that our dedication to provide excellent patient care demands a foundation that incorporates high-quality interpersonal relationships among the team members. We individually and corporately pledge:

1. Honesty
2. Active listening
3. Letting go of expectations about the outcome
4. Flexibility
5. To ask for what we need and to risk vulnerability
6. Self-disclosure which demonstrates trust
7. To treat each other compassionately
8. To be nonjudgmental

What this contract provides for, in fact, is *a safe place:* a nourishing circle of trust designed to promote personal healing, personal growth. Like Dr. Balfour Mount's Partage, the mutually supportive process of this group bears a resemblance to a church in that it has drama, liturgy, regu-

larity (even, in this case, an annual "retreat"), and that it
tends to lift the consciousness of participants above the
purely materialistic and egoistic plane. Peace is being created here, and it is the presence of love as well as peace in
this room that embraces the visitor in an unmistakable atmosphere of "freshness, originality, and attractiveness." The
founder of the UCDMC hospice program was hematologist
and oncologist Dr. E. J. Watson-Williams, who made the
following comments at a National Hospice Organization
meeting in 1979:

> The physician in the modern Western civilization is a
> remarkable person. He or she has been told by medical
> school admission committees that they are intellectu-
> ally superior and inspirationally devoted to the service
> of others, to whom they are irreplaceable, ethically irre-
> proachable, and never wrong.... [The physician] works
> in a tradition that regards illness as a manifestation of
> a bad something, either from within or without the
> patient. It is his job to find out what is bad and then to
> remove it or destroy it. He has learned to treat the
> illness rather than to care for the patient.

Dr. Watson-Williams went on to say—and to teach—that
the best way of educating physicians in hospice work is to
invite them in as members of a group engaged in a task that
is going to be helpful to doctors as well as patients: helping
to provide excellence of care to those whom science cannot
cure. Since that time the UC Davis Medical Center has
achieved a position of leadership in the newly developing
effort to teach hospice care as an integral part of the American medical school curriculum. UC Davis School of Medicine students learn hospice principles today during their
first-year psychiatry course, and also during their fourth-
year course in hematology/oncology. An optional four-
week rotation is also offered, with supervised, hands-on
hospice care. Recent graduates have had these reactions to

the rotation: "A pretty powerful experience. It helped me deal with a lot of my own insecurities about dying patients and what death is all about," and, "One of the most valuable things I did as a medical student."

The hospice itself cared for approximately one hundred patients and families during 1989, with a paid staff of ten and a roster of twenty-seven volunteers. Care was given in the patients' homes except for brief stays in the hospital for specialized palliative care. Funding (of about $475,000) comes, as in most hospices, from a variety of sources, including the medical center itself, but also comes from private donations, memorials, the United Way, and fund-raising efforts by the group. In 1990–91 federal and state funding from Medicare and Medi-Cal was received for the first time. A family conference center, furnished like an ordinary living room, will be provided by the hospice in a new cancer center now under construction at UCDMC; and they will also be working with terminally ill children in collaboration with a Shriners hospital for children soon to be built quite nearby (some children are already being cared for by the UC Davis hospice team). When asked what concerns she had for the future of hospice in the United States, Mary Kennedy replied, "The greatest challenge for hospice will be during the next ten years. This challenge is to maintain the original philosophy and grass-roots commitment of hospice while maintaining a position as a contributing member of the health care system. Hospices must maintain a balance between pragmatism and humanity if we expect to survive. . . ."

Hospice people in general ask today, can we survive the demands and restrictions of regulatory and reimbursement agencies? Can we survive exploitation and/or the threat of takeover by "industry"? Can we survive a full-fledged epidemic of AIDS? These questions all address a central concern: can hospice survive *as itself*—can it remain hospice as we have known it? Possibly not. But if we understand hospice as an organism, powered by an essential force within our society, then this need not be a cause for dismay. Living things change; that is a part of their reality. And in the meantime, people bound up in such a phenomenon as hospice become remarkably determined, and quite marvelously inventive. If one agency will not do, by way of support and/or regulation, they will soon set out to find or invent another. In one western state at this time private insurance companies, rather than the U.S. government, are being asked to provide a per diem for hospice services, and they are beginning to respond to this suggestion. One of the early hospices in the Midwest has been swallowed up by a consortium of five hospitals, with its original medical director now serving as chief of all five; but the hospice team is still there, like Jonah in the whale's belly, with a family practice residency program filtering through. A hospice nurse there of ten years' standing writes, "Each day it amazes me what I learn from the patient and family." When you hear that, you know that hospice is happening.

As to AIDS, hospice in the United States is even now reaching out, creating variations upon its central theme, as we shall see in the next chapter. Hospitals, too, and other health care agencies are absorbing the hospice message in various ways. In other words, hospice per se will not have to bear the full AIDS burdens if indeed this does develop into a massive epidemic; we will all be in it together, and then we will simply do the best we can.

It is the business school ethic (or lack thereof) and the industrial mindset, with its crustacean armor of bureaucracy, that are probably the most poisonous of all threats to hospice. It is possible, as we have seen in Appleton and Sacramento, for hospice to have integrity and autonomy in collaboration with—or under the umbrella of—other institutions for health care. In fact, hospice can do some of its best teaching under such circumstances. However, the hospice manager who does not understand the historical and philosophical basis for the work, who thinks of it instead as a "growth industry," can rather quickly discourage and even destroy the hospice process in many situations. Competitiveness, and the search for divisive political and financial power, have no place in hospice work; it is hospice, instead, that must use wisely "the art of the possible" in finding financial and political support for itself *as hospice.* I believe that this can happen because I see it taking place in the heartlands, and because I see it also reaching out to join a network of like-minded people worldwide.

One of the problems hospice has faced in this decade is that the best care-givers are seldom also the best administrators; they usually need help with organization and paper work, and bureaucracy gets a foot in the door. The patient care coordinator quickly becomes a patient services manager; the director calls for a larger salary and three assistants; each assistant needs a secretary and new office equipment; and soon there is a battery of receptionists at the front desk, there is chrome and wall-to-wall carpeting everywhere, and no one knows what has really been happening with the patients. A letter from a small island off the coast of South Carolina asks:

> What does this have to do with a hospice in a small community with a budget of less than $25,000 a year which has served 43 patients in a year, has 4 bereavement meetings a month, does not bill a single cent to a third party payer and in fact provides payment for medication and additional expense for indigent families, has a nurse and a nursing aide on call, always has at least 1

patient who has no primary care person and who therefore is in greatest need of Hospice, and is available 24
hours a day. Since there is no charge for service, we
never need turn anyone away and can serve every referral. We have no bookkeeper, no computer, not even a
typewriter. What we do have though, is enormous community respect and support. Last spring when 50 people whose spouses we cared for . . . gathered together
in a memorial service to say thank you, we knew we
were a Hospice in the sense that the word Hospice
stands for.

In the ring of these words we hear, again, the meaning of
hospice, the force behind it, and a hint of the deeper reason
why it has not only appeared recently, but widely flourished. The American people are tired of deferring to uncar-
ing institutions, frittering away their power in top-heavy
organizations whose executives are far removed from the
real, the actual event. In the century to come it may become
clear at last that the business of America is no longer business, it is survival. In the twenty-first century survival will
depend upon peace that is not just the absence of war, but
active caring for one another and for the planet we inhabit.
This means that we all need to gather together in a mode
of humility and mutual vulnerability that can help us bring
about the formation of worldwide community. After a great
deal of thought about planet earth, Lewis Thomas once
came to the conclusion that "it is *most* like a single cell."
That observation is now becoming more and more believ-
able. Our computers, faxes, videos, and the international
system of telecommunications now in place may have come
along just in time, in fact, to help us understand how wrong
were the mechanical models of reality of the seventeenth
through the nineteenth centuries. People who insist, still,
upon separating themselves from actuality, behaving as if all
persons and events in the world did not influence one another profoundly, believing that they themselves are not

part of a closely interconnected and interdependent life-system, may soon find themselves toppling under the weight of their own armor, and under the weight of the debts they owe to the earth and to the rest of human society.

What our planet needs now is not money, surgery, chemo-therapy, or prostheses, but healing—achieving of oneness and wholeness. Hospice is linked in organic unity now with a number of other popular movements, here and abroad, that witness to the urgency of that need: the Green movement, the Gaia movement, the many interna-tional movements calling for responsibly holistic and eco-logical perspectives that recognize our interconnectedness, as hospice does. A new and healthier—and a more holy—view of the world is being called for. Douglas Mac-Donald, in recent issues of *The American Journal of Hospice & Palliative Care,* sums up the values of hospice, and its place in this new world view, as follows:

1. "Hospice acknowledges entropy" (accepts death as a reality, acknowledges the disintegration of systems).
2. "Hospice returns human beings to their con-text" (the nurturing matrix of families, friends, teams).
3. "Hospice restores community and full person-hood" ("helps to break false linkages between loss of independent, physical functioning and loss of dignity").
4. Hospice conserves energy by way of its *low tech-nology* and *decentralization of power.* "The more centralized an institution becomes, the more en-ergy is devoted to maintaining the bureaucratic infrastructure and the less to the actual work per-formed."

▲   ▲   ▲

Douglas MacDonald continues:

> Facing the future with a hospice world view means at-
> tempting to heal our society's injuries through a major
> restructuring of priorities, for which entropy is the the-
> ory and hospice the practice. Interdependence and com-
> munity would replace isolation. Human energy would
> supplant high technology. Participation would overrule
> consumerism. Democracy would be substituted for hi-
> erarchy. Efforts would be directed to minimizing the
> energy flow-through and equitably distributing its ben-
> efits. A hospice world view would address itself not only
> to terminal care or to health care as a whole, but to the
> full range of institutions governing the exchange of
> basic resources among human beings. . . .
>
> While there is still time, we must make our way
> back to the central stem of the tree of life, where our
> safety, our spirituality, and the rest of humanity await
> us. . . . The consequences of characterizing entropy—
> or death itself—as a malevolent force are dread,
> denial, and a wounding fragmentation of the spirit.
> How can we ever be whole, if we can never acknowl-
> edge a fundamental aspect of our own nature? But
> Teilhard [de Chardin]'s message and the message of
> hospice, is that we are free to ascribe a healing mean-
> ing to the natural occurrences of our lives. The deci-
> sion to do this is what is meant by faith. . . .

This, I believe, is what hospice 1970–1990 has really been
all about, and this is why, although it may change, it is not
going to vanish. Hospice in our time has been a part of a
spiritual journey, a discovery of new wholeness in the lives
of many, many people—care-givers, patients, and families
alike. The hospice processes we have been observing seem
to flow quite naturally toward larger wholeness in human
community, and in the act of exploring and celebrating that
larger wholeness, we find that holiness has entered in. Hospice in America today, in fact, has been part of a larger
movement in which the concept of holiness is being quietly
stolen out of "church" and claimed as a quality of earth, and

of people, and of all life created. Scientists are among our new metaphysicians, and if they can learn to communicate better with the rest of us, it may be through their eyes that we will finally perceive the whole earth as a liturgical setting. When we do see, at last, the sacredness of our own lives and those of others, when we come to a better awareness of this world's metaphysical dimensions, then—and perhaps only then—will we be able to make peace happen.

William James once remarked that we will not have peace until we discover a moral equivalent for war. At this time in history, perhaps we should be asking ourselves: What is it that makes war so fascinating? It is hard to believe that most people on earth really enjoy killing one another; and war is more than a child's game, in which one has a toy and the other wants it. The great allure of war is surely the intimacy, the trust, and the bonding together of individuals in a task that demands hard work and great courage; and its ultimate fascination is that war asks us all to confront—and master, if possible—our fear of death. But of course, hospice workers do this every day, with a wholly different purpose and different outcome. Hospice work can be seen as the very antithesis of war: as an adventure in compassion, an opportunity to serve the cause of a vital, courageous, and ultimately fascinating peace.

Perhaps we have chosen during this century to begin finding out how to make peace, in part by watching and waking with the dying, because we have seen a purity in them—stripped to the soul as they are, preparing for that final journey—that speaks to us, telling us that this is what we need urgently in our own lives. The dying have their priorities in order, as we say these days; in medieval times it was called being closer to God. This is why we learn so much that is valuable from the patients, although in a secular society we may not always be able to name it. We know, even so, that something in us is being brought to birth as we care for the person who is dying, that the relationship formed is holy, and a witness somehow to the heart and intent of Creation. The hospice process itself may indeed be a way of soul-making, a living and creaturely part of Teilhard de Chardin's great vision appearing now during our own time on earth as a grass-roots, worldwide "conspiracy of love."

14

AIDS

AIDS will become known as the disease that taught a society about humanity, about compassionate care to all human beings.

Mary E. Kennedy, R.N., O.C.N., M.S.
Hospice Director, UC Davis Medical Center

Nothing I do for these [AIDS] patients feels like a waste. . . . Sometimes I feel at these moments that I am being given permission to fall in love with the whole world.

Sue B., hospice volunteer

What follows in this chapter will be to a great extent a mosaic of voices, individual people responding to AIDS from the front lines, or very nearby. I myself have thought of death and dying for too long now in the hospice mode and from a hospice perspective to consider this disease in the abstract—the numbers, the percentages, who should be blamed for what, the various groups and subgroups—or even to place much emphasis upon medical data that in any case are all in flux, sliding and changing continually, even as I write this rather too long sentence. I will hazard a guess that the current epidemic of AIDS will someday be reexamined entirely, that it will be placed later on in a far larger, broader context, understood by future scientists as a part of the growing inability of the twentieth- and twenty-first-century human immune system to defend itself against an increasingly hostile environment. The reasons why that environment is becoming increasingly hostile are another matter, but I expect that AIDS will be heard by future poets and prophets as a cry for help, not just from a few souls in torment, but from an entire planet. In the meantime my own beliefs command me to listen as carefully as possible to the individual, to examine closely the present, the concrete and sometimes messy particular, in the faith that whatsoever is good, true, and lovely here—whatsoever is holy and eternal—will shine through.

William

It was a close, mutual friend who wanted us to meet, but William was living several thousand miles away at the time, and so our first few conversations were by telephone. We didn't talk long the first day—he was under the weather. A safety bar had disintegrated that morning as he was leaving the shower; he'd leaned on it so heavily that he'd taken a bad fall. William was as angry as he was hurt. "I am a survivor," he roared into the telephone, "but this is too much, this is ridiculous. It takes an hour and a half, sometimes two hours as it is, for me to get dressed in the morning. Now I'm supposed to do all that with a fractured skull, too, for Christ's sake." A vivid stream of language followed, in reference to his own situation, the state of the nation, medical bureaucracies in general, and, in particular, what we agreed to call here (it was not a hospice), the Agency. His voice, when he stopped shouting, was pleasant, educated, American, regionally unspecific. He had a nice chuckle. He told me he would be pleased to talk with me from time to time, especially since he spent half of his waking hours on the telephone anyway, a great many of those hours counseling people, particularly those who had just discovered that they were HIV positive. "There is such a need for someone to talk to these people like human beings. Some of them are just kids, so young they don't even know what sex they are yet, and they are already in trouble—God, they are already dying."

I asked him how he spent his time otherwise.

"Smashing up my skull," he said immediately. "I don't lead a boring life. As a matter of fact I attacked a car only yesterday, with my cane. I was trying to cross a street downtown, and I was just a little slow for this slob in a huge Oldsmobile. So she tried to cut me off and damn near wiped up the street with me in the process. A whole crowd of people saw what happened. Well, I am a radical in one way only, in that I am a pacifist, but I went after her taillights with my cane, and everybody cheered. She was ashamed— not when she saw what she had done to me, but when she heard all those people whooping. That really made my day."

I told him he sounded like a dangerous character. He didn't laugh. "I'm a very tough individual," he said, "and I've always had a very high energy level, or I wouldn't still be here. And I am also too mean to die—just too cantankerous. I am not going to oblige anybody on that score, believe me. I get up every morning and sharpen my tongue, first thing."

I asked him what he did next.

"Take my morphine pill and drink maybe a cola. I wait for the stuff to work so I can stand to get out of bed and walk around a little. Sometimes I can't—then I just have to go back to bed and lie there. But on the days when it doesn't hurt too much I get dressed, maybe do errands, go and see one of my doctors—and when I see them, I demand things, I really press them to the wall. I've researched every one of the drugs they want to give me. I found out that some of them might have been bad for me, so I refused to take them. I always demand two opinions—one from the university hospital and the other from a private doctor I go to—and I make my own decisions. I know more about me than the doctors do, and I am still going to be in control of my own life. It's been over four years now since they found out what was the matter with me, because it wasn't at all clear at first. Most of my friends are gone by now—so many. I don't miss my family, I miss the friends that had become my family. It's not that easy to make new friends at this point. I gave up a long time ago using ink when I put names and numbers in my address book. That was a waste—I just use pencil now."

After a pause he continued: "I am in three different research programs, ongoing studies, one in cardiology, one in dermatology—I got the Oscar in dermatology—I am the star in their worst-case-ever video. They have never seen anything like it, and they can't understand why it's not on my face. It's everywhere else, God knows. I tell them it's because I will not *allow* it on my face. I am not going to give up on this one. Well, at least all this may help somebody else if it can't help me. I think it will—at least some data are finally being established at the university.

"So what else do I do? Well, I am a member of the Hemlock Society, and the National Psoriasis Foundation. I keep up with all the latest—buy abstracts of all the big conferences—share my information with anyone who wants it. I run a one-man information service here. I've got lines out everywhere. And I take care of my housemates as much as I can—do a little cooking for them, help them with laundry, sit with them. The Agency people are never available when you need them. One guy in the room above me was screaming all night, the night that he died. It reminded me of when my mother was dying. I was eight then, and they kept chopping little pieces off of her every time she went to the hospital. Finally she was so little there was nothing left of her, but she kept on screaming. After that I got a stash—a lot more than it would take, actually, and some needles, and a chart from the Hemlock Society that tells you how to do it. When the time comes, I'm going to decide, and I am going out in style, not that other way. When it's time, I've got it all planned. I'm going to throw a huge party, helium balloons overhead, the best music, the best food, champagne, and I'll put it all on my credit card. I'll wear my tux—but I've got to have that altered. I used to be six-three without my boots on, two hundred twenty pounds, long hair, a Navaho chief's necklace, lots of turquoise. The girls really used to run after me. I didn't know what was going on for a long time, and I used to date—I even almost got married once. I'm down to one forty-three now. That tux of mine was custom-made, too. I wore it on cruises—dancing all night—everything. When I remember the good times, I think, God, we really did all that . . . and I know I've been lucky. Yeah, when I go, I'm not going to just wither away and disappear. No way. I am going to go out like a flash of light."

William was diagnosed four years ago by a neurologist searching for the cause of his crippling cluster headaches. The next time we talked he described them to me as "so excruciating that I would rather have someone tear my arm off and beat me with it," and listed some of the accompanying symptoms and various medications that had been tried. Nothing had helped very much over the long term, and some of the drugs had extremely disturbing side effects. In fact, during the course of his illness William has experienced so many symptoms, and has had so many medicines prescribed, and has tried so many different remedies, many on an experimental basis, that we soon agreed not to make them a part of this story, which in any case is not about medicine, but about William, a person who has AIDS. He has had access to the best of current treatment for the disease, and that has been disappointing. It is clear that his survival thus far has in part depended on his stubbornness, his inquisitiveness, his acceptance of responsibility for his own care and treatment. Probably it has also been due to the fact that he has, in effect, been running a sort of one-man hospice from his sickbed for the benefit of others. "That really gives me a lot of pleasure," he says. And in the meantime William has been helped in various ways by AIDS support groups bearing a strong resemblance to the beginnings of the hospice movement in this country: networks of care within the community.

James ▲ Yeshua ▲ Maggie

Later in this chapter you will meet James. It was he who told me in August 1988, "The hospice movement came along just in time to show us how to care for people with AIDS, and sometimes I think that had to be a miracle." I have thought a great deal about that statement, and about our usual reliance upon science—or what we conceive to be science—to explain all that is mysterious, when in truth we are surrounded by miracles. We live embedded in a matrix, we swim in a soup of miracles, beginning with the fact that no matter how badly we fail today, the sun will still come up tomorrow morning. I don't know many savants forgiving enough to invent such a program. And what we just as seldom notice on a day-to-day basis about our own society is something equally simple, equally amazing: an unspoken, taken-for-granted set of beliefs upon which we all rely whether or not we have ever set foot in a church, a mosque, or a synagogue. *We know that we are supposed to take care of one another.* And we also know very well that *it is wrong not to.* A miracle. In our own culture this turn of events is called the Judeo-Christian ethic, but that does not mean that it came out of a sociology textbook or a treatise on morals and manners. Actually, it seems to be built-in, and from time to time we find ourselves rediscovering it, experiencing yet again the welling up of a power that is within us, a power that simply will not be held down. It keeps bubbling up no matter what we do. It was this power at work among ancient Jews that caused a tremendous leap of imagination on their part, allowing them to understand suddenly and completely how it feels to be *the other person,* the outsider, and drawing from that some important conclusions. The rational expression of that truly mind-boggling insight followed in Judaic law: be kind to those who suffer and are estranged. *Remember always that you were strangers in the land of Egypt.* Later, Christians were given, not a committee, or a set of rules and precepts about gracious living, but a barefoot man named Yeshua who went around with all the wrong people, sweated and suffered, and in the process, showed the rest of the world how to live. Perhaps the central message that keeps welling up from the source of moral order—which is also the source of dawn and daybreak—is that we are supposed to enter into holy, rather than convenient relationships. On the question of "Creative Caring in the AIDS Crisis" theologian Maggie Ross writes: "For Christians there is but one example of caring: that of Jesus who spent most of his life being ritually unclean because he associated with those people whom 'respectable society' had cast out. Jesus did not demand that people change their lives, or make public acts of repentance, or regard him as morally superior. It was by humbly entering into relationship [with him], by the relationship itself, that forgiveness was offered and received. It was the relationship itself that was forgiveness . . ."

William ▲ Elton ▲ Neil ▲ Lawrence

William was born on October 9, 1952, in the American West, of a well-to-do family with a proud Scots genealogy, plus a grandmother's grandmother from the Blackfeet Indian tribe. His only sibling was a sister ten years older. He remembers his father as an alcoholic, his mother as an invalid. During his early teens he ran away from home, to his sister's. When his father remarried, William was sent to a boarding school in the mountains above Palm Springs, while father and stepmother traveled. The school was small, coed, with teachers from around the world. William was given a splendid palomino parade horse to ride there, and he was happy. The headmistress, he says, was a genius, serenely able to manage a dozen tasks and crises simultaneously. He thought of her frequently later on, when he was working his way up in the restaurant business and in the theater world. "I was never happier in my life than I was at that school. It was a great place, and they were the greatest people. I have contacted them, and they are going to let me plant a tree there . . . no, nothing with a brass plaque in my memory—just a tree. Just the idea of giving shade to someone who passes by is enough for me."

William went to work at nineteen in a restaurant, quickly moving up from lettuce-washer to chef, creating his own gourmet extravaganzas: a garlic soup, for example, with herbs, cream, and brandy—topped, not with croutons, but with miniature puff-pastries. "I was a natural. Everything I did was for the eye as well as the stomach, and I would only use the best, the freshest ingredients. I was really starting to get famous in Colorado. I was working six and seven days a week, twelve to fourteen hours a day, making good money. My father had always worn a diamond ring on his little finger, and they promised me one like it when I graduated from prep school, but they never came through. So with my first savings I bought my own diamond ring—it cost a thousand dollars. I have had more trouble with that ring—it keeps getting lost and then it shows up again. My father died when I was twenty-one.

"Anyhow, I always loved the glitter and glamour stuff—working with lights, colors, fabrics, doing my own designing and engineering. So for about three years in the seventies I worked at a place in the Midwest that did costuming for people way up there in the public eye—people like Elton John, Neil Diamond. Talk about the best ingredients—some of those fabrics were seven or eight hundred dollars a yard, with gold all running through, and patterns in twenty-four-carat gold leaf. When they traveled everything went into fitted containers, lined in silk. God, how I loved doing the magic for those people, making the magic happen. I made a pair of shoes once, with—well, like Tivoli lighting all over them, maybe you remember seeing them, they were quite famous. Elton John—his Shoes of Light? They were really something. But the stuff I had to work with was delivered all wrong—they sent it in these tubes that were impossible to work with—so I bought some flexible gadgets and then I worked for days and days, restringing every one of those thousands of tiny lights, fixing it so it would bend and he could move around in them. Some of the work I did on costumes in those days, I had to do the stitching, say, for bugle beads, from upside down looking in a mirror. God, how I loved figuring out things like that—making the magic happen."

Toward the end of this conversation William said, "By the way, my dearest friend passed away. . . . Not lover, friend. I've never really had a lover in that sense, no one to share my life with. Lawrence was a real friend, and he was getting better. He had gained weight—and then they overdosed him on chemotherapy. When I hear that someone I love has died now, I don't get upset anymore, I don't cry. I don't even bother to cross their names off, sometimes, in my address book these days. Instead, I find myself starting to crumble at the weirdest times—such as I'm watching some stupid cartoon on TV, and suddenly the tears are pouring. Or when I'm talking to someone on a whole other subject. Actually, I'm not feeling so hot right at the present moment." Then he said, "You know, it's going to be a big surprise for some people when they find a few years from now that it's not just the kind of folks they don't like who are dying, when they find out it's *everybody*. Because it is *going to be everybody*."

I told him that I was very sorry about Lawrence.

Fred ▲ John

It is generally considered that there are now more than one million people in the United States carrying the HIV virus, and six hundred thousand suffering from AIDS or ARC. The figures worldwide are even more appalling. The disease in Africa is not at present associated with homosexuality or intravenous drug use, and it is killing women and children, as well as men, in unprecedented numbers. The increasing urbanization of the planet and the enormous increase in worldwide air travel in recent decades have provided easy avenues for proliferation of the virus. In this country, the Centers for Disease Control (under the Department of Health and Human Services) maintains hot lines twenty-four hours a day, in English and in Spanish, for people seeking information about the prevention and transmission of AIDS. The CDC is also willing, when possible, to suggest possible sources of help for those who are already ill. "There's a lot of pain out there," said Fred, a recent hot-line spokesman. "We try to do as much as we can for people. We want to be there for everyone."

Within many communities in this country, however, the stigma attached to AIDS is still focused largely upon the question of homosexuality. Literal readers of the Bible, particularly those self-proclaimed Christians who prefer for some reason to draw their moral precepts from the Old Testament rather than the New, have been some of the AIDS patients' severest critics. A profoundly simple and direct reply to this point of view appears in a recent sermon by scholar, theologian, and pastor, John Paul Engelcke:

> Did God send AIDS? No. The God Jesus reveals is love. He is always on the side of the solution, not on the side of the problem. He heals and saves, rather than condemns and destroys.
>
> God did not create AIDS because he dislikes gays. If he dislikes gays, all he has to do is stop making them. But since Adam and Eve, God produces gays at a standard rate of about 10 percent of the population, year after year, millennia after millennia.
>
> AIDS cannot be God's silver bullet against gays, because it is so sloppy, killing babies, hemophiliacs, and heterosexuals also. If God had targeted gays with AIDS, he would have done a better, cleaner, more expert job. A God of love has no hand in architecturing so nasty a business.

William ▲ Chagall ▲ Big Brother

When we met again, still on the telephone, I asked William about his finances, and the Agency. He said that he had inherited some money from a great-aunt when he was in his mid to late twenties. For three years he had lived with this lady, and had taken care of her, when no one else would.

"Don't ever put me in a home," she begged. And he told her, "You've got it." He cared for her until she died. It was the great-aunt who had brought him on the cruises. After her death there had been some money—quite a bit, for a while—and more travel, and a small art collection, including a Chagall. "I found it is the easiest thing in the world to be a gentleman. I accumulated, then I gave it all away. . . . Well, that's how it's done, isn't it? From time to time I just got rid of everything. It's a great feeling—you don't have to worry about being robbed, or losing things. I don't mind working. I love working, I'm good at what I do. The more stress, the more going on, the better. I ended up running a restaurant again, but of course I'm broke now. Social Security, Medicare, Medicaid, a bunch of other stuff like taxi vouchers, credit cards—it took me three years to get into the computer for all this—and then, the Agency. Low rent for the house, and a person who comes in once a week and purportedly cleans the bathroom. Then I get up and clean the bathroom after them. It wouldn't be so bad except for the really ominous power they want to have over us, and all the bullshit bureaucracy. The head of this organization is making a huge salary, and is obviously more into politics than health care, not to mention compassion. Big Brother is Watching You, here every minute, not to help, but to keep the books straight, making you sign huge documents, searching your room while you are out. Look, I let the people downtown stick me with needles constantly, I have had more lumbar taps, more CAT scans than anybody, pictures taken inside and out from every angle, all for the Benefit of Science and hopefully some other people. I am willing to do that. I even go to a therapist and let him X-ray my unconscious. The only private place I have left is here, where I live, and if I am dying, I think they could let me enjoy a few pleasures now and then, such as not having to tiptoe across the street with my empty pint vodka bottle to hide it in the public trash bin. And then if I call them up to say someone is screaming for help for God's sake or I say the house is on *fucking fire,* then they are always in some *fucking meeting,* they will get back to me later. Sometimes the whole situation here feels to me so empty, sort of like a cushion no one has ever sat on—and I ask myself, should I be here in this room, or am I supposed to be dead already?"

I asked him about possible hospice help, and knowing of my interest, he became polite and evasive. "Very nice people, I'm sure, but it didn't work out. Not here, anyway. Why not? Well, I don't actually remember. I think they wanted to send in nurses, something like that, but it wasn't what we needed. If anybody is the mother in this house, I am. I know what to do here. It's just that sometimes I need help with the stupid things, times when I just don't feel I can do it all."

Scott

It may be that a number of people in hospice work—as well as their cousins in the various AIDS support agencies now proliferating—need to stop their march (it is at times now less than a joyous parade) and begin listening to a different drummer. One good place to begin is with M. Scott Peck's book *The Different Drum: Community Making and Peace* (1987):

> Committees and chairpeople do not a community make. Community-building is an adventure, a going into the unknown. . . . The most successful community in this nation—probably in the whole world—is Alcoholics Anonymous. Through the community of AA and similar fellowships modeled on it, millions upon millions have found meaning in their lives. And all this

> has been done with virtually no organization, the found-
> ers having brilliantly sensed that excessive organization
> is antithetical to community.

Both hospice and the AIDS support organizations began as networks of mutual concern, compassion, and commitment. Let none of them forget, as time moves on, that their fundamental promise to their clients and their patients is "a truly safe place," and that this means, not a business office, not a laboratory, not an institution, but a community. Scott Peck continues:

> Human beings have within them a natural yearning and
> thrust toward health and wholeness and holiness. (All
> three words are derived from the same root.) Most of
> the time, however, this thrust, this energy, is enchained
> by fear, neutralized by defenses and resistances. But put
> a human being in a truly safe place, where these de-
> fenses and resistances are no longer necessary, and the
> thrust toward health is liberated. When we are safe,
> there is a natural tendency for us to heal and convert
> ourselves.

William ▲ Joan

We didn't talk again for a while, and when I next heard from him, William was in a haze of joy, undoubtedly with some measure of chemical assistance, but appropriate in any case, since he and our mutual friend Joan had decided that William should come to Hawaii as her guest for several months. "I can't believe her, I can't believe this friendship, it's one of the most wonderful things that has ever happened to me. It's so wonderful, it actually scares me. I want to cry. Listen, I want to make this the happiest two months Joan has ever experienced. She does so much for other people, never enough for herself. She deserves so much more. Wait until you hear what I've got planned—maybe you can help with the logistics. One day I just want her thinking it's going to be like any other day. And then she'll look out and see the longest limo she has ever seen, there in her driveway waiting all filled with thousands of flowers and half a dozen bottles of French Champagne. Chilled Champagne, chilled glasses, crystal—the very best. And that limo will take her to the most elegant resort you have got out there—and I'll tell her not to pack a bag, she won't need anything, because every single thing she needs is going to be there waiting for her. All she could ever want. A whole wardrobe of new clothes, all hung up in silk bags with her monogram, everything in the world that is totally glamorous. Shoes, cosmetics, stockings, everything. And she can have a facial, a whole body peel if she wants it, a new hairdo, manicure, pedicure—the works. And when she's done with that, they'll have a Jacuzzi for her, and let me tell you that Jacuzzi is going to be all filled with milk and rose petals, because, just for one day, I want Joan to feel like the most glamorous woman on earth. I don't care how young or how old they are, every woman needs that—and it's the kind of thing she would never do for herself. I won't even be there, but I'll have it all set up, and *that will be me, doing it for her.* What do you think? . . . Well, I love women, I have always loved women because I appreciate them, I understand their sensitivity. I may be gay, but women have always, always been my best friends." I asked William if anyone had ever done a thing like this for him, but he didn't hear me—he was on too high a trajectory.

Joan ▲ Sue ▲ Amadeus

Joan is a widow of sixty who lives in an elegantly furnished country cottage with her old dog, Lady, her music, her sewing, and an inherited collection of fine, Czechoslovakian cut glass. She is an accomplished clothing and costume designer, and she is also a retired microbiologist, with med-tech training and a double degree from the University of British Columbia in agriculture and food technology. Joan is a board member of the local hospice, and also of the local AIDS support project, serving as liaison between the two organizations. She is deeply fond of and supportive of William. "However," she told me, "I couldn't have done it if I'd thought, well, I'll just have this dear, delightful man out to visit. The key to it was in very careful planning, and in the really remarkable support I discovered, rather quietly existing here already, in the community."

Joan began preparations by asking William about his needs in terms of diet and general comfort. He requested a grip by the shower that would not fly off as soon as he touched it. That was installed. She then consulted local physicians with AIDS experience, and talked at some length with Sue, public health nurse and leader/coordinator of the local AIDS support group. Joan wanted to have a medical team in place for William, since she lives in a rural area, a considerable distance by air from Honolulu. Sue advised her on various practical matters and insisted that Joan provide for herself during the visit by attending regular, weekly meetings of the AIDS support group. Joan now studied information on home care for AIDS patients, some available locally, some from the National AIDS Information Clearinghouse in Rockland, Maryland. Having had professional experience in the past with measures for control of infectious disease (she had "suited up" for studies of staph outbreaks, and of tuberculosis among Native Americans), Joan found it quite simple and not at all daunting to set up basic household precautions for herself and a guest with AIDS. "There's not much to it," she says. "You start with commonsense hygiene and a good supply of ordinary household bleach. Then you remember that you are not in an ordinary situation. But this is really a very *fragile* virus, compared to some I've worked with—it's the symptoms of the disease that are so terribly capricious."

Joan's guest quarters needed some minor changes, some furniture moved and a few purchases so that William could have privacy without being isolated, a minimum of stairs to negotiate, and easy access to his own bathroom. His bed was placed so as to provide a pleasant view of the garden; a comfortable easy chair was brought in, along with good reading lights and a portable TV. On account of William's very painful skin condition, she searched for and managed to find some extraordinarily soft, natural-fiber sheets and pillowcases for him.

It was not, to Joan's mind, a major undertaking—and yet on later reflection she realized that something rather important had happened in her own life as a result of Will's visit, even before he arrived. Again and again she had been touched, during the course of her preparations, by subtle gestures of support and encouragement she received from unexpected sources. Having lived here for many years, Joan is well acquainted with the efficiency of our "coconut telegraph"—a mysterious process, sometimes terrifying to newcomers—by means of which everyone living up and down our fifty-mile coast knows immediately what everyone else is doing. And yet, without words or signals of which she was aware, since Joan herself is exceptionally discreet, she found herself now in a slightly different relationship with various neighbors, shopkeepers, men and women she was accustomed to seeing in the course of her daily rounds. In a sense, an invisible safety net was being quietly spread beneath her. It was nothing spectacular—a touch here, a gentle suggestion there, now and then a hint of deeper emotion—but she felt a new awareness of many of these individuals, and sensed the possibility of future friendships with them on a far more profound level than before. Of course it was also true that one or two of her acquaintances suddenly became quite preoccupied at this time, or simply stopped calling. "But that's all right," said Joan. "They have their own lives to lead—and I have mine." She was ready to welcome her guest.

On the Mainland, meantime, William's medical condition had suddenly deteriorated. New symptoms had appeared. Now he was not only in crisis, but engaged in a fearsome power struggle with his doctors, who refused permission for him to travel. The visit was postponed once, then again. Toward midsummer Joan undertook the task of designing and producing all of the costumes for an ambitious local production of *Amadeus*. It was a massive undertaking: a period piece that involved transforming a large, miscellaneous group of twentieth-century residents of Hawaii into bewigged and waistcoated, gowned and bejeweled eighteenth-century European courtiers. Joan begged, borrowed, rented, shopped, and sewed by day—then fitted and redesigned by night, constantly frustrated by the fact that materials she needed were not locally available. Opening night began to loom large, with all the usual fuss, stress, and jitters.

Now, William arrived. He was very ill, exhausted from the long trip, but triumphant. He had finally enraged his favorite doctor to the point where the man had shouted at him, "Get the hell out of here and don't come back—I don't ever want to see you again!" He was in a wheelchair when Joan picked him up at the airport with several suitcases full of clothes and medicines, an enormous stack of medical records—which turned out to be a lifesaver later on—and a knapsack filled with charming gifts for his hostess. The following morning United Parcel Service boxes began to arrive. For the local AIDS project William had packed pharmacological information sheets, database search materials, teaching aids, stacks of tapes and informational videos—plus fifty pounds of documents representing the entire proceedings of a major AIDS conference that had taken place recently on the Mainland.

The next parcel to arrive was for the community theater and Joan as costumer—specifically, for *Amadeus.* She opened it, hardly able to believe her eyes. There were yards upon yards of theatrical dazzle and glitter, all the things impossible to find in the local stores: heavy, lustrous European gold braid, bugle beads, faux pearl chains and appliqués, wheels of giant sequins by the yard in brilliant colors, exquisitely made iridescent beading, crystals, teardrops, ostrich feathers, a feather boa, lavish faux diamonds the size of turtles' eggs, emerald cut and faceted so as to capture light from every angle, flashing it back, as the wearer moved about the stage, to the last row in the house. She was stunned. William slept for a good part of the following week, while Joan sewed.

William · Cicely · David

He came to greet me, when I stopped by, walking with great difficulty and leaning heavily on his cane, taller and thinner than I had imagined him. He was dark-haired with fine features, very handsome despite his gauntness, and immaculately dressed. "I can't believe how wonderful this is," he said as soon as we had him comfortably settled on the deck. "It's so beautiful, and Joan has such a healing presence. There's something—I don't know, primal about it—I mean, about this whole experience."

I remembered Dame Cicely Saunders then, so radiantly smiling in her office at St. Christopher's thirteen years earlier, saying to me, *"Healing a person does not always mean curing a disease . . ."* "I worry about my doctors," William said. "They're the ones who really need a place like this to come to. There ought to be a hospice for doctors, don't you think? They have a hard time these days. They should get away, forget everything, sleep, see all this incredible beauty. I can't believe the flowers, the birds, the colors. I'll never forget the one in Washington, D.C., who had to tell me I was HIV positive. It was the first time for her, and she was horribly upset, maybe even more than I was. Especially at the end of the day when I go to my doctors, I can actually see them dying piece by piece, along with the patients. The case loads are so horrible, and it must be so totally depressing knowing that every single person you take care of is going to die."

I told him that death is not the problem—the problem is overload. He sighed and looked around him. "Yeah, not enough recovery time," he said. We sat silent for a while, watching the white and yellow butterflies dancing around the base of the coconut tree, and then I asked him if he would like to tell me how he would plan an ideal hospice for people with AIDS.

"I've had this dream for a long time," said William, "that I was going to win the lottery. And that was exactly what I was going to do with it, build a place, find a place like that. *(Dame Cicely: "Patients are the founders of St. Christopher's. It was through David's eyes that I was given a vision of this hospice in the beginning. As he was dying in a busy surgical ward, we talked for many hours of what his real needs were—not simply for medical care as such, but for someone to care for him as a person, to stand by and honor him for what he was. . . .")* It would be a place where people with this disease could come when they needed to, when they wanted to, but they would not have to stay there all the time. It wouldn't be like a hospital.

You need to feel that it is someplace where you are welcome, where they want you to be, and you have a right to be there. A place where they take you more or less as you are. I would have it be more like a lodge or a retreat, somewhere in the country. And you're going to need a place where the air is good, and you can see things growing, and have some kind of beauty around you. Like here— something like Joan's house, only bigger, a big sort of simple, rough-hewn place is the way I see it, and it definitely ought to be near to some water—there ought to be a lake or a stream, and I see it up in the mountains somewhere. Listen, I don't even have to close my eyes to see this place, I have thought about it so many times, lying there in my room back there on the airshaft, I have got this place all planned.

"As far as running it goes, first of all you have to begin with the personal. Because this has got to be a place where people can have their own space, and be by themselves sometimes, and also be together. People who are sick with this thing can do a lot to take care of each other—I've done it, God knows, so have plenty of others. *(Dame Cicely: "Very often it is the patients themselves who are our best teachers.")* For one thing, it's a good idea because it gives you something to live for. But you have to start at the bottom with the reality, because the reality is the people, and you have got to work up from there. You have got to see people right off the bat the way that they are, and not the way that you want them to be. And you can't start off with a lot of fifty-page contracts, and then let all that stuff turn into a block between yourself and the people. It's not going to work if you do it that way, and besides, all the joy is going to go out of it. No joy, no humor, no future in it for anybody. You'll have to have some professionals living there, just a few, to keep things steady. But the others could

come and go, and there would always be freedom for them
to do that. In other words, it would be saying that we're in
this thing together, and we are going to share whatever
happens from here on out. If I ever do win the lottery, that
is exactly what is going to happen. But it's fairly obvious by
now that I am not going to win the lottery, or anything else,
for that matter. It's too bad, because there was so much I
wanted to do." He looked down at his hands, enormously
swollen, cracked and flaking, and said, "Yo ho, the Heart-
break of Psoriasis."

I told him we should have at least a palomino on this
place, for him. Three weeks ago he would have chuckled,
but now he didn't. He was still looking at his hands. "The
other part of it is touch," he said after a while. "Just touching, and being touched. People need that. I don't mean
sex—I was never very sexually active anyway. Too fastidious, I guess. Actually, I found it boring. But you die a little
when no one ever touches you. When Joan hugged me at
the airport I realized how wonderful that was, and how it
was the first real hug I'd had in a long time. I had thought
of wearing a mask on the plane to protect myself from
bacteria with all that recirculated air, and everyone coughing. I wonder what they would have thought about that.
You can never tell how people are going to react, can you.
Well, I can't stand the way I look, myself, now, and that's
one of the worst things about it. I love beauty so much. It
was beautiful flying over. Blue and green are the best colors"—he was winding down now—"and that's all right, but
people have got to stop feeling that one of them is better
than any other. There are a few people I have to get in
touch with before I die, so I need to get back there and tell
them to stop thinking like that. They have just got to stop
it. I'm not going to say it on the telephone. Besides, I've
already spent too much money on flowers." We had been

sitting for more than an hour on the deck, and it was nearly dark now. "The point is," he said wearily, "just to be human, I guess."

He walked inside very slowly, obviously in great pain, but as I turned away I could see him leaning on his cane, bent over Joan's worktable, where she sat sewing under a bright light. With twenty-four hours to go, she was still stitching gems and braid onto gowns and jackets. On the table between them heaps upon heaps of jeweled trimmings flashed in the light—gold, red, blue, green, silver—all in a shimmering maze of enchantment. Opening night tomorrow! As I left, I thought the two of them looked like a pair of pirates in a cave, sorcerers in a tower, plotting the extraordinary magic that was about to happen.

Merle ▲ *David S.* ▲ *Randy* ▲ *Brenda* ▲ *Paul* ▲ *Sally B.* ▲ *Mary R.* ▲ *Mary K.*

The disease, as Joan remarked, is capricious. According to *The New York Times* of June 12, 1990:

> AIDS is a different disease than it was last year [said Dr. Merle A. Sande, chief of medicine at San Francisco General Hospital]. In gains already made against the disease, drugs are helping people live months or even years longer and are gradually controlling the pneumonia that was originally the most devastating infection to strike AIDS patients. But this progress has led to a new plateau of complications. During the precious extra time granted them, more people with AIDS are now falling prey to several cancers and a bewildering array of secondary infections that most victims in the earlier stages of the epidemic did not live to get.

It is this plateau of complications that presents one of the most difficult challenges to our hospices today, since most have undertaken to care only for patients with limited life expectancy. Government reimbursement policy, reflecting this assumption, now limits Medicare reimbursement for hospice care to six months; but persons suffering from AIDS may go into crisis, then enjoy a reasonable quality of life for indefinite periods. Another difficulty has been that most hospices require home care patients to have a primary care-giver in residence; but many persons with AIDS (in the stricken, gay communities, for example) live alone, or with others who are unable to help manage their care, and among these are many estranged from their families and communities of origin. A related, extremely serious problem has been that the epidemic in this country thus far has targeted persons already vulnerable, isolated, and/or stigmatized: hemophiliacs and others needing blood transfusions; infants born into poverty; homosexual males, and intravenous-drug users.

"Epidemics threaten the ties that bind communities together," Deputy City Attorney David Schulman of Los Angeles writes in the Spring 1988 issue of *Nova Law Review.* David is the nation's first full-time government AIDS discrimination lawyer. He continues:

> Events such as AIDS remind people of epidemics past, of battles of each against all. . . . But today . . . civil rights reminds American Society of something else. An archaic form of the word "remember" is "re-member," to bring all members back into the whole. Civil rights enable American citizens to re-member those who are unpopular, those who are disenfranchised, even those who are frightening, remembering that in a democratic society all are members of the whole. . . .
> It is useful in this regard to consider how our response to AIDS might have been different had the epidemic broken out among white, middle-class, happily married mid-Western businessmen.

Many observers have felt that the responses of the government and the medical establishment to AIDS have been unpardonably reluctant and ineffectual because of unadmitted distaste for this disease's target populations. In relation to the gay community, Randy Shilts's book *And the Band Played On* (1987) has been the most massive, eloquent— and elegantly documented—cry of outrage to date, charting the progress of our understanding of AIDS, and leveling the charge that information has not been properly developed or effectively put to use on account of establishment homophobia. The fact that this book has been a best seller in the United States for some time is perhaps a harbinger of change.

How have hospices in America responded to AIDS? A sincere effort to help has been made by many hospice leaders. Hospice care-givers have not shied away from the task; they are not by nature fearful, bigoted, or morally judgmental people. The new strategies called for—especially the need for residential facilities for patients lacking care-givers at home—are finding creative response from hospices in many areas. Private as well as public funds are being aggressively sought by hospice people on behalf of better care for those with AIDS, and creative liaisons for the purpose are being formed with other agencies. For example, the AIDS Action Alliance of Central Florida was responsible for helping to secure a $350,000 grant from the state for a planning study to determine how HIV infected/affected persons would be cared for in the future throughout the community. This alliance was chaired by Brenda Horne, who also serves as director of the Hospice of Central Florida.

AIDS patients now constitute 3 to 5 percent of this hospice's patients. A few are being cared for now on an inpatient basis at Hospice of Central Florida's residential facility, Martin Andersen Hospice House. Brenda Horne says, "We developed a policy statement as soon as AIDS came along, saying that we would not discriminate against people with this disease. We are very proud of remembering our roots and our commitments here. We don't turn our backs on anyone, period. If we can't help them for any reason, we go out looking for someone who can; no one goes away from here empty-handed. We are a big organization today, but we haven't forgotten that hospice has to start with the heart. We have broken things down into a series of small teams that can work closely together and keep the intimacy—so we can get to the patient, love and accept that patient as an individual. That's what it's all about. We have a wide-ranging board, mixed as to race and sex, personal background and spiritual commitment. Right now we have a target program for more volunteers from the black community, and we're advertising in the local Hispanic newspapers for a bilingual nurse. No man is an island here. And I see two hundred ten real heroes every day—those are our care-givers."

Brenda was one of the original volunteers of Hospice of Central Florida, which opened in April 1977 in the home of a local physician (Daniel C. Hadlock) as Hospice Orlando. At the time, they had only one paid staff member, ten volunteers, and a small service award from the city. They managed to care for sixty-three terminally ill patients and families during the latter half of 1977—quite an ambitious beginning. Brenda Horne has seen this acorn grow until, as director of Hospice of Central Florida, she now (1990) heads an organization with 110 paid staff members, some 210 patients per day, and a budget of $5 million (70 percent from Medicare and Medicaid, 11 percent from private insurance reimbursements, and 15 percent by donation; and the hospice is now seeking an endowment).

There are other heartening hospice stories involving AIDS, in many communities. A few hospices have always welcomed, whatever their illness, the homeless and those with no care-giver at home. This, in fact, has been seen as the particular calling of Hospice of St. John in Denver, established in 1977 by Father Paul von Lobkowitz of the Order of St. John of Jerusalem. Here, "the hospice and its staff become a part of the patient's extended family. We live together trying to live life to the fullest." Hospice of St. John accepts AIDS patients. *(William: "In other words, it would be saying that we're in this thing together.")* Connecticut Hospice (formerly Hospice, Inc., of New Haven) cares for those who have no support at home, many of whom have been AIDS patients, in a three-bedroom cottage recently added to its compound in a pleasant, suburban neighborhood. Hospice medical staff and specially trained volunteers work with the resident cottage director, a Roman Catholic priest. Approximately 4 percent of this hospice's patients have AIDS. "No hospice could *be* hospice and refuse to care for AIDS," says the Rev. Sally Bailey, staff art therapist. "Such care broadens [our] outlook and increases [our] vision of the meaning of hospice care in American society." Mary Runge, director of Appleton Community Hospice, says, "There should *never* be a . . . hospice or any health care facility that refuses to care for persons with AIDS/HIV infections. I feel very strongly about this. We will not hire anyone . . . who refuses to care for persons with AIDS. If staff has a fear, we support them, educate them, and help them through this. Our expectation, however, is that all staff will care for persons with AIDS." Of forty-five patients currently cared for by this hospice, two have AIDS.

From the University of California at Davis Medical Center, Mary E. Kennedy, hospice program director, reports that of seventy-two patients in 1989, two had AIDS, but that during the first two quarters of 1990, nine AIDS patients had been admitted to their program. She goes on to say: "The AIDS crisis has a specific meaning for our society which is not yet apparent. The lessons may be more obvious from a position fifty years hence. I think the lessons surrounding AIDS are embedded in a healing process. AIDS will become known as the disease that taught a society about humanity, about compassionate care to all human beings who are suffering and dying, regardless of diagnosis."

Joe ▲ Sally Y. ▲ Pat ▲ Cyra ▲ James

Critics of the hospice performance in regard to AIDS point out that the number of persons with AIDS now receiving hospice care is a very small percentage of the total AIDS population. As my knowledgeable friend Joe put it recently, "Virtually all hospices say that they will accept AIDS patients, but the number of them actually doing it—or caring for them in any significant proportions—is minuscule. For one thing, most of them want their Medicare reimbursement. And then you have a sociological problem here, where they are silently saying—we don't want *those people* anywhere around our nice, white, straight, middle-class patients. And our nice little volunteers wouldn't be happy about it either."

"On the other hand," says Sally Yoder, a seasoned observer of the hospice scene, "you have got to face the fact that there are also a whole lot of people with AIDS who don't want a bunch of Girl Scouts and do-gooders coming around to see them either." Sally has owned and managed Rainbow House, a small, private convalescent home in San Rafael, California, for many years; she has worked with the terminally ill, sometimes in collaboration with Bay Area hospices; and she has trained hands-on care-givers as a volunteer at the local (Marin County) AIDS support project. "But there's no way to judge this situation on an across-the-board basis," Sally says. "The responses I see are completely different, neighborhood by neighborhood. *Block by block,* they are different. Some hospices, some communities—some individuals for that matter—are knocking themselves out trying to help, and they are doing a great job. Others aren't doing diddlypoop. That's the way the world is. Look at what happened during the Plague in the Middle Ages. Some people behaved themselves, others didn't—but what we ought to remember is, "good" people, "bad" people, it didn't make a bit of difference, half the population was wiped out before it was over. I do the best I can for people who are hurting, not because I am a do-gooder, but because they are human beings and I care about them. What gets me madder than anything else is the number of people and institutions that don't care a damn about this epidemic and won't pay any attention. How are you going to toilet-train *those* people is what I want to know. Well, when it all gets to be too much for me, I go out in a boat by myself, and I go fishing."

Pat Kelley, training director of the Northern Virginia AIDS Ministry, points out another problem: "Many people with AIDS tell us that they prefer to have very aggressive treatment in the acute phases with the hope that they will have a period of comparative wellness afterward, and maybe in that time someone will find out a cure for them. But because hospice care has so much to offer that is very appropriate for these individuals, some of us in hospice recognized the need for us to be sharing our knowledge and skills with other health care workers and care-giving organizations." Thus, hospice leadership has moved out in some cases to meet AIDS sufferers on their own turf, so to speak, in various new and innovative coalitions. In northern Virginia, concerned clergy from the Episcopal Church teamed up with hospice people and with staff from Whitman Walker Clinic, a large organization serving the gay community in Washington, D.C., to offer a variety of services to those with AIDS. Pat, who had served ten years as a home care nurse and nursing education coordinator at Hospice of Northern Virginia, has seen this group grow over the past three years to become nondenominational and truly ecumenical. Direct financial help as well as practical assistance, counseling, and hands-on care have been provided during this period to about 200 patients and families. Some of the special aspects of hospice care, according to Pat, that are particularly appropriate for AIDS patients are as follows:

▲ Hospice care is for the patient and family, and as we all know, AIDS is an illness that affects families and friends as well as the one who is sick.

▲ We consider family as whomever the patient describes as family, and long before taking care of persons with AIDS, we cared for many families that did not have the traditional family structure, including gay couples.

▲ We have experience in helping people in crisis, especially in helping those who are dying make difficult decisions and in helping bring about reconciliations in families that have been troubled or estranged.

▲ We are experts at symptom management, so when diseases cannot be cured we have much to offer in making a person as comfortable as possible.

▲ We never limit our attention to physical needs, symptoms, and pain. Our holistic approach is invaluable when caring for persons with AIDS as they and their families often have to struggle with emotional, social, and spiritual issues.

▲ We know a great deal about grief, both the whole

process of grieving and how to help others heal through their grief. There is extra pain involved for those grieving the death from AIDS of someone they love, and our knowledge and skills are invaluable here.

▲ We recognize the need to help staff deal with their stress and grief. Working with people who are dying and their families means that we will all absorb some of the sadness, and hospice programs build in, and emphasize the need for, staff support and stress management.

"In fact, the Northern Virginia AIDS Ministry really did grow out of hospice," says Pat, "and we are taking many of the skills we developed in our hospice years and using them to help our community face this new challenge of AIDS." Present and former hospice workers are members of board, staff, and volunteer groups serving this AIDS ministry; and education for the community, as in hospice programs generally, is an important part of their effort. Taking up one of St. Christopher's founding principles *(Dame Cicely: "Very often it is the patients themselves who are our best teachers.")*, Pat, with Penny Lane, another former hospice worker, has developed a program for young people in the area. Not only are they given the facts about HIV infection, but they also hear directly from persons with AIDS as to what it is like to cope with the disease. "I can see it making a difference," she says. "Suddenly it becomes real to them, and they are really willing to listen." Other AIDS support groups in the United States have also taken many of their cues from hospice.

The director of client services for the Marin AIDS Support Network is James Tomlinson. After pre-med training and

a double M.A. in counseling and health education at JFK
University in Orinda, California, James, now forty-one,
worked as a medic at the Berkeley Clinic and Children's
Hospital, San Francisco; he participated in some of the earliest research on the AIDS virus and also worked in private
practice as a counselor before being hired in 1987 by the
Marin AIDS Support Network, which was then in development. A sturdy and personable fourth-generation Texan,
his accent softened by early years spent in Alabama and
Georgia, James has strong gifts in administration as well as
the ability to think like a visionary, and speak in the plain
language of experience. I asked him to describe the processes of his group, as a basis for comparison with their
hospice cousins.

"We're helping about two hundred individuals now,
double from two years ago, and that takes very careful
planning," he says. "I spent the first couple of months at
MASN just reading files, updating, reorganizing. Now I
have everything color-coded so that I can find what I want
in various categories very quickly, and match up the clients
with our services. After that, I worked on training volunteers, while I slowly, and methodically, developed our contacts in the community.

"It was a question at first of befriending people, telling
them our story, then approaching them with ways in which
they could help—for example, for the Marin Community
Food Bank to help provide some basic staples for our clients. We've had a very fine response from licensed psycho-
therapists in the community. They participate in the Marin
AIDS Mental Health Project by providing free counseling
to our clients, and we in turn train them in psychosocial
issues of HIV disease and AIDS, and act as a referring
agency. I've been finding ways to work with other professional groups in similar ways, people like massage thera-

pists, people who can help with transportation, personal care—even pet care, because we feel that the bonding between people and their pets is so important for their wellbeing. And all this has got to be done in a way that leaves everybody feeling good about it. You can't just go in and demand things from people, you have to involve them in the process of thinking it through, finding a way together. If they say, 'We can't do that,' you say, 'Okay, I understand you can't do that, but let's see what we *can* do,' and you keep on talking. I try on principle to give everyone a comfortable space to be in—and I am also *strongly* convinced that it's not going to work if you try to sell people on an idea where they have to give in to you. Sometimes you can negotiate a very simple detail that turns the whole situation around—and that makes all the difference.

"You have to keep thinking in terms of: this is a need I have identified, and somewhere out there is the answer to that need just waiting to be found. For instance, I read one day about corporate jets providing seats on their return flights from one place or another, when otherwise those seats would have been empty, donating them for people who are ill—they call those 'angel flights.' And I thought, there must be empty airport limousines going one way between here and the city, and maybe they could take some of our clients to see their doctors. I am working on this program now. It's good public relations for people to do this sort of thing, and so there are benefits all around. You always look for the win-win situation.

"Then sometimes I think: I need such and such, and there's got to be someone, or a group out there, already convinced of the need to help, so that I don't even have to convince them. All I need to do is find the right group and come up with a plan. How about getting a group of churches together on this project? If they gave us a donation, they wouldn't get to see the direct results of that, and they wouldn't know what specific good it's doing. On the other hand, we could do something satisfying for their members, because, for example, we need another person to work in our office, and we could name that the 'Honorary So-and-So Position' in the agency. Now, if just a small amount of money could be collected each month from each of, say, ten or twelve churches in the county, and they pledge to do that on a regular basis, then we could go ahead and fund this position. People need to feel that they are participating. And it's important to give them something they can point to and say, 'This is the result of our donation.'

"It's not just a matter of logic and brainstorming— thinking of needs and resources and putting them together. Most of the time it's also a matter of getting out of my own way and allowing what needs to happen, happen. The more I get myself out of my work, the more successful it becomes. . . . Is the work addictive? Well, that's the addicting part of it for me: I am given opportunities every day to achieve something, even though it sometimes looks as if it is going to be impossible. But it is only my own limited understanding of the situation that makes me perceive it that way."

I told James it sounds as if he is doing a good deal more than taking care of sick people. Perhaps the Marin AIDS Support Network is really offering a ministry, of sorts, to the entire community. Could he tell me anything about the sociological problem others had mentioned? (Marin is largely an affluent, white, middle-class county, although it has never been particularly conservative—as Cyra McFadden and others have noted.) "I haven't told you yet about our volunteers," he replied. "They are absolutely incredible. I am continually amazed by them. Some of these people are the individuals who tend to get stereotyped as 'the middle-class white woman' or 'the successful businessman,' and there they are, helping, providing care. People from all walks of life have stepped forward, asking to be involved. Some may have been very comfortable, others may have a life filled with AIDS already. And they will do all sorts of things, all of them equally important: clean a home, give a ride, or maybe end up holding someone's hand through the night, night after night. And what often happens is that in a special way they end up falling in love with a person, and then there is going to be a painful loss. This is a huge emotional risk. It takes tremendous courage to do this work—and they are doing it."

"How about burnout?"

"I hope our volunteers learn—I try to create a space as a therapist so that they can learn—that they will not get burned out unless they fight their feelings by holding on to them. They need to let it happen—let it flow through, instead. If you hold on to *anything,* even the muscles in your body, that's where it's going to start hurting. If you learn how to be open, you can create just enough of a filter there for your own protection—and you don't need to armor yourself from what is happening, or from what you are feeling. Most people aren't so afraid of death as they are afraid of life—the *experience* of life. They think it's going to overwhelm them, but it won't—only the resistance will. Death is just another part of experience as a whole, the part where you let go completely. The important thing is, remembering to be present—and that's something everyone really knows how to do. We just have to be reminded. And that's what this work is all about—self-forgetting, which is sometimes disguised as self-discovery."

Sue B.

A message from Sue in New Haven, 1987: "I am working with gay and black AIDS patients now, and yes, it was frightening at first. But I was brought up in a home where there was not very much touching, or affection expressed. And I feel such permission now, to touch and to hold— because they need it so. And it is possible always, no matter how ill they are, to make that deep connection, person to person, that is the great thing. And a kind of holiness comes over the simplest of acts, so that helping a person to eat, or even just doing up a button, seems totally important. Time doesn't matter because nothing I do for these patients feels like a waste. And an energy begins and it comes through, a sort of current—I don't dare say where it comes from, though I think I know—but sometimes I feel at these moments that I am being given permission to fall in love with the whole world."

Francis

When St. Francis embraced the leper, was it in order that the leper—by the grace of God—might be healed, or was it the leper, by the grace of God, who healed Francis?

David S. ▲ Rachel ▲ Bill ▲ Lisa ▲ Joanne ▲ Tom ▲ David R.

Their dining room table was spread with a lavish feast of exotic, Mideast delicacies (how William would have loved it) when I visited Deputy City Attorney David Schulman and his family in Los Angeles one summer evening in 1988. His beautiful wife, Rachel, a talmudic scholar and author, had prepared this feast for the eyes, for the soul, for the stomach. Dr. Bill Lamers and his wife, Lisa, were also with us, and our conversation went on late into the evening—

about books, about hospice, about law and religion, about the wave of AIDS beginning to appear then in the drug-ridden ghettos of our inner cities. We thought aloud together then, and on later occasions, about a question that stayed with me as I traveled in the United States during the next few months, meeting others equally concerned: *how could hospice best help with the next, oncoming wave of AIDS?* On the one hand, there was the cherished hospice tradition of *hospitality* to all who were ill and suffering; on the other, the hard-earned medical expertise of the modern hospice organization, with its focus upon intensive personal care and support for the dying patient and family. The continuing, aggressive treatment of disease called for by many AIDS patients was not a part of the traditional hospice contract. Should that contract be changed? Most thought not. Instead, hospice should share its attitudes and processes freely with other groups and agencies. It was regretted by many that hospice in the United States thus far had been largely a white, middle-class phenomenon, depending heavily upon efforts by family members as well as trained volunteers. An article on hospice ethics written by Dr. Joanne Lynn in 1985 had pointed out quite rightly that the new federal funding encouraged home care primarily for those whose needs "can be predicted to remain low . . . [that is,] families with . . . physical, emotional and financial resources." But these are exactly the resources so often lacking where there is poverty, drug abuse, and despair.

In Texas, church people expressed their fear that in a massive, urban epidemic, a comparatively helpless population might be seriously mistreated in the name of hospice. They already perceived exploitation of the Medicare hospice benefit by institutions seeking profit. "This is one step away from government-sponsored euthanasia," a furious clergyman said. "And when AIDS really hits, it's going to be *profitable warehousing and genocide.*" Only the pressure of enlightened public opinion will be able to help us avoid such abuses.

Government funding has given hospice technical legitimacy, with ground rules (however basic) and a measure of financial support. However, hospice attitudes cannot be bought, or made to function by the HCFA (Health Care Financing Administration) rulebook, so it was interesting to find during my travels that the religious and philosophical base of hospice was resurfacing now in concerted efforts toward better AIDS care: a training film in Philadelphia funded and directed by Episcopalians; private citizens in New England and New York, moved by their own religious beliefs, both Christian and Jewish, to provide housing for destitute AIDS sufferers; Roman Catholic nuns caring for unwanted AIDS babies in California; and support groups across the country being founded and funded by people whose various faiths would not allow them to turn away from human suffering.

Other linked groups and communities also offered their help. The so-called "San Francisco model" of AIDS care relying upon the buddy system and informal networking functioned well for a time because of the strength and determination of the gay community in that city, and the heroic efforts of some medical practitioners. However, it was so exhausting for participants that few believed it could meet the threat of a larger, urban epidemic. Would it be possible, some hospice people wondered, for lean and mobile but highly trained hospice medical teams to be stationed in the future at crisis locations, so as to demonstrate their knowledge of palliative care for AIDS and HIV-related conditions? Could demonstration of their teamwork, their respect for one another and for their patients, set a useful example? Could their teaching of skills and sharing of humanitarian attitudes help to rebuild the shattered communities of the inner city? And if so, how would such efforts be funded in a nation already dealing with a calamitous budget deficit? *A Passion for Excellence* (1985) and other recent books by Tom Peters have been suggesting that the leaner the team, and the less bureaucracy involved, the more likely it is that it can accomplish much with little money. Why not try it? Variations upon this idea have been placed before the public recently by myself and David Schulman, among others—evidently to no avail.

But in the end, of course, the problem does not belong to the inner city, or to *those people* anywhere—it belongs to all of us, and to our planet. AIDS is merely a sign, an omen. A new consciousness, and actions leading to a new, global ethic, are being called for by prophets such as David J. Roy, director of the Center for Bioethics (Clinical Research Institute of Montreal). At the Fifth International Conference on AIDS in 1989, he said

> We will face catastrophes again, catastrophes similar to the HIV epidemic, if we do not come to grips with the realities of the place of our species in nature, on a planet that we share with a host of viruses and bacteria. The place of our species? We will surely invite a catastrophe of a quite different kind if we fail to ensure that the place of our species is where those threatened with deep loss will find dedicated, sensitive and civilized care. . . . The consciousness of human global solidarity, with its implication that human beings *do* have a claim on us *just because they are human,* needs to be realized in particular concrete endeavors before it expands to become the ethos and the foundation for a new global ethics. . . . HIV infection and AIDS challenge us . . . to demonstrate the germ of a new world community, within which inequities regarding the basics for human life and dignity [are] deemed to be utterly intolerable.

Joan ▲ *William*

During the summer there had been three distinct crises, each different from the other, all extremely painful and debilitating. The last and most recent problem had involved an acute cellulitis. His right leg had become so swollen and infected that there were fears he might lose it, or indeed, lose his life before the situation could be brought under control. Joan's carefully selected medical team went into high gear during these periods, and Sue came to the house, making herself available twenty-four hours a day, to help with William's nursing when needed. Every day of his visit had not been spent in misery, however. There had been "windows" of comfort and enjoyment, and during most of the past seven weeks, Joan had been able to keep up her usual obligations—errands, board meetings, the theater—leaving William for short periods of time to rest or entertain himself. Whenever she left the house, Joan found on returning that he had prepared some charming surprise for her—perhaps only a few flowers, or a single blossom from her yard, but those perfectly chosen, and arranged with great elegance. And it seemed that whenever she arrived feeling tired after an hour or two of dealing with "relatively boring, inconsequential matters on the outside," William had summoned an extra touch of magic to please her: the dining table, for example, would be splendidly set, with candles here and there, in the dining room and on the deck, all shimmering in their faceted glass containers. She had never seen her house more beautiful, and I thought that despite the stress and anxiety she had experienced over the past few weeks, Joan herself was also looking not only beautiful but relaxed and content. William's continued weight loss showed particularly in his face now, with cheekbones more evident; but his expression was as determined as ever, and his eye had an extra glint of triumph in it, I thought—almost a glitter. It was the look of a man who has faced death quite directly in recent days, and stared it down once more. In a burst of determined energy he was packing his things now, to go back to the Mainland.

"I'm here for some reason," he said to me the last time I saw him, as we sat together on the deck. "I don't know if I've completed the task yet. Sometimes I feel it's like a certain test that I have to pass, and I don't know if I have passed it. Then I think about infinity, space, time. We can't be all that there is, can we. Can people invent heaven? I have a little place in my mind where I go, and that is my heaven. Look, my immune system is way down—yes—but most people's defenses are *too quick*—my God, look at the Persian Gulf situation, look at South Africa. The only thing in the world that really matters is your compassion for another human being, whether it's her, or him, or whoever. People have got to find a better way of settling things than this, they've got to start being kind to one another instead. Is that so impossible? I look at the news these days and it gives me a kind of heartache, and I feel a pain that's like, worry for the whole world."

Two days later he was on the plane, and after a week I stopped by Joan's house to hear her own thoughts on the visit. We had agreed that this would be at most a two-hour discussion, but as it turned out, it lasted more than twice that long. Before it was over there had been tears and laughter shared—together with joy, amazement, anxiety, anger, and a wide-ranging discussion of the anomalies and paradoxes—the truly infuriating frustrations—of the AIDS situation as the bureaucracies are handling it in the United States today.

"It was wonderful beyond words," she told me. "It was also awful at times, and that was exactly what I wanted to share with William, the whole spectrum, because this is *his reality.* I care deeply for this man. I respect him very deeply. William is a person of dignity, a person of very great strength. I have enormous admiration for him, and I didn't want and didn't ask for a textbook situation with nothing but pretty pictures and apt solutions in it. As someone said, life is not a problem to be solved, it's a mystery to be lived. It was sharing the mystery, the reality of William that was important to me. He has to go through this all the time—I don't, you don't. We can walk away from it, but—this splendid man, it is absolutely devastating to me what he has to go through. The ups and downs, for one thing, never knowing what it will be like when he wakes up in the morning, whether his mouth will be filled with fungus, or a leg or an arm suddenly swollen twice its size and so painful that he would like to tear it off and throw it away. Not knowing whether he will be blind. The arthritic pain, the suppurating skin, the rashes, the ghastly headaches—all the rest of it. I have never witnessed such pain. . . . Well, he copes with the pain as best he can with a whole collection of medications, and I rather think often the mix is not right, or he loses track of what he has taken—as who wouldn't, under the circumstances. There were times when I felt that the medications themselves were causing difficulties, and he likes his vodka, too, as, my goodness gracious, who wouldn't. Can you *imagine?* We talked about it. One of the many things I love about William is that he is so very approachable, such a reasonable person under most circumstances. He's tough, but he is also a very gentle person, incredibly sensitive. Of course, there were a few times when I wanted to punch him out—but this is natural, when you care."

I said that any houseguest who stays more than two months ought to be punched out on a regular basis, didn't she think, just by way of showing affection?

"That may be true. But in William's case I was not eager to see him go, and I would have been perfectly happy to have him stay on here, as long as he himself wanted or needed to. We postponed his return, and I canceled his ticket at one time, in fact, so that he'd understand that there was absolutely no pressure. William is important to me. And this is a man who did so much for me, and for this whole community—in the midst of his illness and his debilitation, the beautiful things he brought for the theater, the research he had done, the things for the AIDS group—he will be reimbursed for those, by the way—and all the teaching he did. I can tell you that they were absolutely electrified by those offerings, and by his presence. And there was all his thoughtfulness to me—all the very real nourishment he offered day after day to his care-giver. We shared so much. There were so many wonderful laughs, so many things that were so touching. One day we just sat down and cried together, because he was hurting so, physically and emotionally and spiritually, from this horrendous illness. I felt so close to him then, and I always will. This is in a very special way a sort of love story. We haven't known one another for very long—we met through friends on the Mainland, you know but right from the first there has been such a bond, such an extraordinarily deep bond between us. But, you see, the flare-up of his leg was really quite serious, and very frightening. William felt the need to get back to his own community, his own doctors. Also he was running out, or else was completely out, of some of his medications. It was a real wrench when he left, but I was laughing and crying at the same time. I was so terribly worried about him, and yet, to tell you the truth, I was also laughing to beat the band because of the most ludicrous thing that went on, just as the visit was ending."

Joan tried several times to begin telling this part of the

story, but exploded into laughter each time. Finally, wiping away tears, she managed to say, "I don't really know how to put this, it was all so ridiculous." Then she began laughing again, and by this time we were both laughing, even though I didn't know what was so funny. Again she wiped away tears and said, "You must understand that this man is quite a mover and a shaker, sick as he is—as director of operations, as master of ceremonies, he is really *formidable.* He had just been through a very dangerous crisis, after all, and he had a long and tiring trip ahead of him. But William was determined to orchestrate all sorts of fanfare and celebration in connection with his departure. He had spoken of a party with helium balloons flying over the house, and the entire neighborhood invited—well, I thought that was a bit much, and he certainly wasn't up to it. But people were in and out, there were telephone calls, messages, visitors, cocktails at noon—as you know, that is *not* part of the usual routine here, and I kept getting out the herb tea, but it always seemed, as far as William was concerned, that that was not going to be the ticket. Then *more* visitors, masses of flowers, leis to be made for every single person he knows back on the Mainland, all to be handcarried, of course, in a huge box about five feet long, and I could just see myself trying to get him through the airport alleys and turnstiles in a wheelchair with that. But no, then there were *more* flowers, more cocktails, more entertaining, boxes and boxes to be packed as well as all those suitcases, and of course, William is extremely fastidious. He insisted on doing all of this himself, because everything has to be done just so—he is a magician, after all—who am I to interfere with his procedures—and I had never, *ever* seen him display such energy. I really became frightened for him—I didn't know what pills he might have taken, and so for safety's sake I

decided early in the evening"—she began laughing again—
"that the vodka bottle really ought to be removed from the
scene. I stood out on the deck with it, thinking, where am
I going to put this thing, and I suddenly realized that I was
so furious—I mean, I was *furious,* at the pain, the suffering,
the misery of this terrible virus for so many people, and I
was *furious* at the *damned* government for not doing more
about it sooner. And for still not facing the fact that this is
an epidemic—just giving piddling amounts of money for
'education about AIDS'—well, how about those who have
already got it? How about the care-givers, the hands-on
people? I was *furious*—they're not getting the support—it's
only given for prevention. What do they think they are
doing? Protecting the 'innocent' against the 'guilty,' I suppose, and what kind of a judgment is *that*—who do they
think they are, some kind of primeval Jehovah? Haven't
they ever read the Book of Job? And can you believe, there
are actually some insurance companies discriminating
against groups that are working so hard giving hands-on
care—and some of those *damned* companies won't give insurance for anybody who gets near the patient? *How can you
care for people without getting close to them?* This is insane! What
kind of a country is this, anyway? What kind of people are
we? And then I thought, I am *furious* at William for being
happy at this point, in spite of everything—having such a
high old time of it when he is *leaving,* when he is *dying,* for
God's sake—this is intolerable! This splendid man is going
to die—how *dare* he be cheerful about it!

　　"And at this point I wound up and I threw that bottle out
into the dark as far as I could throw it. I don't believe I have
actually thrown anything so hard for years. Certainly, not
nearly that far. Really, I was quite surprised at how nice that
was—I mean, what a perfectly delightful feeling. Of course,

I did check first, to make certain it wasn't a glass bottle. I wouldn't want anything like that on the ground, in an area where so many people go barefoot.

"But, you see, what was so *funny* was—I found out the next morning that the vodka bottle had landed up in the coconut tree.... Yes, right out there where no one driving by in the early morning on their way to work could possibly fail to see it. They start going by at five-thirty in the morning, dozens of people. Oh dear, I thought, when I spotted it at eight-thirty, did I really do that? How absolutely extraordinary! Well, there goes my reputation. And William was sitting there at breakfast on the deck with the coconut tree right behind when I noticed it. He was just as cheerful as could be, damn his hide—I had hardly slept a wink all night, and here he was all dressed for the trip and looking better than ever. But, you see, the tree was directly behind him—it was right there—and I was thinking, oh dear God, don't let him turn around. I was not about to go out there and start climbing a coconut tree in full view of the neighborhood at that point in my day. It's not an easy tree to climb under the best of circumstances. So I just sat there looking at it over William's shoulder—honestly, I thought that breakfast would go on forever—and I kept thinking, oh please God, don't let William turn around and see that idiotic thing up there—*what under the sun is he going to think?*"

15

GLOBAL VILLAGE: 1990

A lamp am I
To thee that beholdest me. Amen.

A mirror am I
To thee that perceivest me. Amen.

A door am I
To thee that knockest me. Amen.

A way am I
To thee a wayfarer. Amen.

Now answer thou to my dancing . . .
Apocrypha: The Acts of John

On the crest of the Pacific Rim, little more than one degree from the equator, there is a new, white city: the island republic of Singapore. "Instant Asia," it is often called in the glossy tourist brochures, or, more prosaically, "The Place Where East Meets West." However, even on relatively brief acquaintance, the island city reveals itself as something far more substantial and interesting. With all its flaws—including first and foremost an execrable climate—Singapore is a vigorous, heart-lifting city, a truly global village offering many an intriguing glimpse into the planet's future. The faces, the voices here are a marvelously rich mix: primarily Chinese, Malay, and Indian, but also Indonesian, Filipino, European and British, Australian, North and

South American. There are 2.7 million people living in peace together on an island of only 221 square miles. And the government has plans to accommodate 1.3 million more.

On a midsummer afternoon of my visit, an occasional jet streaks by overhead, practicing for next week's celebration of the young republic's twenty-fifth year of independence. In the distance from time to time parachutists plunge, then pause and sway like clusters of exotic flowers opening over the marina. The sky sustaining them is a vivid, lustrous gray, and I wonder if it is any cooler up there.

Dr. Cynthia Goh of Singapore's brand-new Hospice Care Association has joined me on a terrace downtown. The heat has been so fierce all day that at four o'clock the trees lining the wide boulevards look defeated, and anxious little knots of tourists stand melting and dripping below us, laden with parcels at the crosswalks. "It's awfully warm today," Cynthia remarks sympathetically, looking, herself, crisp as a salad. She is young and very pretty, in her page-boy's cap of sleek, dark hair with bangs and an engaging smile. As she begins to tell me in a quick, clear British accent about hospice progress in Singapore, she reminds me suddenly of Dr. Sylvia Lack, who helped to bring a dream to fruition in the United States half a generation ago. Something about this fresh, very feminine energy is captivating; it is so blithely unselfconscious and at the same time so sage, so competent.

"It's all quite exciting, of course, but I hope you understand that hospice here is still in its infancy," Cynthia is saying. "It has been a grass-roots thing. . . . How did it start? Well, some of us were terribly stubborn. We simply insisted on moving ahead." She grins. "We rebelled—refused to be held back by the usual, conservative forces. We are finally well under way now, with the Association, our Hospice at

Home program caring for about two hundred patients in this, our first year of existence, and a number of suitable, inpatient beds available. We are officially registered—oh, that means the Registrar of Societies knows we are not going to do anything *seditious*—and we have even managed to discover funds. The Hospice Care Association began, as you may know, with a rather large group of medical professionals and lay people volunteering.

" . . . Yes, Mike Galazka [executive director of the Hospice Education Institute] was out here, and told us that the number of medical professionals was quite unusual. For quite a time we were living hand to mouth, not knowing how we would survive—literally—the next day, or whether a home could be found for us. The first meeting of our committee took place in my living room, for example. Our first office, for lack of other space, was in Dr. Anne Merriman's master bedroom. Anne was marvelous—we never could have done it without her.

"There had been previous efforts here in Singapore. A coalition of churches tried to set up an inpatient hospice in 1987, but things went wrong, and it soon closed. That was a very sad business. As far back as 1976 the Rotary International, Lions, and other public service people wanted a hospice, and they had funds, and even a doctor who was interested. But it didn't work out. There were several reasons, but in any case the time was not right. There has been a feeling of unease here, stemming from an ancient situation that was quite a scandal. You won't be able to find it today, but in the mid-seventies the government had just finished razing the site of the old 'Death Houses'—they were down in a place called Sago Lane, which was known as 'Death House Row.' The whole street is gone today, completely wiped out. I myself had to go into the National Archives to find a photograph. Sago Lane was a really horrible place where people who were destitute went to die. They stayed in rented rooms provided by old, outmoded charitable organizations, and conditions were Spartan—no medical care—and coffin-makers living and working, hammering away, in the same street. There were stories about some of the old people who had nothing at all, actually sleeping in their own coffins. Later on, Singaporeans wanted to forget all this, disassociate themselves. And so, a place for the dying was not a thing to mention, and hospice was actually a dirty word here for quite some time."

There is a sprinkle of rain, a gust of hot wind, and a riotous outburst beside us: brilliant songbirds, *hwa mei*s and crested bulbuls, all thrashing and clamoring at once in their swaying cages. A wide awning is cranked down above our heads by invisible hands. Steaming darkness closes over the city.

"As for my part in our group, I am president now, since Anne has left Singapore, even though I have always thought a nurse should run hospice," Cynthia continues. "I grew up in Hong Kong, and went to study medicine in London. As a medical student I was at St. Bart's. I qualified in 1974. That is where I met my husband, who is also a physician—a surgeon. Hak and I were both there at medical schools. We might never have met, otherwise. He is Chinese too, but from a town a thousand miles away, in Sarawak, North Borneo. Do you know where that is? His family is from Mukah, Sarawak. It's now a part of East Malaysia. We were married in Hong Kong and then worked in England. After that, I left medicine entirely for five years while having young children. We have a boy now twelve years old, and a girl of ten. We came back to Sarawak together when our daughter was very little, but stayed only a year and a half since I was held to a tourist visa and thus could not work. There were other difficulties there for us too, and so we came on to Singapore. When our youngest was eighteen months I began training again, and by that time, of course, I had to do it from scratch."

"*Composing a Life,* as Catherine Bateson put it? That's a book about the strength of women in being flexible, persistent—transforming the obstacles. . . ."

"Yes, but I was extremely lucky. We had an amah—the same one who had cared for me as a child. She came to help while I did internal medicine and took postgraduate exams. She is retired now. Then it was time for me to choose a subspecialty. For a while I studied with Dame Sheila Sherlock—this was in 1985—who is one of those amazing—well, you know those *great English Dames!* I think she was the first female professor of medicine in the U.K. Dame Sheila is a liver specialist, and naturally wanted to make a liver doctor out of me.

"But in the meantime, the sisters at St. Joseph's Home here in Singapore had set up two wards for the terminally ill, with sixteen beds in them. They are a charitable organization, Roman Catholic, run by the Canossian Sisters. They were being staffed at the time by volunteer doctors, general practitioners, and doing as well as they could, but they were distressed by their inability to control the patients' pain. Then one day Sister Mary Tan, who was in charge there, heard a talk by Dr. Anne Merriman—she is a geriatrician—about the care of the terminally ill. Anne is a Catholic herself, very energetic, a great traveler. At this point, she has gone off to start a hospice in Nairobi! Anne is a Liverpudlian, trained in Ireland, very articulate, forceful, passionately determined about hospice, and she agreed to help out part time at St. Joseph's. Then, in August of 1986, they got hold of me. While at St. Bart's, I had seen the need for better pain control. I had also heard lectures, seen books and articles telling of better methods, but at the time did not see them being used. . . . Yes, I had visited St. Christopher's, but only very briefly. I remember those brilliant paintings everywhere, done by Marian Bohusz, who of course is now Dame Cicely's husband. . . .

"I served as a volunteer with Anne, initially. We did rounds together at St. Joseph's, to see how the other worked, and found we got along very well, agreed on most decisions. After that we split up, and began alternating. A local G.P. group filled in for us on the days when neither of us visited. They could do death certificates, for example, to spare us the long drive out there, but we were always on call, twenty-four hours a day. Just to give you an idea of attitudes here at that time," she says with a glint in her eye, "an article in the *Straits Times* in July 1986 mentioned 'a place' where people who were dying could be well cared for—but the word *hospice* did not appear, or anything about the concept. Still, one hundred forty people wrote in asking about it, saying that they were interested, so the sisters decided to have tea parties—"

"Tea parties?"

"Yes, a whole series of them, for all who were interested, to meet and discuss. It worked. A lot of people came. None of us knew one another beforehand, but as soon as we were all there we looked round at each other and said, why not organize? So we did. But we wondered where in the system we could fit. Two possibilities suggested themselves: the Home Nursing Foundation, which is funded by charity and staffed by the Ministry of Health, and the local Cancer Society. I myself saw hospice as a natural extension of the Cancer Society, though they were reluctant at first. After a time they agreed to take us under their wing temporarily until we could stand on our own two feet. So in March 1987 our group became the Hospice Care Group of the Singapore Cancer Society, and donors began writing in, asking, can we designate these funds for hospice? So, right away, this confirmed the great need.

"Anne gave some talks meantime—did that P.R. sort of thing, but keeping a relatively low profile—while I concentrated on getting on with the work. Suddenly everything began to fall into place. A grant came in from a charitable foundation to pay a nurse's salary for us, full time, for three years. We hired Chua Lee Kiang—you will meet her—as nurse-coordinator, and she is still with us. Unfortunately, Lee Kiang was used more and more in that situation to do administrative work rather than nursing, which was a disappointment. However, when we left the Cancer Society to go out on our own in 1989, they very kindly let us take Lee Kiang with us—and also her salary! From the beginning we had many, many referrals, from relatives, friends, nurses, doctors—we took referrals from anyone at all, and we made the patient's *need* the basis of acceptance. It was a struggle, but somehow we always managed to find volunteers, and never had to turn anyone away."

The lights on the terrace have been lit by now, and moths fly against them. Rain spatters inconsequentially from time to time on the awning above us, and the heat of the day continues. On an evening such as this it is hard to imagine what it must have been like, only twenty years ago, in those rented rooms on Sago Lane. I think of the old women I have seen on the streets of Chinatown, Chinese, Indian, Malay, with their sparkling eyes, their raucous laughs, and their gnarled, walnut hands. The frail old men, smoking, with their stick-thin arms, their very clean, short-sleeved shirts. And the odor of old, downtown Singapore that is made up of dried fish, hot sesame oil, coriander, dust. Even the dust of Chinatown smells of the sun's baking, and of interminable heat.

▲ ▲ ▲

"People have been suffering quite unnecessarily here," Cynthia says, "so pain control has been our first priority. We needed to change basic attitudes, and this was very difficult. We ran course after course to train volunteers, and separate ones for doctors and nurses. We began working in conjunction with the College of General Practitioners, which of course helped to lend us respectability. The physicians' courses were given on Sunday afternoons, and forty-two doctors—all sorts and all ages—came to our first course, and sixty to the next! Those lasted four weeks. Nurses came a hundred at a time to our weekday-evening classes for them, eight sessions each. That was when I *really* learned hospice medicine. You learn your subject best, don't you think, when having to teach it?

"Naturally, it was very heavy going, and we were all exhausted. But I think by doing it, we have actually managed to change the nature of medical practice here in Singapore. And now that we are caring for patients, of course, word of mouth helps. Singaporeans are beginning to hear that dying patients *can* be kept comfortable! Our main focus now is on the Hospice at Home program, but we also work on an inpatient basis, in liaison with St. Joseph's, and with the Assisi Home, which is the charitable section of Mt. Alvernia, a private hospital. The private insurance situation here is difficult. Few people can afford it, and many of those feel that it is bad luck to buy it because then something is sure to happen. And although there is supervised saving toward health care taken from most people's wages, the government does not want a socialist state of affairs here, with everything taken care of. Both the Assisi Home and St. Joseph's care for patients who have very little money to offer, or none at all."

▲ ▲ ▲

"After Sago Lane, doesn't it strike you as ironic that the finest care for the dying here in Singapore is probably being received, at present, by the destitute?"

Cynthia leans back in her chair and flashes a merry smile. "Well, we have always said that we do not discriminate against the rich! But actually, we had a *very* wealthy man out there at St. Joseph's Home not long ago, caring for him. We were afraid that he wouldn't like having all those, literally, dozens of people around him, but he rather seemed to enjoy all the commotion.

"As to why we left the Cancer Society, that decision came in 1989. We needed a doctor full time, more nurses, and a less unwieldy, hierarchical structure. As a hospice group we needed to work closely together as a team, with freedom to be more innovative. Also, we had come to feel that hospice should not be restricted to cancer. We saw AIDS upon the horizon, and knew that those patients were going to need our care. It was really quite frightening. We had no funds whatever, and tax-exempt status was bound to be problematic. But again, somewhat to our amazement, everything fell into place. We were able to get a provisional budget from the Community Chest, and their support has continued. Then, with a carefully placed letter or two, we also found encouragement at the Ministry of Health. They are now putting a roof over our heads. They're about to donate a large part of our rent, in a building they own. And so, after all, we do now share premises with the Home Nursing Foundation. Our offices need a coat of paint, and various rearrangements, but we have been too busy thus far, getting on with the work."

"What about the place that failed—the coalition?"

"It stopped providing hospice service in less than a year. And that was because their administration did not understand what hospice is about. They simply did not see the principle behind it. All sorts of backup help had been promised to the nurse who ran it, and then did not materialize. Anne and I did all that we could to help. Others did also. Nurses who had worked all day on their regular jobs would volunteer, tired as they were, for night duty there. We discovered later that some of them had been giving money out of their own pockets to help the patients who could not pay. And it was an impossible situation in other ways too. Although it looked ideal—a lovely old building, over two dozen beds—it was in a rather isolated place, and rather dark at night, with a columbarium and a memorial chapel in its compound."

"Rather a gloomy spot, I should think." *Bones and ashes. . . . Do ghosts roam more often in Singapore than in New Jersey? Are there more of them in Bali than in Alabama, or is it only that they are painted, danced, storied, and costumed—even celebrated, after a fashion—so much more freely in this part of the world? Those Balinese landscape paintings, for example, with miniature sprites and demons peering out from behind every tree. . . . The elfin-eared trickster figure of Han dynasty sculpture, showing dead souls the way to the afterworld, making absolutely certain that they get there without lingering. . . .*

"As you know, there are many different cultural groups here, and many differing belief systems. Just to begin with, we have Muslim, various sorts of Christian, all rather different from one another, Hindu, Buddhist, Taoist, and the old Chinese ancestor worship which is something quite different again. The rites and ceremonies of these various groups are as a rule quite helpful to our patients and families. We haven't as yet got a systematic bereavement program in place, but we do keep in touch, and we try to involve people's pastors if they have them. If not, of course, then it is a little more delicate.

"Our interdisciplinary team has only four now, but it will have six full-time, paid positions: a physician, two nurses, a social worker doubling as coordinator of volunteers, an office administrator, and a general dogsbody for the odd jobs. All but two of our twelve-member council are actively involved in patient care. They include, for example, an oncologist, a cleric, a retired schoolteacher, a housewife, all different sorts of people, and all serving as volunteers. Dr. Vijay Sethi, consultant in radiotherapy at Singapore General Hospital, who is now our honorary secretary, has been very much involved, also as a volunteer, and is a great asset to us. ["It was the patients who brought us together," Dr. Sethi tells me the following day, "and that is how it should be."] My husband has been useful too. Hak teaches hospice principles, sees some of the difficult cases for us. He heads his own unit at the General Hospital now, and works directly with Lee Kiang, if one of his patients is terminally ill, toward possible hospice help.

"There has been an enormous growth of interest in hospice lately, all through this part of the world. When we had our conference called Update in Hospice Care '89, people came from all over—including two very nice, very determined ladies from Borneo! Some of them went home and started their own hospice groups; one in Penang and another in Kuala Lumpur. I flew up to K.L. recently to meet them. Well, I am afraid I must be off now—the family expects me. . . . Yes, the children are old enough now to be very helpful, and they are awfully good, too, at keeping me sane. I do hospice things mainly Mondays, Thursdays, and Fridays, but I am spending as much time as possible now in the lab, preparing to write my dissertation. That makes a marvelous contrast. I walk in and as soon as I have closed the door behind me, I am in an altogether different world, one that helps to keep the other parts of my life in balance. The work in the lab," she concludes, gathering up purse and parcels, "is because I am now a molecular biologist—that is my employment, you see."

In a pleasantly green, residential neighborhood, but beside busy Dunearn Road that leads into the city, Singapore's Hospice Care Association has a home now on the ground floor of a square, three-story Ministry of Health building. Their designated space inside is rather bleak and cavernous at the moment, but markers on the floor describe future partitions: doctors', nurses', and coordinators' offices; a large room for seminars and volunteers; two smaller "quiet rooms"; a tea pantry. Dr. Anne Merriman left her houseplants here before departing for Nairobi, and they appear to be doing well.

Two offices already enclosed, and mercifully air-conditioned, are sparsely furnished with desks and office equipment. Boxes of paper and other supplies are stacked on the floor. Wall surfaces are as yet unfinished, and everything needs paint. But telephones are ringing and being answered. The hospice physician is out seeing patients in their homes. The nurse-coordinator, Chua Lee Kiang, is on one telephone, discussing a patient's diagnosis, while the office administrator takes a message on the other. The social worker is studying reports, and a volunteer has just stopped by to see how things are going.

A place that feels right, immediately, for it is plain that this is hospice. Signing the guest book, I think of Hospice of Marin in California during its earliest days—books and records stacked in grocery boxes, a single chair, a table, and on the wall, a telephone. One doctor, one nurse, only a few patients, but those being beautifully cared for. One day thirteen years ago in that rented room Dr. Bill Lamers pulled out a treasured book to lend me, Medical Work of the Knights Hospitallers of St. John of Jerusalem, *the story of hospice long ago, in faraway places. It was a story of compassion and nobility, of suffering, hardship, the leper with his bell. Now we have come full circle, it seems, for the question being asked on the telephone by Lee Kiang at the moment is whether or not the hospice patient in question has active leprosy. And I note that the signature above mine in the guest book is that of a visitor from the Hospice Association of Witwatersrand, South Africa.*

The volunteer who has stopped by is Mr. L., a cheerful, well-dressed businessman, middle-aged, who became interested in hospice after helping his mother through three bouts of major surgery, and his father through a serious stroke. "I saw the need for home nursing then," he says. "An old friend of mine, a teacher I have known for twenty-six years, suggested one day that I should come to this volunteer training for hospice, just give it a try—no obligation. But I am comfortable, being involved in this type of social service. I used to stop by St. Joseph's Home sometimes in the morning—it's near where I live. There is a priest who says mass out there every morning at six-forty, and I would try to go for mass, and then just stay with the old people there for a while, wheel them around a little, talk with them. That was no trouble for me. But you make time for people, your mere presence helps them feel better—I found that to be true.

"You know, some of the elders here in Singapore, the older folks, their forefathers believed that cancer was a punishment from God. Many of them still believe that, so they think it is bad luck to get near a person with cancer—and also they think they might catch it. This is the old, conservative element here. Then the young people in business today wanting to make it big—I see a lot of that, too. They entertain at home, it's part of getting ahead, and they don't want anyone sick to be there. That is bad luck in another way—it spoils their image. One person I visited was a very successful man with a good income, and he had helped his kids for years. But when he got cancer most of the children moved out, leaving the house scarcely furnished. He was a nice old man; I enjoyed being with him. That was no trouble. It seems to me that everybody in the world ought to have someone with no motive, a person just willing to be there if they are needed. I appreciate the opportunity to see this kind of thinking, reminding me constantly to care and share. If I can help a person feel better, then that is the satisfaction I derive from this work. Quite frankly, I am not just trying hospice—hospice is trying me!"

"Our volunteers are warm people, very supportive of us, as well as of patients and their families," nurse-coordinator Chua Lee Kiang tells me later. "It will take time to finish our offices, but we feel that we must tend to first things first." The Singapore Polytechnic Institute has donated odds and ends of furniture, and other volunteers do what they can toward refurbishment. One volunteer is helping with the cost of renovations in memory of his father, who received hospice care. This is authentic hospice process, and it is also typical of the creative drive, determination, and optimism one finds again and again in this thriving, hard-working city. The present offices of the Hospice Care Association formerly housed a family planning clinic. "They did such a good job, they put themselves out of business," says the hospice physician, Antony Tam, a recent immigrant from Hong Kong. With comparative wealth and security, the population here has stabilized itself, then decreased enough so that Singaporeans are now being encouraged to have more children. Foresight and system are visible everywhere: in the city's high-rise, low-cost housing; in its public transportation system, one of the finest in the world; in its plenitude of parks, ponds, and reservoirs. Green, open spaces on the outskirts of the city are zealously guarded; and especially in contrast with other Southeast Asian centers of population, Singapore is amazingly clean.

And yet as recently as the early 1800s, this same acreage was marsh and jungle, a haven only for pirates, traders, and fishermen. As late as the 1850s, tigers swam across the Straits of Johore from the jungles of the Malay Peninsula and prowled freely here, killing many people each year. Memories of the British colonial period, the opium trade, and the opium wars are still fresh; and it has not been forgotten that 138,000 British troops died here within a few weeks during World War II, many as prisoners of war of the Japanese. Spotless as it now appears to be, this is indeed a place of many ghosts, many memories.

The time for hospice has arrived here, it seems, as a natural part of the young republic's process of growth, maturation, and healing. Despite the offshore oil rigs now scarring its outer harbors, it is obvious that Singapore's true wealth lies in its population of pioneers and innovators, entrepreneurs and skilled technicians. Something of the sort was suggested recently on television by Prime Minister Lee Kuan Yew: "I would wish that both people and leaders [of the republic] recognize that their human resource is their only resource, and therefore maximize it . . . by nurturing [one another] so that everybody can make the maximum contribution." This is the language of civilization; it is also hospice language. In such an atmosphere it seems very likely that the hospice concept, and this well-founded Hospice Care Association, will survive.

"But how did you yourself learn hospice medicine?" I ask Chua Lee Kiang, searching as usual for the golden thread, half expecting her to say that she has been in England, studying with Robert Twycross or Dame Cicely. But no, it seems that the thread this time must be traced via Australia. Lee Kiang, a calm and pleasant young woman with two young children and a "very supportive" husband, trained at St. Vincent's Hospital in Sydney, where the nuns ran a hospice called Sacred Heart. She also attended courses taught by Dr. Rosalie Shaw of the Palliative Care Unit at the General Repatriation Hospital in Hollywood (near Perth), and by Joy Brann of Cottage Hospice in Perth. By 1988 Lee Kiang was working as the only paid hospice staff in Singapore, with the Hospice Care Group of the Cancer Society. "I've learned most of my hospice medicine on the job, taught by Dr. Anne Merriman, Dr. Sethi, and Dr. Cynthia Goh." Her telephone rings again, and as she reaches to answer it, Lee Kiang says, with a grin, "In my opinion, it's not morphine that is addictive—it's hospice."

The following day—as hot as any other, though a light rain is falling—I make my way to Mt. Alvernia Hospital, one of the two institutions now offering inpatient hospice care in the city. As we pass the broad, green lawns of the Singapore Polo Club, my elderly taxi driver suddenly remarks, "Plenty horse in there." By way of continuing this pleasant conversation, I compliment him on the dazzling array of decorations all over the city, for the coming Independence Day. There are literally thousands of red and white Singaporean flags everywhere. He nods, appearing to appreciate my comments, so I ask him please to explain the white crescent moon and the five white stars on the Singapore national flag; do they stand for Singapore's various cultures or religions? At this, the driver looks extremely unhappy. I am afraid that I may have said something, unintentionally, to offend. But at last his face brightens, and he says, "Five stars, very good hotel." I explain as best I can that I didn't mean hotel, I meant the symbols on the national flag, but again he is sad and downcast. After another block or so, light dawns: "You want to buy flag? My sister sell flag—I show you." The dialogue that follows is fairly excruciating, but I finally arrive, in a steaming downpour, at Mt. Alvernia Hospital.

In a garden setting, elegantly maintained and overlooking a handsome, tree-fringed reservoir, this private hospital is owned and managed by an order of Roman Catholic sisters, the Franciscan Missionaries of the Divine Motherhood. A fifty-bed section of the hospital is separately managed on a charitable basis for those with limited means. This is the Assisi Home, until recently limited to the care of the chronically ill and a few traumatic-injury patients, but now the unit is in transition. Since 1988 new long-term-care patients have not been accepted so that twelve terminally ill patients could be received and given skilled, palliative care.

"How is need determined?" I ask Staff Nurse Cher, who has met me at the head of the stairs in the Assisi Wing. Matron of the Home, Sister Eulalia Yeo, is in England just now, attending a Hospice Education Institute workshop. Nurse Cher is petite, quick, and intent, with a shy, warm smile—and she speaks excellent English! We sink into comfortable chairs in the sudden chill of an air-conditioned staff office, where an administrative assistant struggles silently with a large computer. "Patients and/or families may refer directly to us, or they may be referred by their doctors," says Nurse Cher. "Many are referred by the hospital's social worker. We have a six-bed hospice ward for women now, and another of six beds, on a different floor, for men. We try to bring in those who have the greatest emotional and social need, those for example who have no one at all to care for them at home. And yes, of course, those for whom pain is a major problem. There is a subcommittee of the Home in charge of Assisi admissions, and of course Sister Eulalia keeps them fully informed.

"When we hear of need for this sort of help, one of us goes to the patient, and we introduce ourselves, and talk with them for a while, just getting to know them. We feel our way along at this point. One of the difficult things is that patients sometimes don't know—don't have an understanding of their condition. That means we must have a very careful interview. Before coming in, the patient usually has to give consent. We also interview the next of kin and explain what we can do for the patient—and what we do not do."

"For example, no heroic resuscitation?"

"Yes, that would be very unusual here. Once the patient enters the actual process of dying, we don't believe in stopping it unless there are very special circumstances. We do promise to keep the family informed at all times. We explain to them that they are part of our program of care, that they must come in and visit the patient and be involved. Then the patient's family is asked how much they can afford to pay, and we make an agreement. Cancer patients are often at the end of their financial resources, and if they have nothing to give, then we do not expect anything.

"Of course, you should understand that there are some who would not call what we do here *hospice.* We are working with the concept, toward it, but hospice itself is just beginning here. Sister Eulalia attended the first hospice conference here, arranged by the Singapore Cancer Society about three years ago, when Dr. Twycross came. He had the medical information and statistics. I felt he was also a very humane person, who spoke of things straight from his heart. We had a great deal of encouragement and help also from Dr. Merriman. About six of our staff have done training with the Hospice Care Association, and I also went to a three-month multidisciplinary course in Perth. I spent some time with the Palliative Care Unit of the Repatriation Hospital, and also with Cottage Hospice in Perth. The hospice people in Australia have done a great deal for us. Sister Geraldine at St. Joseph's also trained there. Hospice is really quite international now! For example, people came to the Update '89 conference from the U.K., Japan, Australia, Malaysia, and Thailand. Also from New Zealand, the Philippines, Hong Kong, and Taiwan.

"It is different from other nursing, and for me personally, it is very much more rewarding. I had been in general nursing before, with six months in oncology and some administrative experience as well. This work is much more personal. Families of hospice patients nearly always return to see us, for example, and thank us, after the funeral. We feel close to them, and that rarely happens in the acute care situation. There is such a great need in society, I think, for people to care for one another. There is such a hard road ahead for many terminally ill patients. They need our help and support, and they should have it. By touching a single life in this way, and then another, I believe we can make a difference. And I believe that what we do lives on afterward, in the lives of their friends and families."

Later, in the hallway, we meet Sister Bernadette of the hospital's pastoral care team. "Some people ask whether they have to be Catholic to come here!" Her eyes sparkle with good-humored outrage. "Absolutely not! We care for anyone at all, no matter what their faith—or lack of it. We do not proselytize about our own faith. We don't even introduce prayer unless it is requested. The point of our being here is simply to show the patients that they are important to us as individuals. It's a matter of just being there for them—letting them know that we care, that we are *glad* to share their burdens." A leaflet describing the pastoral care services here includes this statement, adapted from Isaiah 46:

> I will be your God throughout all your lifetime.
> Yes, even in your sickness, sorrow or uncertainty . . .
> Yes, even in your moments of joy and happiness . . .
> Yes, even when you feel lonely, or thrown among
>   strangers . . .
> Yes, even when your hair is white with age . . .
> I made you, and I will care for you.

Staff Nurse Cher and I walk the wide, immaculate hallways. It is a quiet place this afternoon, remarkably peaceful, and even without air conditioning here, the heat at the moment is not oppressive. The six-bay wards on either side are pleasantly spacious, and each bed has a ceiling track around it so that curtains may be drawn for privacy. All of these are open now, and several beds are empty. "We have had several deaths in the past few days," Nurse Cher quietly explains. In the hospice ward a patient stands, fully dressed, beside her bed, evidently packing up some of her belongings. We are introduced. Mrs. C. is a retired schoolteacher.

"Are you leaving?"

"Yes," she replies. "I have to go for my chemotherapy. My daughter is coming for me in a little while—she should be here now. I'll stay over at the other place, you know, for a few days, but then I will be coming back here."

"How do you feel?"

"Fine now, just fine," she says cheerfully, "but tomorrow I am going to feel terrible." She laughs—a tall, sturdy-looking, gray-haired woman with a broad, intelligent face and rimless glasses. "That chemotherapy makes me so sick, I can't believe it," she continues. "Look at this bump on my forehead. Last time I had it, I was so sick that I fainted and fell down, and look what happened to me. What a mess. Doesn't it look terrible?" On her left temple is a thin, dark scab about two inches long. "Well, I'll be back here in another week and feeling fine again. This is such a nice place. Did you know they had a birthday party for me here last Monday? I was sixty-five years old. Isn't that terrible? I can't believe I ever got to be as old as that!"

"Don't tell anyone how old I am," says Nurse Cher, laughing. But as we continue to chat of this and that, I notice a small, dark haystack of a head popping up in the bed most distant, by the window, and a thin arm waving.

Mrs. C. leaves the floor, striding firmly, carrying her own overnight bag, and now it is time to find out who my new friend might be. I cross the ward, sit at the edge of her bed. We smile at one another for lack of any other common language. "Hello."

Who are you? I'm sure that I must know you, although it's impossible that we've ever met before. Is it only that I myself feel so at home here, because this is hospice, and because I am so glad for a chance to be with the patients?

This little one is all eyes, all bones by now—the rest of her so frail, so emaciated. . . . Eyes very black, short hair even blacker, sticking out every which way, limbs carrying no more flesh than a bird's claw. She could be seventeen, thirty-seven, seventy. "Hello."

But who are you really, what has your life been until now? Are you Chinese? Filipino? Japanese? Malay? Indian? Or a mixture, perhaps, as I am a mixture of Scots, French, English, Welsh, Irish, plus—I believe and hope—a touch of African? Hand in hand now, we two could imagine that we hold the world between us. Maybe in microcosm we do. If blood could speak, what travels the two of us could have, through the galaxies!

"Hello."

"Hello." She can see me now, but from farther away than before, since she has made herself tired by waving.

"How are you?"

"Hello."

"Hello." Both of us need earphones and simultaneous translations, not so much between languages as between distances, times, probabilities, coefficients. *Beam me up, Scotty.* Her weightless hands now resting, one in mine, one in Nurse Cher's are insubstantial as smoke, but she smiles and smiles—and those great black eyes are blazing.

"She understands a little English," says Nurse Cher, "if you speak slowly."

"Well . . . you have beautiful eyes,"

She smiles again, and after a time turns toward Nurse Cher. "Kind. Very kind," she whispers, and not in response to the compliment. Rather, she needs to convey to us both what has happened here. It has been a miracle, her eyes tell us. She has been lifted from her place of torment by the kind, the very kind lady here in white. Her pain is gone at last, and with it, her terror. She gazes first at one of us, then the other, evidently seeing us now from a vast distance, but with joy so intense that it is like a benediction. "Love was closer to the surface and easier to convey," Gregory Bateson wrote of his own near-death experience. "At the same time there was a feeling of aloneness which was like looking out from some high peak after the exertion of climbing. . . . When death is close and utterly sure . . . then it becomes possible to see with a new clarity and the mind can soar."

In silence for a few moments the three of us share this clarity, this high place of love and mutual aloneness.

Later, in the men's ward, I discover an elderly Chinese gentleman propped up on pillows, also looking curiously familiar. *Well, now, who are you? I know for a fact I've seen you before, somewhere.*

Mr. W. has the clear, smooth skin of a baby, and he sits quietly, gazing at the world around him with benign and wondering eyes. Tubes up his nose are bringing in oxygen to ease the discomfort of his advanced lung cancer. He is well over eighty, very ill, very deaf, but his hand wraps mine in a grip that is warm, and still remarkably powerful. Kingdoms, empires are shaped by such a hand. Nurse Cher puts her lips to his ear and shouts, first in English, then in his own Chinese dialect. He nods agreeably, looking me over, taking my measure, but does not speak. Never mind. That does not matter. He is amused, I am amused, and after a few moments, we are utterly delighted with one another. His enormous dignity reassures, envelops, realigns me, a dignity so profound and so confident that in a little while our eyes are beginning to say to one another, shall we play at being clowns?

Yes, let's. On the other hand, perhaps we already have, and today is a memory. But memory tickles—I am tempted to do a buck and wing, stand on my head, make funny faces. What is it? There's something, I'm sure, having to do with theater in all this. Charlie Chaplin? The Godfather? Alec Guinness?

Much later, after a number of bad jokes on my part about bird's nest soup (while a volunteer spoons up broth for him), I realize suddenly that this old Singapore charmer is really Sir Laurence Olivier. That is to say, he is Sir Laurence's Chinese brother—the one the family didn't know about. I'll never tell, but honestly the resemblance is amazing. It haunts me later in the day, and only the next morning does it occur to me that it was Olivier's great gift and genius to be able to look like, sound like, anyone at all, if he put his mind to it. Why, Laurence Olivier could make himself look Asian, or Roman, or Irish. . . . And then, all in a heap, in a thunderclap, I have got it: *Oh, Susanna! Oh, don't you cry for me, sang my beautiful Irish grandfather while we played silly games (he was going to Alabama, I was the banjo on his knee), and then one day when I was six he didn't tell me where he was going, and he didn't take me with him. He just went to the hospital all by himself, and died.*

"I look at each person I meet," says hospice physician Antony Tam, "as a gift with unique wrappings—a gift filled with surprises, waiting to be opened." Dr. Tam, a trim, energetic, and youthful thirty-nine, has come recently onto the Singapore hospice team from Hong Kong, where he served on the first Executive Committee of their Society for the Promotion of Hospice Care. Hong Kong hospice people, he tells me, are now building an independent inpatient unit, and have already been providing a home care program and community education—something like one hundred fifty talks per year. This hospice started with strong leadership from a group of Maryknoll sisters and individuals such as Lucy Chung—a nurse who went to England for hospice training—and president of the Hong Kong College of General Practitioners, Dr. Peter Lee. Conservative elements in government, media, and the public have been slow to respond to the need for hospice, although cancer in Hong Kong is recognized as their number one cause of death. However, having attracted the support of the prestigious Keswick Foundation and other respected local powers, hospice leaders there have high hopes for the future.

The political situation in China has been instrumental in moves made in recent years by the Tam family: Antony's brother, sister, and parents are all in the United States now. However, together with his wife and child, he has "made a commitment to Singapore." In hospice work Dr. Tam finds an opportunity to practice a kind of medicine combining his lifelong interest in the hard facts of science with his strong sense of the value of human beings—their emotions and intuitions, their creativity, their processes in relationships. He also sees in Singapore the hope of drawing upon the best of many cultures so that hospice may become a part of a new and richer world synthesis.

"The English hospice tradition," he says today, "is an excellent model in that it represents an open offering of knowledge. People like Anne Merriman in Nairobi and Sister Gabriel in Hong Kong give you their experience freely. They don't play the game of 'I had to steal this knowledge, and so now you are going to have to do the same.' You are welcome to have anything they know, take it, and use it. English medicine, of course, has been excellent too; but in hospice, medicine isn't going to be the whole story. The Americans have done better teaching and service thus far, I think, in the whole question of personal relationships, the care of the family as a unit, the psychology surrounding dying, death, and bereavement. That includes Dr. Bal Mount in Montreal, by the way. Montreal was a bible for Sister Kenny and others in Our Lady of Maryknoll Hospital, Hong Kong's first to start a palliative care program. Bal Mount handles this kind of thing with grace, with real humility. He's not saying, 'I'm telling you this because we are so great,' but just, 'We started doing it this way because we recognized that there is a problem.' His keynote address at the First Annual American Conference on Hospice Care [June 1984] was very important, very fine. Here he was facing different life-styles of families, showing that a hospice care-giver explores when allowed, facilitates where possible. It is not helpful to be judgmental: there is no ideal way to live; there is only his or her own way to be encouraged. And Mount is also saying that a hospice staff is not supposed to be just one more gathering of authoritarians; they have got to work together democratically, as a team.

"I did some work myself in the United States that has been valuable: in family reconstruction, role-play of family scenes, and how family as the unit of care is lived out. I attended a four-week workshop in Crested Butte, Colorado, led by the late V. Satir—an integrated approach, learning to be more fully human and helping people to change, especially in the context of families. There I met a Trudeau Award family physician from Calgary who said I was lucky to have learned about these tools so young. The approach is at the same time conceptual, kinesthetic, contextual—getting your right brain connected to your left brain *and* to your body; learning to listen to the body as well as the intellect. Most people are brought up to despise the body. Poor homo sapiens! With the rapid advancement of the technological sciences, we have tried too hard to be objective, and have ended up getting objectified instead— persons becoming numbers in big institutions, pornography, violence, mass murder. Most people today are only half alive because they ignore the right brain, when what the world needs is the whole person, the whole individual—and the readiness, receptivity, willingness to get in touch with one another. Joyful acceptance of the self is necessary before we are ready to love others."

Dr. Tam scribbles notes for the listener as he speaks, and draws quick, expressive diagrams by way of further explanation, all the while tossing out a cornucopia of book titles, names of articles, people, places, and descriptions of illuminating experiences. Now, beginning to talk about the meeting of Eastern and Western medicine, he demonstrates the origin and development of some characters in Chinese calligraphy: picture writing, a method of communication that is both abstract and intuitive, both intellectual and sensuous.

"Eastern tradition," says Dr. Tam, "has many things of value to offer to world medicine in general, as well as to the development of hospice protocols. To begin with, we have a point of view, part of a very long tradition telling us: *work with nature, use nature wisely, but don't disrupt nature.* Too often Western science, Western medicine disrupts nature. My own people for centuries were part of the Yellow River culture in China, always close to nature and close to the land"—he makes a quick list labeled *Right Brain,* including *concreteness, sense of space, "woman," earth, intuition, feelings, sixth sense, artistic, Zen, etc.*—"and this was true since the time of the Han and the T'ang dynasties. Then my uncles were killed, and my grandfather had all his money stolen. I understand how some of the old Chinese people here in Singapore feel. When they are sick, they still expect doctoring as they knew it in their youth. They want you to show your experience by predicting symptoms after taking the pulse and looking at the face—never mind a long medical history. Many have had their language as well as their culture taken. . . . Yes, many families here can't communicate, because the new generation has to speak English. And there are five different Chinese dialects here, three major, two minor, and all very different—so, a great many barriers. Many of the old people want to keep their traditional ways, for example their traditional herbal medicines. Some of these were in use a thousand years before Western medicine found the same ingredient and called it by a different name. Many of these remedies can be very helpful in palliative care. Unfortunately the media and 'Western' physicians are disproportionately exposed to regretful patients who felt cheated by spending money—pressing for a cure—after being disappointed in Western medicine. We need both

Eastern and Western traditions just as we need both East and West to make the world whole, just as we need both right brain and left brain working in order to have a whole person. This calls for a bigger effort from the community to enable more G.P.s, more family doctoring, so that people in crisis can have one professional to coordinate all the services needed. In fact, one objective of our Hospice Care Association is to do just that.

"I see it as the hospice physician's job to bring peace of mind to patients, along with physical comfort. That takes intuition as well as knowledge. A doctor needs to live in the stomach as well as the head—and it often takes learning from, and knowing about, more than one tradition. For example, an elderly man was pacing at the entrance of the ward recently while his wife gasped in a coma, having suddenly and unexpectedly taken a turn for the worse. He was in a state of panic. And I knew that in his culture, his tradition, the funeral ceremonies could be so elaborate, with so much to pay for—music, food, processions, all the relatives, the friends, entertaining and so on—that he was overwhelmed. How could he pay for all that? He was retired, and had used up savings on his wife's chemotherapy. So I said to him, 'Your daughter will help you—it will all work out. Would you like to take this precious time to relate to your wife? Let her know you are with her, tell her how you feel about her.' When he heard that, he cried. And with my hand still on his back helping to support him, he moved at his own speed back to his wife. I brought up a chair so that he could sit close beside her, and I think, then, they both found peace of mind. His wife expired a half an hour later."

"Is it very different for you here in Singapore?" I ask. "Do you find yourself homesick at all?"

Dr. Tam answers, smiling, "Well, you see, that is a time

to use some interiority. If I am at peace with myself, then everywhere is home."

And today at last I will be seeing Sister Geraldine, Sister Mary, and the people at St. Joseph's. Looking out at the city from my hotel room, I see that a marvelous change has come about: the sun sparkles sharply this morning on the leaves of the coconut palms, the green lawns below are dense with shade, the streets are glittering and vibrant. A few moments later, on the sidewalk, I realize that I have just gone out of my mind and forgotten that the hotel was air-conditioned. The weather out here is not sparkling, it is blazing; the heat comes down like hammers, and the lawns are not dense with shade, but with impenetrable humidity. St. Joseph's Home is supposed to be in a place called Upper Juron Road. According to the map there is such a road, but according to my driver, there hasn't been one for a year or so: Upper Juron Road has been bulldozed over. At last, after meandering for some time among blank-faced high-rises, we spot a side road with a sign saying ST. JOSEPH'S HOME.

As I walk in, whipped by a wind so hot it is scouring, squadrons of jets go screaming by, barely overhead. Low buildings, a parking area, a covered walkway. A white habit, a round face calmly smiling in all the tumult, turns out to be Sister Mary, the Home's Matron. "Hello! Hello!" we shout at one another as still more jets go shrieking by, then we move toward the center of the complex where there is a large, enclosed courtyard with ranks of old people sitting, standing, sagging in wheelchairs around a central garden. The wind dies and the light blazes down, thick with the fragrance of Singapore cooking. A large sign on the wall of the courtyard says, OUR HOUSE IS OPEN TO GOD—FRIENDS—GUESTS—AND SUNSHINE. Sister Rita, cheerful and welcoming, brings me rambutans and a merciful glass of cold water. We are standing, chatting in the tea pantry, when Sister Geraldine comes in. My first reaction is astonishment. Having heard and read of her work with hospice patients, I had expected a person very much older—had an idea fixed in my head, I suppose, that she ought to be bent and gray as Mother Teresa. Instead she is young and very lovely, rather pale, with a voice almost as soft as a whisper. Immediately one is aware of a deeply modest sort of simplicity about her, and then, more gradually, a tensile strength, an inheld radiance. She is very serious indeed— and also, from time to time, as I soon discover, extremely funny.

We walk through the courtyard together to an open pavilion, a reception room with flowers, chairs, and sofas, all simmering at sauna heat. The jets begin ripping yards of silk out of the air just above us again, and we both burst out laughing. When we can speak, finally, Sister Geraldine begins to tell me about St. Joseph's. There are ninety-six beds for the elderly here, sixteen for hospice patients. And yes, she finds it works well to care for her hospice people here among the elders. At first some were upset a little, when several patients died, but then they came to understand that. "And there is a beauty in this because we are more like a family. I let the old people who are not ill participate, when possible, in the care of the dying. If they are able, I put some of them in a position of responsibility—they can call in an emergency, they can help by sitting beside a dying patient, or giving them a sip of water if needed. This is very satisfying for them, it helps them to feel needed. Sometimes the patients say, 'Oh, you shouldn't be doing this for me—I should be helping you, instead,' but, you see, this helps to bring us all together. Then, too, when the old people see those a great deal younger dying, for example, of cancer, it helps them to accept their own situation. They think, I have had a long time to live, after all, and here is another person going much sooner. I think too that the gentleness, the warm hospitality that is true of the nurses in general in a home for old people fits very well with a hospice program.

"My own training began before I joined the order in 1982. I was then already an oncology nurse. The Canossian Sisters is an order founded by an Italian noblewoman in the eighteenth century, Magdalene of Canossa. She was a remarkable person who gave up everything she had, wealth and family, to help the poor. She was canonized in 1988. Pastoral work, education, and nursing are the main concerns of the order. Six years before I joined, I had a personal experience that influenced me greatly. A close friend had leukemia, and she committed suicide. She simply could not cope with the illness, the chemotherapy. I didn't know what to say to her at the time—I didn't know how to help her. Then, after her death, her mother was grieving and grieving, and oh, then the mother also committed suicide. You see, I felt I had failed them both, and I knew that I had to do something about this, become more aware, learn how to help people in such a situation. For a long time I kept this story privately to myself, but then I came to understand that it needed to be shared.

"We are in a cradle area of hospice, here in Singapore. Sister Rita and I went for training in palliative care to Cottage Hospice in Australia. Dr. Cynthia Goh visits here every Friday"—she beams at the thought—"and we have a very good relationship, very open. We work very well together. The buildings here are owned by the Catholic Welfare Services, but they give us autonomy in management. And because they support us, we are very fortunate in being able to care very well for people who have no money at all. This is an unusual situation, of course. One woman I remember broke down and cried when we told her that she would not have to pay anything. I myself do bedside nursing and counseling, and education in the hospice concept is one of my priorities. Some patients, of course, need counseling more than others, but it is a real joy to me to be able to share in this way. Every single person who comes to us here is unique, each one is such a priceless gift, and I am always thinking"—her face lights up again—"I wonder what this one is going to be teaching me?"

Sister Geraldine speaks very gently, very lovingly of her patients; the merriment bubbling up from time to time is directed at herself. "You see, I try to ask each patient, how can I support you? And their life stories are always so full of insight for me. For instance, there was a traveling man who came here, a man who went on many ships, and he was forty-nine years old and dying. Actually, I think he may have been some sort of gangster. He had at least three or four wives in different parts of the world, and he was covered with tattoos on his belly and on his arms—well, you know, various pictures. So I asked him how I could support him at this time in his life, and I started sponging him. And when I saw the tattoos, I was a *bit* scandalized, I admit, but I did not show it. He said to me, 'Aren't you scandalized, Sister? Can this mean that you accept me? After seeing all of this, do you still accept me?' You see, that is what most people are worrying about, and he was no different.

"So I told him, 'I look past all of that, because what I am looking at, and what I am seeing, is the person inside.' At first he could hardly believe me. And the poor man with all those wives, not one of them would come to his bedside when he was dying. I telephoned two of them myself and asked them, but they would not. Oh my, what a terrible rejection that was for him!

"And I have helped patients to write letters. One man

wanted to write twenty-two letters at the end, and we sat up all night doing it. But of course we sometimes have to set limits with our patients, and it is the patients themselves who have taught me this. I remember one who was very unreasonable and demanding, and I knew that he was testing me—all the more so, probably, because I am a nun. One morning it was, 'I didn't want boiled eggs, Sister, I wanted to have them poached,' and when I took this away and brought him poached eggs, he got really angry and yelled at me, 'How can you be so stupid—I can't eat these, I wanted them fried.' This went on four times over, and I was thinking what I would do about the situation, when he suddenly said, 'Sister, why don't you bawl me out, please—then I'll feel better.' So I understood that what he wanted was my response. And I shared my feelings with him *quite frankly,* and after that we did well together. He was a very nice person, really, and later this same man began to question himself, and question what his life had been about. He was one of those who began asking questions about God, and the meaning of everything, wanting to read something. . . . Of course, we don't force anyone here to become a believer, but sometimes they ask for our prayers, or the families say, 'This is rather frightening—we would feel better if Sister is there.' . . . As for medication, where there is pain we have them on a round-the-clock schedule. We start with low dosage, bring it up to the level of comfort, maintain it. Reliable patients are encouraged to medicate themselves so as to maintain a sense of independence. Come, I will show you, and we will meet some of the patients, and the old people.''

Down the corridors, through the courtyard, in and out of the sleeping rooms, into the dining space that merges with pantry and kitchen (enormous pots, stewing and steaming in the breathless heat), Sister Geraldine makes her way gently among human beings so helpless and forlorn, so unable, many of them, even to sit up in their beds or wheelchairs, or to respond in kind to her touch, her smile, her greeting, that this is like a scene from a medieval Inferno. Here are the rejects of present-day society—the much too old, the much too poor, the derelict, the repellent, the dying, the wholly incapable. However, this is not the way they are seen here. The Canossian Sisters give their attention to a different drummer: *Go out quickly into the streets and lanes of the city, and bring in hither the poor, and the maimed, and the halt, and the blind. . . . Go out into the highways and hedges. . . .*

And at this moment, as I shall always remember her, Sister Geraldine moves about the courtyard delighting, admiring—bringing attention to this one and that of her charges, who are her treasures, calling each one by name. I learned later that she does not live in an air-conditioned retreat house, or even a tidy dormitory down the street: she lives here. "Oh, yes, I have a little room, right here with the old people." So the truth is that this is not, in fact, a warehouse for the unwanted: it is the sisters' home, a castle shared, a palace to which the Canossians invite their most honored guests. Viewed in this way, everything changes: *Behold, I shew you a mystery; we shall not all sleep, but we shall all be changed. In a moment, in the twinkling of an eye. . . .* And now in the light of the ancient metaphor, so rich in human history and remembrance, this moment can become for the visitor a wholly different set of events, a different journey entirely, so that, walking in once more from the parking lot with better eyes this time, we find ourselves entering, rather than a blazing courtyard, a vaulted and tapestried chamber, dim in torchlight, where pilgrims are greeted, welcomed, embraced—given rambutans and cold water—or, if we are now amid icy mountain passes, steaming mugs of cider and wine. So seen, the courtyard under the screaming jets becomes a musty, wood-hewn, straw-covered hospice hall once again, where the frail and weary gather while dust is washed from their feet, where the sores of the leper are bathed in healing waters.

What is happening here at St. Joseph's in Singapore has happened again and again over the centuries, in many cultures; and there are people unknown and unnamed, by the thousands even now, all over the world, laboring like these sisters to give help, comfort, and surcease of pain. To these who know how to love, each human being is a gift and an opportunity, not only for service, but for joy. They see the dying as travelers on the greatest of all journeys. Are they foolish, all these loving, giving, hardworking people? The wisdom of the ages says no, they are not. In fact, there are many who believe that these very same weary, desperately needy, and road-worn travelers will be brought in time (carried, if they can no longer walk) into the great hall of the lord of the manor, where the poorest and least desirable of them all will be led to the seats of the highest honor; that they will be placed there, along with their canes and their walkers, their trusses, their IVs and their prostheses, their bandages, bibs, spit pans, and plastic guards against incontinence, to share, beyond time into eternity, in the greatest of all Wedding Feasts. *And God shall wipe away all tears from their eyes, and there shall be no more death, neither sorrow, nor crying, neither shall there be any more pain: for the former things are passed away. And he that sat upon the throne said, Behold, I make all things new.*

CLINICAL APPENDIX

HOSPICE: CURRENT PRINCIPLES AND PRACTICES

by
Michal J. M. Galazka
Executive Director
and
Karen B. Hunter
Projects Director
HOSPICE EDUCATION INSTITUTE

(Portions of the text have been excerpted or adapted from *Notes on Symptom Control in Hospice & Palliative Care, Revised First Edition, U.S.A. Version,* by Dr. Peter Kaye [Hospice Education Institute, 1990] by permission of the Hospice Education Institute.)

I *Competence, communication, and compassion are the hallmarks of hospice.* Good hospice care (also called palliative care) is characterized by:

- ▸ a multidisciplinary team approach to coping with the many problems faced by dying people and those who love and care for them
- ▸ a focus not only on the dying person, but also on his or her family and friends as the unit of care
- ▸ emphasis on the quality, not the quantity, of the dying person's life
- ▸ assurance of continuing support for family members and care-givers during their bereavement
- ▸ the dying person's involvement, to the fullest possible extent, in decisions relating to the type and location of care.

Over the past generation, hospice has taken its rightful place in the mainstream of medical care by developing and demonstrating sound principles and clinical practices of good care for people with far-advanced illness. *Hospice care is intensive, active care, demanding the highest professional skills and personal commitment of each member of the hospice team.*

Hospice team members traditionally include:

▶ *nurses,* who usually have the most contact with patient and care-givers, and who frequently take primary responsibility for coordinating the team's efforts

▶ *physicians,* who must be skilled in symptom management, and who must often learn both the clinical skills necessary for good hospice care and the interpersonal skills necessary to work as part of an effective multidisciplinary team

▶ *social workers, psychologists, and counselors,* who offer special skills in caring for the social and emotional needs of dying people and their care-givers, and by supporting other members of the hospice team

▶ *clergy,* who can offer valuable spiritual and religious support to patients, care-givers, and members of the hospice team

▶ *art therapists and music therapists,* who are playing an increasingly important role in encouraging the dying to seek the challenge and solace of expression through art and music

▶ *physical and occupational therapists,* whose special responsibilities to the patient are to encourage and facilitate activity and increase independence, and to remind other team members of the importance of rehabilitating the whole person, even in the presence of far-advanced illness

▶ *dietitians and nutritionists,* who specialize in planning balanced diets, enhancing taste and texture of foods, and (occasionally) in suggesting appropriate use of nutritional supplements

▶ *pharmacists,* who are crucial to hospice teams because most dying people require the concurrent use of several medications ("polypharmacy")

▶ *trained volunteers,* who, as full members of the hospice team, offer their personal and professional support to patients and care-givers.

II *Good communication—and the reassurance it brings to patient, care-givers, and hospice team members—is often the single most important ingredient in successful hospice care.*

Hospice involvement needs to begin early in a terminal illness, allowing the hospice team time to make plans, build trusting relationships with patient and care-givers, and educate and empower them to share in all aspects of physical and emotional care.

Hospice team members should encourage open communication among the patient's family and friends. Relationships may be strained by fears, old wounds, embarrassment at discussing sensitive topics, or the mistaken urge to try to withhold vital information from each other. A meeting with patient, family members, and close friends can encourage the sharing of information, emotions, and fears. Children should be included in family discussions.

Team members must learn to communicate clearly and effectively with each other, and with the patient and care-givers. *Listening is the most important communication skill of all.*

III *Skilled physical symptom control is the linchpin of good hospice care,* around which other key services to patient and carers revolve, and without which the many psychological, social, and spiritual needs of patient and care-givers cannot easily be met. Many patients suffer needless pain because doctors and nurses are simply unaware of what to do. A study at St. Christopher's Hospice of 6,677 patients admitted between 1975 and 1985 showed the following as the ten most common physical symptoms on admission:

Symptom	%
Weight loss	77
Pain	71
Loss of appetite	67
Breathlessness	51
Cough	50
Constipation	47
Weakness	47

Nausea/Vomiting	40
Edema/Ascites/Pleural effusion	31
Insomnia	29

Psychological and spiritual problems, though not included in the table, are almost always troubling to people with advanced disease, and to their care-givers. Hospice team members must always remember that psychological and spiritual issues may often be couched in physical terms. The many drugs needed in good hospice care should never become substitutes for the discussion, reassurance, and counseling needed by anxious patients and care-givers. Writing a prescription for benzodiazepines or antidepressants is not an adequate reply to the difficult questions asked by a dying patient.

A *Weight loss:* Both patient and care-givers may worry about poor food intake, and it is important to explain that weight loss is the result of illness rather than poor diet. With weight loss, the patient's previous body image is lost, which may be frightening. New, well-fitting clothes can boost morale. Current photographs of the patient with family members and friends can show that this "new person" still belongs.

Loss of appetite: Anorexia occurs in about 65 percent of hospice patients. It is important to consider oral thrush, nausea, constipation, and hypercalcemia as possible causes, and to treat these problems. Steroids (dexamethasone 4mg per day or prednisolone 30mg per day) help about 80 percent of patients with anorexia. Metoclopramide 10mg before meals can help if anorexia is due to small stomach syndrome. Attractive preparation and serving of small portions of favorite foods, preferably with strong tastes, can help. A dietitian can give advice about a balanced diet, and suggest possible use of nutritional supplements. (Ensure Plus or Sustacal in small sip feedings can replace eating for patients unable to manage normal meals.)

Often no physical cause for anorexia can be found. Psychological factors are important, and anorexia may reflect the patient's morale. *Care-givers and visitors must be discouraged from forcing unwanted food on weak patients.* Invasive nutritional support is *inappropriate* for hospice patients. Measures of nutritional support (such as enteral tubes and IV hyperalimentation) that may be appropriate (ordinary) in patients undergoing treatment aimed at cure or enjoying general well-being, become inappropriate (extraordinary) in far-advanced disease, and should usually be avoided. Such measures do not add to the dying person's comfort, and may cause unnecessary distress. The decision to remove a tube or IV line is simply one of patient comfort: if the patient wants a tube or IV line removed, it should be removed. If the dying person is unconscious, professionals should gently explain to family members and care-givers that tubes and IV lines do not significantly prolong life or add to the patient's comfort.

The main problems of reduced food intake are the related psychological concerns of the patient, care-givers, and professionals. A reduced diet does not shorten prognosis in advanced disease. For an inactive patient with advanced cancer low food intake does not cause hunger. Patients' concerns about lack of appetite often relate to worries about having a serious disease and facing death, and need to be understood as expressions of spiritual anguish. Professionals all too often focus on technical methods of nutritional support rather than on the more difficult issues of emotional and spiritual distress in facing up to the impending death of the patient. *Caregivers sometimes feel that feeding is all they can do to "help," and they must be taught other methods of supporting the patient.*

B *Pain:* Many cancer patients assume they will have severe pain and are relieved to learn that 30 percent of cancer patients have no pain. Nevertheless, severe pain too often remains one of the most inadequately treated symptoms of advanced cancer. *Severe pain is a medical emergency.*

Pain in cancer patients can be cancer-related, treatment-related, or unrelated to the cancer. Cancer patients can suffer pains unrelated to the cancer, such as headache, arthritis, or angina. Even a patient taking large amounts of morphine may occasionally need acetaminophen for a mild headache, for example.

Cancer pain is relatively easy to control in most patients. *Pain control involves three steps: detailed assessment, a plan of management, and continual monitoring.*

Determining the likely cause of each pain is the purpose of an initial assessment, usually accomplished by a careful history and physical examination. (In one survey, 34 percent of cancer patients had more than four different pains.) Determining the severity of pain is secondary, as this is useful only in monitoring response to treatment. Generally, *pain is what the patient says it is, not what the doctor believes it ought to be!*

Use of a body chart (see below) improves communication. Ideally, the chart is filled in by the patient at regular intervals, with the doctor and nurse present.

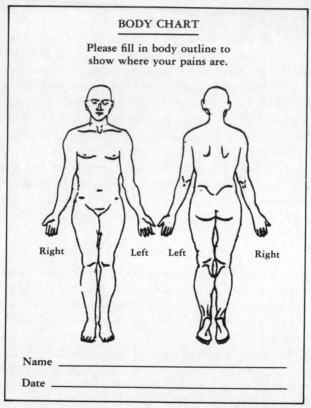

BODY CHART

Please fill in body outline to show where your pains are.

Right   Left   Left   Right

Name _____

Date _____

The patient should be given a "drug card" listing all medications to be taken, the times of day each should be taken, and the purpose of each. This fosters good communication, improves patient understanding, and is an important step to successful prescribing and effective pain control.

DRUG CARD

Cynthia Spencer House

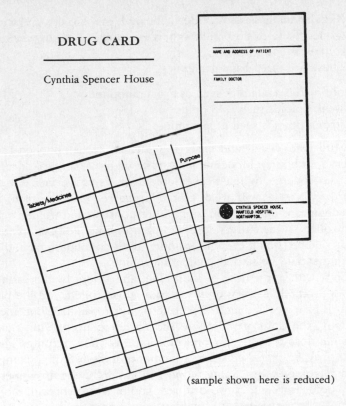

NAME AND ADDRESS OF PATIENT

FAMILY DOCTOR

CYNTHIA SPENCER HOUSE,
MANFIELD HOSPITAL,
NORTHAMPTON.

Tablets/Medicines

Purpose

(sample shown here is reduced)

There are two basic types of cancer pain:

- ▶ continuous visceral or soft tissue pains, which usually respond *well* to opioid analgesics
- ▶ variable pains (bone, nerve, pleuritic, colicky) which tend to respond *poorly* to opioid analgesics.

Continuous pain needs continuous relief. Regular analgesia is most likely to keep pain away. Prescribe analgesics regularly "by the clock." *Never* prescribe PRN (as needed). The goal of pain control is a pain-free and alert patient.

Management options for pain control include morphine (or other opioid drug), coanalgesic drugs, radiotherapy for bone pain, nerve block, and psychological interventions.

Regular analgesia should ideally be oral, easy to take, and with few side effects, so the patient can live as normal a life as possible once pain is controlled.

There are three basic analgesics:

► nonopioid analgesics such as acetaminophen
► weak opioids such as codeine
► strong opioids such as morphine.

Mild pains need mild analgesics such as acetaminophen (1g every four hours). Moderate pains respond to weak opioid drugs such as codeine. When weaker opioid drugs prove ineffective, *start oral morphine.* If weak opioid drugs reduced the pain, it usually means that the pain is opioid-responsive, and will be well controlled on the correct dose of oral morphine. For example, if oral codeine (60mg every four hours) does not abolish pain, the patient should be started on oral morphine.

Start with a low dose of morphine, and titrate by increasing doses promptly in steps until the pain is controlled, and the patient is pain-free and alert. If a patient who is pain-free becomes drowsy, the dose of morphine should be reduced. The usual starting dose for 4-hourly oral morphine is 5mg to 10mg. The dose may be increased every four hours in steps: 5mg, 10mg, 20mg, 30mg, 45mg, 60mg *(or more as needed).* Mild drowsiness may occur for the first two or three days of treatment with morphine. About 30 percent of patients experience mild nausea for a few days after starting morphine.

Always start a laxative and an antiemetic at the same time as morphine or any of the opioids, strong or weak. Almost all patients on regular opioids need daily laxatives, but antiemetics can usually be withdrawn after a few days.

Once the patient's pain is well controlled on 4-hourly oral morphine, it is possible to stop the 4-hourly morphine and change to an equivalent dose of controlled-release morphine sulfate (MS-Contin or Roxanol SR) every 12 hours. (Do not use 4-hourly oral morphine and 12-hourly morphine together. It is unnecessary and tends to confuse both patient and care-givers.)

There is no known opioid superior to morphine. Pain that does not respond to carefully titrated doses of morphine will not respond to other opioid analgesics. Using several drugs from the same group simultaneously (morphine with another opioid drug, for example) is illogical and ineffective. The analgesics *not* suitable for management of chronic pain include dihydrocodeine (constipating), pentazocine (dysphoriant effect), meperidine (too short-acting), and methadone (too long-acting).

"Morphine myths"—tolerance, addiction, respiratory depression—have contributed to the poor management of cancer pain and untold needless suffering. These myths are based on single-dose studies in animals and humans without pain. *Chronic pain prevents these side effects.*

Patients and clinicians commonly fear that morphine tolerance will occur. Tolerance (needing higher and higher doses with diminishing analgesic effect) does not occur when oral, rectal, sublingual, subcutaneous, or intramuscular morphine is used to control visceral or soft-tissue cancer pain. The fear of tolerance is based on the clinical misuse of morphine for pain that does not respond well to morphine, such as bone pain, nerve pain, or colicky pain. (Morphine is not effective for these, but the ignorant tend to try higher and higher doses of morphine—a very inefficient way to try to achieve pain relief.)

The dose of morphine may increase for the first few days or weeks as the dosage is titrated, but once a pain is controlled by morphine, the patient can stay on the same dose for weeks or months. The longer a patient is on morphine, the more likely he or she is to have a *decrease* in dosage. If the pain remains constant, the correct dose of morphine (the one that controls the pain without causing drowsiness) can remain constant for weeks, months, or even years in some cases. If pain is reduced, the dose of morphine will need to be reduced. If the pain increases, the dose of morphine will need to be increased.

Patients with chronic pain *do not* and *cannot* become addicted to morphine when it is used correctly to control their pain. This is clinically proven by observing patients whose pain is suddenly abolished (by a nerve block, for example), where high doses of morphine used for several months can be stopped with no withdrawal effects.

Respiratory depression does not occur when morphine is correctly used to control pain. As long as the dose of morphine is titrated, and the dose reduced if drowsiness occurs, there is no danger of respiratory depression. When pain is controlled by other means (such as a nerve block), the sudden reduction in pain requires reduction of the morphine dose, and careful observation of the patient.

Never prescribe opioid agonist/antagonists (buprenorphine, nalbuphine, pentazocine) with opioid agonists (codeine, morphine).

Avoid fixed mixtures of drugs (such as the obsolete Brompton's Cocktail), because the correct dose of one component will usually result in inappropriate doses of the others.

Intravenous (IV) infusions of morphine are often used if a patient has a permanent indwelling IV catheter. This route can be effective, but has one major disadvantage: tolerance sometimes develops to morphine administered by the IV route (either infusion or bolus). Higher and higher doses are needed, and pain can escape control. Transferring to oral morphine, or occasionally to morphine by continuous *subcutaneous* infusion, gives better pain control with lower doses. (The reason for tolerance to IV morphine, *but not to morphine given by other routes,* remains unknown.)

The continuous *subcutaneous* infusion of drugs by a small battery-operated portable pump or "syringe driver" (usually weighing less than 12 ounces and smaller than a Sony Walkman), is a major advance in hospice care, particularly for control of symptoms at home, and for use during the last hours of life when the patient may be unconscious. Continuous subcutaneous infusions are rarely needed for pain control alone, and are especially useful for control of nausea and vomiting. (A continuous subcutaneous infusion of drugs can also be useful in the symptomatic management of malignant intestinal obstruction, avoiding nasogastric suction and surgery.) Morphine, cyclizine, haloperidol, methotrimeprazine, and scopolamine can be mixed together in one continuous subcutaneous infusion. (Do *not* use chlorpromazine, prochlorperazine, or thiethylperazine: they cause skin irritation.)

It is wrong to use morphine (or other opioids) without proper assessment of the pain. Morphine is not effective, or only partially effective, for variable pains such as bone pain, nerve pain, pleuritic pains, and colicky pains.

Bone pain and related nerve compression pain account for 40 percent of cancer pain. The pain is typically worse on movement, often well localized, and tender to pressure. There may be a dull ache, even at rest. (Bone pain is occasionally vague and poorly localized with no bony tenderness.) There can be radiating pains due to nerve compression in the arm, leg, or around the chest.

Palliative radiotherapy is the treatment of choice for bone pain whenever possible. A *single* radiotherapy treatment of 800cGy can be just as effective as multiple treatments. Eighty percent of patients obtain partial or complete pain relief within one to two weeks.

Nonsteroidal antiinflammatory drugs (for example, naproxen 500mg two times a day) are the first-line analgesics for bone pain, and reduce or abolish bone pain in about 80 percent of cases. About 10 percent to 20 percent of patients complain of dyspepsia, which can sometimes be controlled by adding ranitidine 150mg two times a day.

Nerve pain, sometimes called deafferentation pain, occurs in an area of abnormal or absent sensation, and often presents as a continuous burning or aching pain, numbness or tingling, with stabbing pains occasionally superimposed. It can be severe and continuous, often disturbs sleep, but can fluctuate in severity. Nerve pain is poorly understood and difficult to treat. The nature of this pain must be explained to the patient, emphasizing that it is caused by nerve damage, and not by tissue or organ damage.

Though nerve pain responds poorly to analgesics like acetaminophen and morphine, a trial of morphine is important because some nerve pains respond partially, especially if there is a deep, aching component to the pain. (An element of soft tissue pain can also be superimposed on the nerve pain.)

Tricyclics can be effective; imipramine is the drug of choice. The aim is to increase the dose as quickly as possible to 100mg to 150mg per day (it is unusual to need more than 100mg per day). The speed of increase in dose depends on the severity of pain and the degree of supervision, but a useful guide is:

Day 1	10mg to 25mg
Day 3	25mg to 50mg
Day 7	50mg to 100mg
Day 10	100mg to 150mg

Elderly or frail patients need lower doses. Side effects (especially a dry mouth) often limit the tolerated dose. Onset of relief is unusual before Day 4 or 5, and unlikely using only 25 mg.

Anticonvulsants can sometimes relieve the severe stabbing pains of neuralgia. The useful drugs are clonazepam, carbamazepine, valproic acid, and phenytoin, in that order. No one particular pain syndrome responds to a particular drug. Ideally a trial of each drug should last from four to six weeks, but with severe pain and a short prognosis, the period may have to be reduced to one to two weeks.

Membrane-stabilizing drugs (flecainide 100mg two times a day) have been used to treat the pain of malignant nerve infiltration. Clonidine (25 micrograms three times a day increasing to 100 micrograms three times a day) has been successfully used to control nerve pain. A trial of high-dose steroids (dexamethasone 8mg per day for ten days) may be indicated, especially if other drugs have failed, and can occasionally produce a dramatic response.

A nerve block—the insertion of a needle close to a nerve to inject a solution causing a temporary or permanent neural blockade—can help a small number of hospice patients whose pain is uncontrolled by drugs, psychological intervention, or radiotherapy. The most useful nerve blocks include the celiac plexus block (for pancreas and liver pain), paravertebral block (for chest wall pain), epidural steroids (for nerve root irritation), epidural local anesthetic (for pelvic or leg pain), psoas compartment block (for hip or lumbar root pain), and intrathecal neurolysis (for perineal pain).

A reversible diagnostic block should be performed with a local anesthetic, to establish distribution of pain and observe side effects, *before* neurolytic agents are used to give a long-lasting blockade.

Nerve blocks are an adjunct to other treatments. They can reduce, but rarely abolish, pain. *It is essential that the actual nerve block procedure be painless.* (Anticoagulant therapy is an absolute contraindication to nerve blocks.)

The dose of morphine should be reduced or stopped following a nerve block, and the patient observed for 24 hours. Morphine requirements may decrease as pain lessens. Drowsiness and even respiratory depression can occur if the patient remains on a higher dose of morphine than is required for the pain. Promptly retitrate morphine doses (using an initial low dose and increasing every four hours as necessary) following a nerve block.

Nonpharmacological methods of pain control, when used in conjunction with (not as substitutes for) adequate doses of opioids and other useful medications, can play a very important role in helping to achieve good pain management. The patient's pain threshold can often be raised by relaxation exercises, meditation, art and music therapies, and recreational and diversional activities. "Good company" is often the best therapy of all.

Common problems not listed above, such as a sore mouth, eyeglasses or dentures in need of adjustment, a blanket too heavy or a room too warm, often thought to be minor, are not minor at all, can cause considerable distress, and need prompt attention.

The multifaceted pain of advancing cancer is an all-encompassing experience that requires interventions on several fronts. Effective control of physical symptoms lays the foundation for psychological and spiritual support of the patient and care-givers. Spiritual distress is universal as disease progresses and death approaches. Anger and fear are common. Companionship through secure and open relationships is an essential part of supporting the dying person as he or she strives to make some sense of the past, cope with the pain of the present, find some hope for the future, and thus begin the difficult task of letting go.

To achieve good pain management, careful medical, nursing, and psychosocial monitoring of the patient, and regular review of medications and treatment plans, is essential. Hospice nurses and physicians should review the patient's condition, effects of current medications, and proposed treatment plans *on a daily basis.* Other members of the hospice team must pay equally careful and continual attention to the psychological, social, and spiritual needs of the patient and care-givers. *The hospice team should meet regularly.*

C *Breathlessness:* Dyspnea is reported in about 50 percent of all cancer patients on admission to hospice care, and in 70 percent of those with lung cancer. (Dyspnea is a symptom, not a sign. A patient may have difficulty breathing and yet have no abnormal physical signs.) Only about 5 percent to 10 percent of hospice patients have dyspnea that severely limits their mobility.

Sudden onset of dyspnea suggests arrythmia, embolus, or left ventricular failure due to a myocardial infarction. Onset over hours or days suggests infection or effusion. Gradual onset over weeks suggests tumor growth or anemia (or rarely multiple pulmonary emboli).

Episodic shortness of breath is usually due to hyperventilation. Any patient with both dyspnea and cancer is prone to episodes of anxiety. However, episodic shortness of breath can occasionally be due to arrythmias, bronchoesophageal fistula, or pulmonary emboli.

Appropriate intervention by a skilled physiotherapist, respiratory therapist, and/or relaxation therapist is usually the key to successfully managing patients with dyspnea. These professionals can transform the life of patients, enabling them to cope psychologically and extend their range of day-to-day activities. Breathing exercises, relaxation techniques, and teaching the patient and care-givers how to clear secretions by gentle shaking of the chest wall may all be involved. Reassurance from trusted care-givers and hospice team members is effective, as is explanation. Anxiolytics (diazepam 2mg three times a day) can help if used in conjunction with relaxation therapy and breathing exercises. (If the patient already feels drowsy, use haloperidol 3mg to 5mg two times a day.)

Morphine reduces the inappropriate and excessive respiratory drive that is a feature of dyspnea. It reduces inappropriate tachypnea (rapid breathing) and overventilation of the large airways. A low starting dose of morphine (2.5mg to 5mg orally every four hours) is often sufficient if a patient is not already taking morphine. Doses above 10mg to 20mg every four hours are unlikely to give further benefit. Morphine can be given via a nebulizer.

Bronchodilators are very important because many patients have an unexpected airways obstruction that can be reversed. Slow-release theophylline and aminophylline can reduce dyspnea both as bronchodilators, and also by improving ventricular function by peripheral vasodilation. Nebulized local anesthetic can reduce dyspnea and cough in some patients, particularly those with bilateral diffuse disease or lymphangitis carcinomatosa. A week's trial of high-dose steroids (dexamethasone 8mg per day) is considered if dyspnea has not responded to other measures.

Oxygen therapy is rarely helpful in chronic dyspnea. Blood gases are often normal, and relatively few patients are breathless due to hypoxia (end-state fibrosing alveolitis and COPD are exceptions). Most patients should be weaned from oxygen once other methods are instituted.

In severe dyspnea even at rest, the patient needs to know that he or she will not be left alone. An electric fan or humidifier near the bed can help, as can careful positioning of the patient (45 degrees usually feels most comfortable). On the very rare occasions when a patient remains very distressed despite all possible measures, it may become necessary to give morphine and diazepam in doses high enough to obtain relief, even if this causes drowsiness or unconsciousness.

Scopolamine (0.4mg IM every 3 to 4 hours or 0.8mg to 2.4mg per 24 hours in a continuous subcutaneous infusion) is a very useful drug for the terminal bubbling that may occur in the last few days or hours of life. Secretions in the large airways are occasionally distressing to the patient, but more commonly the patient is unconscious and the bubbling "death rattle" frightens the care-givers. (Sucking out secretions is effective only for a short time. Turning the patient sometimes reduces the bubbling noise.)

D *Cough:* As a troublesome symptom, cough is surprisingly uncommon. A persistent irritating cough without sputum production can be difficult to manage. The usual causes are bronchospasm, pleural effusion, or bronchogenic carcinoma. Treatment for bronchospasm includes albuterol (by nebulizer or inhaler), slow-release aminophylline, or steroids. A pleural effusion is treated by aspiration; by instillation of either cytotoxics or sclerosants (doxorubicin or quinacrine) following aspiration for rapidly recurring effusions in a relatively fit patient; or by talc pleurodesis in patients in good general condition and a prognosis of two or three months or more.

Radiotherapy may be indicated if there is a large untreated carcinoma. Oral steroids (dexamethasone 4mg to 8mg per day) can reduce wheeze and may reduce cough due to a large bronchial abscess. A humidifier can help, as can simple linctus.

Opioids are the most powerful central cough suppressants. Codeine linctus 5ml to 10ml four times a day may be sufficient. Oral morphine, starting with 2.5mg every four hours, increasing to 5mg, 10mg, or 20mg every four hours, will suppress cough in patients not already taking morphine. For patients already taking morphine, methadone linctus (2mg in 5ml) three times a day can sometimes help to reduce cough.

Nebulized lidocaine 2 percent, used for 10 minutes every 2 to 6 hours (maximum of 10ml per 24 hours), can bring dramatic relief. Numbness of the mouth may persist for about 30 minutes after each treatment, so the patient must not eat or drink during this time.

In the last days or hours of life, if the patient is too weak to cough up secretions, atropine 0.6mg up to four times per day can reduce bubbling without causing sedation. (For terminal bubbling, use scopolamine as described above.)

E *Constipation:* Constipation is one of the most frequent problems for patients with advanced illness. In a study of 200 patients admitted to an inpatient hospice, 75 percent needed rectal measures (suppository, enema, or manual evacuation) within the first week.

The most frequent cause of constipation in cancer patients is the use of opioids without adequate doses of laxatives. When taking a history from the patient, be sure to ask whether laxatives were started simultaneously with opioids or only after constipation had occurred. Alternating constipation and diarrhea is usually due to incorrect use of laxatives (intermittently rather than regularly) in a patient taking opioid drugs.

Other causes of constipation are a low-fiber diet, dehydration, anticholinergic or diuretic drugs, depression, hypercalcemia, or reduced defecation due to weakness, confusion, or pain.

On examination, the abdomen may appear distended. Fecal masses (which indent on steady pressure) may be palpable in the left iliac fossa. The colon is usually moderately tender. In severe constipation, the cecum can become distended with pain and tenderness in the right iliac fossa. It can sometimes be difficult to decide whether abdominal masses are fecal or neoplastic.

An empty ballooned rectum on rectal examination can be a sign of impaction of feces higher up in the colon. If the history is suggestive of constipation, the patient should have high enemas. Severe constipation can present as spurious diarrhea, with small amounts of liquid feces leaking past the fecal mass. If rectal examination reveals a large claylike lump in the rectum too big to pass through the anal sphincter, this needs to be removed manually. This is a painful procedure, and the patient should be given morphine and diazepam.

Constipation can cause anorexia, nausea, vomiting, abdominal pain, rectal pain, anal fissures, confusion, abdominal distention, and sometimes even obstruction. Pain tends to be colicky.

High doses of laxative need to be started simultaneously with any opioid analgesic. Prescribe both a fecal softener and a stimulant laxative (Peri-Colace or Senokot-S) whenever starting opioids. If maximum doses of laxatives are still ineffective, add oral magnesium sulfate 5mls to 10mls (taken with plenty of water) in the morning. If the patient has fecal masses palpable throughout the colon, he or she will need either oil retention enemas or soap and water enemas to soften the feces, followed by phosphate enemas to stimulate the bowel. Patients can still become severely constipated on inadequate doses of laxatives.

The bowels should move at least once every three days. If a patient goes longer than three days without a bowel movement, he or she should have a rectal examination, and a suppository or microenema should be considered.

F *Weakness:* Almost all patients with advanced cancer complain of generalized weakness. Sudden onset of specific weakness suggests a neurological deficit. Sudden generalized weakness may be due to adrenal failure or septicemia. A trial of steroids and antibiotics may occasionally be indicated. Exclude hypokalemia as a cause of weakness. Stop any unnecessary hypotensive drug.

There is no drug that restores strength. Blood transfusions do not help. Steroids (dexamethasone 4mg per day) do not improve strength, but can induce a feeling of well-being.

Exercise seems to be the natural antidote to weakness. Many hospice patients can benefit from physical therapy. Mobility and independence can often be improved once symptoms are controlled and the patient regains confidence. Even small improvements boost morale.

G *Nausea/Vomiting:* Nausea and vomiting occur in about 60 percent of patients with advanced cancer, but tend to be intermittent. It is important to stop nausea and vomiting as soon as possible.

Causes of nausea include drugs, oral thrush, brain metastases, anxiety, gastric irritation, small stomach syndrome, intestinal obstruction, constipation, hypercalcemia, uremia, low-grade urinary tract or pulmonary infection.

When taking a history, try to discover if there is a pattern to the nausea. Does it occur after certain drugs, after meals, on movement, during intervals of anxiety, or with certain smells? Ask about epigastric pain (consider gastritis), pain on swallowing (consider oral thrush), pain on standing (consider mesenteric traction), thirst (consider hypercalcemia), hiccup (consider uremia), heartburn (consider small stomach syndrome), dysuria (consider urinary tract infection), and constipation.

There are usually several causes contributing to nausea (for example, anxiety, a new drug, constipation, and the smell of cooking from the next room could all play a part). Think in terms of a nausea threshold (analogous to a pain threshold) and consider several ways of raising the nausea threshold. Nausea can become a conditioned response.

Drugs that can cause nausea include opioids, nonsteroidal antiinflammatories, antibiotics, digoxin, estrogens, and many others. Stop as many drugs as possible.

Nausea related to morphine can occur when the patient is taking more morphine than is required. Thirty percent of patients experience mild nausea for a few days after starting morphine. An antiemetic (prochlorperazine 5mg three times a day, or haloperidol 0.5mg to 1.5mg at bedtime) can be prescribed to prevent this nausea. Only about 1 percent of patients are intolerant of morphine, and suffer severe, persistent nausea and vomiting despite appropriate antiemetic treatment. These patients need an alternative opioid analgesic (hydromorphone, oxycodone, buprenorphine, methadone), although these drugs, too, sometimes cause nausea. Nevertheless, true morphine-related nausea can be abolished in an individual by changing to an alternate opioid.

Anxiety causes nausea, and nausea causes anxiety. Relieving anxiety (often by sharing worries and fears) can help to reduce or abolish nausea.

If uremia is causing nausea and vomiting, explain to patient and care-givers that uremia cannot be cured, but chlorpromazine can usually relieve the nausea and vomiting.

Palliative radiotherapy does not cause nausea unless the field includes the celiac plexus. Chemotherapy may cause nausea.

The oral route for medication is effective for prophylaxis. *When a patient is feeling nauseated, or vomiting more than two or three times a day, oral absorption is reduced and suppositories or injections are needed for at least 24 hours before starting oral antiemetics.* A continuous subcutaneous infusion is useful for severe nausea and vomiting, to avoid repeated injections.

Choose an appropriate antiemetic. Antiemetics can be divided into three groups. Anticholinergic drugs, including scopolamine, cyclizine, and promethazine, act mainly in the vomiting center in the midbrain. Antidopaminergic drugs, including prochlorperazine, thiethylperazine, haloperidol, chlorpromazine, and methotrimeprazine, act mainly on the chemoreceptor trigger zone (CTZ) in the medulla. Gastrokinetic antiemetics, including haloperidol, act on the CTZ and also increase gastric emptying and gut peristalsis.

Haloperidol is effective as a twice-a-day regime. Chlorpromazine may be more suitable if sedation is needed or if hiccups are troublesome. Metoclopramide is useful if poor gastric emptying is a problem. Cyclizine is particularly useful is there is an element of motion sickness, or as a logical addition to a drug acting at the CTZ. Methotrimeprazine in a continuous subcutaneous infusion is the most powerful antiemetic, but can cause drowsiness.

Try full doses of one antiemetic before changing to another. Sometimes a patient will need two (and rarely three) antiemetics for good control. It is logical to combine antiemetics that act at different sites. (Do not combine haloperidol and metoclopramide.)

A trial of high-dose steroids is considered in three situations: raised intracranial pressure, hypercalcemia, and malignant pyloric stenosis. Steroids can have a direct antiemetic effect, and commonly reduce or abolish nausea in advanced malignancy. They should be tried for severe nausea resistant to antiemetics.

H2 receptor antagonists (ranitidine 150mg two times a day) should be considered for nausea, especially if there is a history of peptic ulceration or if nausea is associated with heartburn.

A celiac plexus nerve block should be considered for intractable nausea resistant to other treatments.

Vomiting with little or no nausea can occur in regurgitation (usually seen in cancer of the esophagus with total dysphagia), malignant pyloric stenosis (try dexamethasone 8mg per day by IM injection to reduce peritumor edema and improve gastric emptying), and raised intracranial pressure. (In fact, in advanced disease due to cerebral primary tumors or cerebral metastases, both headache and vomiting are uncommon.) It may not be possible to abolish vomiting, but patients will more readily tolerate occasional vomiting when free of nausea.

H *Edema/Ascites/Pleural effusion:* About 20 percent of terminally ill patients develop ankle edema (excess fluid in tissue spaces). Common causes are fluid retention (due to steroids or nonsteroidal antiinflammatories), immobility, abdominal pressure (often due to hepatomegaly), and protein deficiency.

Consider stopping or changing drugs that cause fluid retention. Encourage exercise, which reduces ankle edema because the calf muscle acts as a pump to improve circulation and reduce venous back-pressure. Use full-length compression stockings for active patients, especially if diuretics cannot be used. Leg elevation is effective only when legs are raised to the level of the right atrium, perhaps by having the patient lie in bed from 30 to 60 minutes with pillows under the legs. Increased dietary protein is helpful only if serum albumin levels are low, if recent diet has been poor, and if the patient still has a good appetite.

Diuretics are the mainstay of treatment, but resulting urinary frequency can be troubling for very ill, weak patients. Give diuretics early in the day, and use caution in men with prostatic symptoms. A combination of a loop diuretic (potassium-losing) and a potassium-sparing diuretic is useful to minimize the need for potassium supplements. For resistant edema, the dose may have to be increased to furosemide 80mg two times a day, or bumetanide 2mg two times a day with spironolactone 200mg two times a day. Avoid IM injections, which are poorly absorbed.

Ascites (free fluid in the peritoneal cavity) causes abdominal distention and pressure. Symptoms include abdominal discomfort, inability to bend or sit upright, leg edema, dyspnea, and heartburn.

Low doses of opioid analgesics are useful for the feeling of tightness and discomfort. High-dose diuretics (spironolactone 200mg per day with furosemide 40mg per day) usually begin to work within five days, and the ascites resolves over two to four weeks in about 70 percent of patients. Girth measurements should be taken twice weekly. If there is no decrease after one week, increase doses to spironolactone 200mg two times a day with furosemide 120mg per day. Follow up carefully to avoid dehydration.

Paracentesis (which can easily be performed in the home using bupivacaine 0.5 percent as a local anesthetic) is a useful emergency measure when a patient has a tense ascites causing severe discomfort, dyspnea, or inability to sit up. If the patient has a short prognosis, paracentesis (to relieve symptoms quickly) is more helpful than starting diuretics.

A peritoneovenous shunt can effectively control malignant ascites. The shunt can be inserted under local or general anesthesia, and can remain patent and effective for months and years, producing excellent palliation of symptoms even though the abdomen is not totally emptied of fluid. (The insertion of a shunt is contraindicated if the fluid is viscous or loculated.)

Pleural effusion is the collection of fluid in the pleural cavity. It does not necessarily indicate a short prognosis. The usual history is increasing dyspnea over a number of days, sometimes with a dry cough or pleuritic pains. A pleural effusion should be left untreated in a patient with advanced metastatic disease (and a known diagnosis) if it is not causing breathlessness. Simple aspiration of 500ml or more of fluid under local anesthesia at home will often relieve dyspnea, but fluid tends to reaccumulate over one to seven days.

Cough due to a pleural effusion can be treated as explained above in the section on coughs.

Chemotherapy (for breast cancer, oat-cell carcinoma of the lung, or lymphoma) may effectively prevent recurrence of a pleural effusion.

I *Insomnia:* Insomnia lowers the patient's pain threshold, exhausts care-givers, and is a common cause of breakdown in hospice home care arrangements. Sometimes simple remedies—a warmer blanket or a small night light—can be effective. Temazepam (15mg to 60mg at bedtime) is the most useful drug for night sedation for most patients.

Insomnia may be due to symptoms (pain, sweats, incontinence, cough, itch), anxiety, or depression. Fear and loneliness are worst at night. Recurrent nightmares can make patients fear sleep, as can their fear of dying during the night. These anxieties need to be gently discussed.

Boredom and lack of activity during the day can worsen insomnia; referral to an occupational or recreational therapist is useful.

If the patient is depressed, a sedative oral antidepressant (amitriptyline 25mg to 100mg nightly two hours before bedtime) may help. Hypnotics should be short-acting (temazepam 15mg to 60mg at bedtime). The maximum recommended dose of one hypnotic should be tried before changing to another.

If anxiety is the main problem, oral chlorpromazine is very effective for some patients. An initial dose (10mg to 25mg) at about 5:00 P.M., followed by a second dose (25mg to 50mg) at bedtime is often successful.

If the patient is waking to take 4-hourly morphine in the night, it is usually possible to achieve longer-lasting analgesia by doubling the dose at bedtime. Alternatively, change from 4-hourly morphine to 12-hourly MS-Contin.

J *Depression:* Sadness is natural in dying patients; it must not be confused with depression.

Reactive depression often responds to good symptom control and communication. Endogenous depression, however, though not common, can be difficult to diagnose in terminally ill patients because the usual indicators of depression (disturbed sleep, anorexia, weariness, constipation, reduced libido, emotional lability) are also common symptoms in patients with advanced illness.

The best clues to true depression include a history of depressive illness, an expressionless face, an inability to enjoy formerly pleasurable experiences, low self-esteem, persistent guilt, and delusions about the nature of the illness. Chronic pain can cause depression. (Comments about suicide are not necessarily depressive. They may be the patient's way of saying, "I want you to know what I am going through.")

Antidepressants usually take two to three weeks to take effect, although a response can occur in seven to ten days. They should be started at low dosage and increased quickly to a maximum tolerated dose (usually the patient's dry mouth is the limiting factor). Even in very ill patients large doses can be well tolerated, so use as high a dose as prudently possible. Amitriptyline 25mg to 150mg at bedtime also has sedative properties; a similar dose of imipramine is less sedating. A useful guide to increasing daily doses is:

Day 1	10mg to 25mg
Day 3	25mg to 50mg
Day 7	50mg to 100mg
Day 10	100mg to 150mg

(*Note:* Elderly or frail patients need lower doses. Side effects often limit the tolerated dose.)

Good care for the dying and the bereaved must include management of physical symptoms, careful attention to the complex social, emotional, and spiritual needs of patients and care-givers, and education that empowers patients and care-givers to participate fully in the patient's dying process as caring partners.

NOTES

Introduction

xii (not the ultimate tragedy) Cousins, N., *A Celebration of Life* (New York: Harper & Row, 1974).
(hard medicine) Personal communication, August 26, 1977. Used by permission.

Chapter 1

3 The petition of the citizens of London is cited by Mary Rotha Clay in *The Medieval Hospital of England* (New York: Barnes & Noble, 1966), p. 236.
I am indebted throughout this work to Henri Nouwen for his development of the concept of *hospitality* in *The Wounded Healer* (New York: Doubleday, 1972), and, at greater length, in *Reaching Out* (New York: Doubleday, 1975).

6 Military terminology, interestingly enough, appears quite frequently in modern medical thought, e.g., "the magic bullet," "the war on cancer," etc.

7 (Thomas) *The Lives of a Cell* (New York: Viking, 1974), p. 98.

9 (Aries) *Western Attitudes Toward Death* (Baltimore: Johns Hopkins Press, 1974), p. 57.

11 (Riesman) *The Story of Medicine in the Middle Ages* (New York: Hoeber, 1935), p. 1.

12 *Agen hine:* literally, *again servant.* Anglo-Saxon law stated that the visitor was a guest for three days, then a member of the staff. Three days was the traditional period of hospitality, after which the relationship was apt to change; and ancient proverbs reflect an ambivalent attitude about the

host-guest relationship, ranging from the Chinese, "The host is happy when the guest is gone," to the Czech, "A guest in the house: God in the house." One of the most charming is the old Welsh rhyme:

Hail, guest, we ask not what thou art;
If friend, we greet thee, hand and heart;
If stranger, such no longer be;
If foe, our love shall conquer thee.

13 These statutes for care of the sick appear in *Medical Work of the Knights Hospitallers of St. John of Jerusalem,* ed. Edgar Erskine Hume (Baltimore: Johns Hopkins Press, 1940), pp. 28, 29.

14 (Saunders) "And From Sudden Death . . ." *Frontier,* Winter 1961 (reprint), pp. 3, 5. Marya Mannes, so often a prophet in advance of contemporary thought, was one of the first American writers to discover the existence of the modern hospice in England; see her work, *Last Rights* (New York: William Morrow, 1972).

Chapter 2

15 Dieter Jetter is quoted a number of times by John D. Thompson and Grace Goldin in their comprehensive and handsomely illustrated work, *The Hospital: A Social and Architectural History* (New Haven: Yale University Press, 1975); the passage quoted here appears on pp. 34–35. The quotation from Tolstoy is from "The Death of Ivan Ilych" in *The Death of Ivan Ilych and Other Stories* (New York: New American Library, 1960), p. 97. The plea of the patient entering a London hospice is recalled by Dr. Cicely Saunders.

Drawings and models of early Greek *asklepieia* and Roman *valetudinaria* appear in Thompson and Goldin; medical procedure is described by Riesman, op. cit., and by Mary Risley in *House of Healing* (New York: Doubleday, 1961).

22 Dr. Martin G. Netsky's moving article about the death of his mother appears in PHAROS, April 1976, pp. 57–62.

24 (Emperor Julian) Cited in Risley, op. cit., p. 93.

26 (Liegner) "St. Christopher's Hospice, 1974," *JAMA*, 234:-10, Dec. 8, 1975, p. 1048.

27 (Rabbi Moses ben Maimon, also known as Maimonides) quoted in the *Bulletin of the Institute of the History of Medicine*, 3:585, 1935; cited in *Familiar Medical Quotations*, ed. Maurice B. Strauss (Boston: Little, Brown, 1968).

(Snow) *A Death With Dignity: When the Chinese Came* (New York: Random House, 1974), pp. 95, 104.

Chapter 3

29 (Pirsig) *Zen & the Art of Motorcycle Maintenance: An Inquiry into Values* (New York: William Morrow, 1974), p. 13.

(Clay), op. cit., p. 207.

(Nouwen) *Reaching Out,* p. 65.

34 The prayer, cited by Hume, op. cit., p. 111 (quoting Leon le Grand, "La Prière des Malades dans les Hôpitaux de St. Jean," Paris, 1896) begins:

> Seigneurs Malades, pries pour pais que Dieu la mande de ciel en terre;
>
> Seigneurs Malades, pries pour le Fruit de la Terre que Dieu le multiple en tell maniere que sancte eglise en soit servie et le peuple soustanu,
>
> Seigneurs Malades, pries pour l'apostell de Rome et pour les Cardennaus et pour les patriarches et pour les archevesques et pour les evesques et les prelats. . . .

Since our habits of speech are a powerful influence on our behavior, it is interesting to imagine what subtle changes might take place in a modern hospital if staff should refer to patients as "My Lords" (using the same word generally used to refer to the Supreme Being) and implored their aid daily in matters considered to be of crucial importance.

Hume (pp. 50, 56) says that the incurably ill were set apart for the first time at Rhodes and that the eleven gallery rooms were evidently used for those in isolation and for pilgrims.

38 Descriptions and illustrations of early English hospices are

to be found in Clay, op. cit. The price of a swan on the market in London in 1338 and other fascinating glimpses of medieval life are to be found in abundance in *The Knights Hospitallers in England: Being the Report of Prior Philip de Thame to the Grand Master Elyan de Villanova for AD 1338,* ed. Lambert B. Larking (New York: AMS Press), 1968.

41 (Brother Roger) "Frontiers of Pharmacology: The Middle Ages," *MD Magazine,* August 1976, p. 92.

42 (Beaune) Founded by a wealthy benefactor in 1443, the Hôtel-Dieu at Beaune has the charm of a nobleman's country villa, with turrets and balconies facing into a central garden-court. Its "Hall of the Sick" with carved, vaulted roof over gracefully curtained cubicles and a stained-glass window above the altar at the far end is perhaps the most beautiful room ever designed for patient care; and because of the quality of the art as well as the architecture, this place of healing has become a much admired museum. For detailed description and illustrations, see *Les Villes d'Art Célèbres: Bordeaux, Dijon, Beaune* by Charles Saunier (Paris: Libraire Renouard, 1925), pp. 146–54.

44, 45 (Maggie Ross) From an unpublished monograph, "Compassion and Common Sense: Creative Caring in the AIDS Crisis," Oxford Diocese Working Group, 18 March, 1987, pp. 1, 5. Quoted by permission of the author.

Chapter 4

47 (Phillips) The Seven Laws of Money (New York: Random House, 1974), p. 1.
(Paper work) It is rather mind-boggling to contemplate the superstructures of medical bureaucracy in comparison with the procedure of the Knights Hospitallers in ancient Jerusalem: "It is the custom in this palace or hospital that every pilgrim should pay two Venetian pennies for the use of the hospital. If he sojourn there for a year he pays no more, if he abide but one day he pays no less": *Palestine Pilgrim's Text. Soc.,* Vol. XII, pp. 106–7, cited in Hume, op. cit., p. 17.

Chapter 5

65 (Risley) op. cit., p. 166.

66 The young mother's case was reported in *The New York Tribune,* April 25, 1860: cited by Gert H. Brieger, ed., *Medical America in the Nineteenth Century* (Baltimore: Johns Hopkins Press, 1972), p. 234.

69 (Public opinion) H.J.C. Gibson, quoted in George Rosen, *From Medical Police to Social Medicine* (New York: Science History Publications, 1974), p. 11.

71 Two sources of detailed information about nineteenth-century workhouse conditions are Risley's *House of Healing,* and *The Hospitals, 1800–1948* by Brian Abel-Smith (London: Heinemann, 1964). Both quote the work of reformers who made on-site investigations and reports at the time, horrified to discover situations where people not only starved and suffered untold physical miseries, but were treated with utmost contempt. It was not unusual, in such places, to find inmates forced to wash in their own urine, denied the simple amenities of fresh water, soap, and lavatory paper simply because they were not considered to be truly human.

75 The statute against vagabondage is quoted at greater length by Risley, op. cit., pp. 158–59, and includes the directive that "all persons are empowered to take idle children from vagabonds and retain them as apprentices until the boys become twenty-four years of age and the girls twenty years; if they run away before the end of their apprenticeship, the masters can recover them, punish them with chains, and enslave them again. . . . Masters are authorized to put a ring of iron around the neck, arm, or leg of their slaves . . . for a surety of keeping them." This law, impossible to enforce, was shortly thereafter rescinded; and in any case should not be taken to represent the policy of Edward VI, who was very young at the time and caught in a power struggle between ambitious advisors, large landowners, and chiefs of state.

(Humanitarianism of the successful) George Rosen, *A History of Public Health* (New York: MD Publications, 1958), p. 137. The humanitarianism of the successful is also likely

to be tempered by their realization that if the helpless cannot be held accountable for their condition, then no moral
superiority accrues to those who have "done better."
("Uneconomic aberrations") John Langdon-Davies, *Westminster Hospital* (London: John Murray, 1952), p. 16.
(Selection of patients for teaching and research) Abel-
Smith, op. cit., p. 46.

78 (Nightingale) From *Notes on Hospitals,* cited by Risley, op.
cit., p. 193. George Pickering's delightful book, *Creative
Malady* (New York: Dell, 1974), gives a detailed account
of Florence Nightingale's psychosomatic ailments, taking
the view that they gave her the privacy and freedom she
needed for her creative work.

82 A number of readers of the first edition of *The Hospice
Movement* have asked me about my traveling companion on
that night flight and have wanted to know what book he was
reading. Of course, he was an angel. The book he had
brought with him was a New Testament, in Greek, and it
is my own opinion that the passage that so amused him was
John 4:17–19.

Chapter 6

83 (Holden) "Hospices For the Dying: Relief From Pain and
Fear," *Science,* July 30, 1976, p. 390.
(Phillips) St. Christopher's Hospice: Annual Report, 1975–
1976, p. 36.
It should be noted that quite near the spacious lawns and
gardens of St. Christopher's immediate neighborhood there
are crowded areas far less affluent. Residents here are also
considered to be very much a part of the hospice community.

96 (An oral mix) Diamorphine (heroin) was used in the Hospice Mix at St. Christopher's until May 1977, since it was
legal to do so, and there are physicians who feel that it has
certain technical advantages in some cases. However, this
presented a problem in translation of English pharmacology
to other countries where heroin is outlawed even for the
treatment of the terminally ill. Diamorphine is, in any case,

transformed into morphine within the body very shortly after administration. Therefore, in May 1977, after a series of careful studies, morphine in suitably large amounts was substituted for diamorphine in the St. Christopher's mixture across the board, with no difficulty being noted. For further information on this question, see R. G. Twycross, "Choice of Strong Analgesic in Terminal Cancer: Diamorphine or Morphine?" in *Pain, The Journal of the International Study of Pain*, 3:2, April 1977, pp. 93–104. Also, see Clinical Appendix, pp. 341–363.

Dame Cicely had first seen the regular giving of oral opioids at St. Luke's Hospice between 1948 and 1957, and they could trace the system back to about 1935, soon after the so-called Brompton's Mix was introduced. Further information on development of St. Christopher's medication system will be found in "The Evolution of the Hospices," by Dame Cicely Saunders (a reprint from *The History of the Management of Pain*) published by St. Christopher's Hospice.

104 (Budget, St. Christopher's) Total expenditures in 1989 were £3,129,695, with legacies received amounting to £911,610 for the year. "St. Christopher's Hospice: Annual Report and Year Book 1988–1989," p. 42.

Chapter 7

118 The patient described here as "Mrs. Kent" was, at the time I met her, far closer to death than I (or perhaps she) realized. After being discharged once again from St. Christopher's she went to stay with a close friend, who wrote me, "Mrs. ——— has now returned home, which is what she and her 'extended family' always wanted. The lounge in my house has been turned into her bedroom. The hatch in the kitchen is permanently open and even in her now very drowsy state she hears, and warms to, the familiar noises of our daily routine. And the care, the all-enveloping and strengthening care, given by St. Christopher's Out-patients' service, continues. . . ." And later, "She died peacefully and surrounded by both her own and my family, on the evening of January 31st, 1977."

122 The experience of the woman known here as Lillian Preston
     is reminiscent of the writings of an ancient Venetian, Louis
     Coronaro (1464–1566) who reported at the age of ninety-
     five: "At this extreme age of mine, I enjoy two lives at the
     same time: one, the earthly, which I possess in reality; the
     other, the heavenly, which I possess in thought. . . . And I
     hold that our departure from this world is not death, but
     merely a passage which the soul makes from this earthly life
     to the heavenly one, immortal and infinitely perfect."
     (Coronaro) *The Art of Living Long* (Milwaukee: William F.
     Butler, 1903), pp. 110–111.

Chapter 8

127 (Fletcher) "The Patient's Right to Die," *Harper's,* 221:-
     1325, October 1960, p. 141.
132 (Eliot) "Little Gidding" from "Four Quartets" in *The Com-
     plete Poems and Plays* (New York: Harcourt, Brace and
     World, 1934), p. 139.
140 The senselessness of pain in incurable disease is a subject
     discussed by many writers on modern hospice care: see
     works by Saunders, Twycross, Lamerton, and others in Bib-
     liography; also, L. LeShan, "The World of the Patient in
     Severe Pain of Long Duration," *Journal of Chronic Diseases,*
     1964:17, pp. 119–126.
     (Dickinson) in *Final Harvest: ED's Poems,* ed. T. H. Johnson
     (Boston: Little, Brown, 1961).

Chapter 9

146 (Belloc) *The Cruise of the Nona* (Boston: Houghton Mifflin,
     1925), p. 161.
147 Quotations from Jonathan Edwards in this chapter are from
     his "Images or Shadows of Divine Things" (edited by Perry
     Miller) in *Colonial American Writing,* 2nd ed., ed. Roy Har-
     vey Pearce (New York: Holt, Rinehart and Winston,
     1969), pp. 370–75.
149 (Keeping patients at home) In 1977 it was clear that a
     majority of cancer patients (67 percent) wanted to die at

home, whereas only 20 percent achieved that wish (see Claire F. Ryder and Diane M. Ross, "Terminal Care: Issues and Alternatives," *Public Health Reports,* Jan/Feb 1977). Those who were affluent, with the ability to hire suitable caretakers, and the lower income group, with Medicaid help and comparatively cohesive family units, were most often able to stay at home. However, in 1990, with ever escalating medical costs, and with further disintegration of family relationships due to drugs, poverty, and disease in the lower income groups, hospice is needed more than ever by our entire society.

151 (President Carter's campaign speeches) Quoted in "The Health Cost Crisis," *Medical World News,* Feb. 21, 1977, pp. 57–72.

See Colin Murray Parkes, *Bereavement: Studies of Grief in Adult Life.* Middlesex: Penguin, 1975; and "Effects of Bereavement on Physical and Mental Health—A Study of the Medical Records of Widows," *British Medical Journal,* August 1, 1964, pp. 274–79.

156 (Sylvia Lack) Dr. Lack is now (1990) Director of the Chronic Pain Program at Gaylord Hospital, Wallingford, Connecticut.

175 (The young musician, Jim Burnham) Hospice staff arranged shortly after my visit to contact this patient's father, who came from out of state—though in poor health himself at the time—to see his son for the first time in fourteen years. At this meeting, the two were reconciled. Then, on August 23, 1977, I received a call from the hospice letting me know that the patient was near death. Among his last words were a request that I should use his real name in this book. I telephoned him and promised him, just before he died, that I would.

Chapter 10

181 (Tennyson) *Idylls of the King* (New York: Airmont, 1969), p. 251.

182 (Wigglesworth) Cited by John B. Blake in *Public Health in the Town of Boston, 1630–1822* (Cambridge, Mass.: Harvard University Press, 1959), p. 4.

(Arrest and deportation of a Widow Paige and her family)
Ibid.

184 Benjamin Franklin's delight in his methods of raising funds for the founding of Philadelphia General Hospital is described and documented by Thompson and Goldin, op. cit., p. 97.

185 ("A Cup of cold water . . .") From *The Papers of Benjamin Franklin,* cited by Thompson and Goldin, ibid., p. 97.

188 On the corporate power of hospitals at the turn of the century, see "The Use and Abuse of Medical Charities in Late Nineteenth Century America," by Gert H. Brieger, *American Journal of Public Health,* 67:3, March 1977, pp. 264–67.

194 (Deborah Allen Carey) From *Hospice Inpatient Environments,* New York: Van Nostrand Reinhold Company, 1986, p. 21.

Chapter 11

196 (Congreve) From the preface of *The Book of the Craft of Dying and Other Early English Tracts Concerning Death,* ed. Frances M. M. Comper (New York: Arno Press, 1977), p. xxxv.

(Spenser's *The Faerie Queene*) (l:X:xxxvi) shows the troubled hero taking refuge in a traditional hospice setting:

> Eftsoones unto a holy hospitall,
> That was foreby the way, she did him bring;
> In which seven Bead-men, that had vowed all
> Their life to service of high heaven's King,
> Did spend their daies in doing godly thing.
> Their gates to all were open evermore,
> That by the wearie way were travelling;
> And one sate wayting ever them before,
> To call in commers-by that needy were and poore.

198 (Juiraros) Robert W. Habenstein and William M. Lamers, *Funeral Customs the World Over* (Milwaukee: Bulfin, 1963), p. 22. For information about death customs of Navajo, Mexican, African, and many of the Asian groups mentioned in this chapter, I am indebted to this work.

200 (Solzhenitsyn) *The Cancer Ward* (New York: Dial Press, 1968), p. 97.

(Byrne) *Destiny Bay* (Boston: Little, Brown, 1928), p. 28.

201 (Newly released soul) In the Indonesian archipelago there is an often found belief that souls of the departed go to the land of souls by ship, and the "Ship of the Dead" figures in their textiles and other art forms: Frits A. Wagner, *Art of Indonesia* (Singapore: Graham Brash, 1988). Modern-day Balinese have a series of elaborate rituals to help the spirit on its long journey to "the other world." According to a contemporary observer, "They are not certain when the spirit is really released, so they are always careful, believing that from limbo, or purgatory, the spirits can still cause *big* trouble": private communication with Fr. N. Shadeg, Sanor, Bali, 1990.

In Ireland, too, there is an ancient belief that departing souls make their journey by ship, over the "Western Sea" to *Tir N'an Og*, the Isle of Eternal Blessedness: Private communication with Patricia Kelley, October 1990.

(Bonhoeffer) The verse "Death" from the poem "Stations on the Road to Freedom," in *Letters & Papers from Prison* (New York: Macmillan Publishing Co., Inc., 1976), p. 371.

204 (Moody subjects) *Life After Life* (Atlanta: Mockingbird Books, 1975), pp. 48, 9.

(Kübler-Ross) *McCall's,* August 1976, p. 136.

A patient of Dr. Cicely Saunders, after telling of a "near-death experience," then reported, "Quite recently I have been ill again, and then I did think at one time that I was going back to where I had been before. I seemed to know where I was, and I can remember thinking suddenly, 'I've got something to do. I must arrange my elder son's bar mitzvah,' nobody else *could* do it, as my husband is not Jewish, and I dreamt—I'm sure it was a dream—that I said 'If it's all the same to you, Lord, I can't go just yet, I've got something to do' and I seemed to hear in my dream a laughing voice saying, 'Well, if you think you are the only one who can do it, stay.' And then in the dream I heard the most beautiful voice—I've never heard a voice like it, nothing in my life—saying, 'I wouldn't have you come to Me fretting.' " (Private correspondence. Used by permission.)

207 (Death as a journey) Carl Jung writes: "In my rather long psychological experience I have observed a great many people whose unconscious psychic activity I was able to follow into the immediate presence of death. As a rule, the approaching end was indicated by those symbols which, in normal life also, proclaim changes of psychological condition—rebirth symbols such as changes in locality, journeys, and the like" (in "The Soul and Death," from *The Meaning of Death,* ed. Herman Feifel [New York: McGraw-Hill, 1969], p. 10). In a near-death experience of his own, reported in *Memories, Dreams, Reflections* (New York: Random House, 1965), Dr. Jung felt freed of the "box-system" of three-dimensional existence and entered a realm of spiritual ecstasy, "a non-temporal state in which present, past and future are one." His nurse told him afterward, "It was as if you were surrounded by a bright glow" and, "that was a phenomenon she had sometimes observed in the dying, she added" (pp. 289–97).

(Ars Moriendi) From *The Book of the Craft of Dying* (op. cit.) pp. 93, 96.

209 (Jacob) *Science,* 196:4295, June 10, 1977, p. 1166.
("Go, go, go, said the bird.") T. S. Eliot, "Burnt Norton," op. cit., p. 118.

In *Heaven: A History* (New York: Vintage Books, 1990) authors Colleen McDannell and Bernhard Lang suggest that "the ways in which people imagine heaven tell us how they understand themselves, their families, their society, and their God. . . . Heaven can be used as a key to our Western culture" (p. xvi); "Near-death experiences, in effect, describe the gate of heaven and not the interior. . . . Scientific, philosophical, and theological skepticism has nullified the modern heaven and replaced it with teachings that are minimalist, meager, and dry" (p. 352).

211 ("Dying is the experience of a lifetime") These were the last words of Marian Murdock Rattray, Marin County, California, September 5, 1976.

Chapter 13

222 (Thomas) Op. cit., p. 147.

(Fr. Tom O'Connor) "The Power in Care," St. Joseph's Hospice: Annual Report, March 31, 1989, p. 15.

225 (Elderly blind man) Ibid., p. 3. Dr. Richard Lamerton, former director of the Domiciliary Care Service at St. Joseph's, is now the medical director of Hospice of the Marches in Brookfield, Tarrington (England). For updated material on St. Joseph's I am indebted to J. A. Scott, Esq., secretary (private communication, June 26, 1990): St. Joseph's budget is £3.5 million annually, half from the National Health Service, half from gifts. Of some 1350 patients annually, 280 are served in their homes, 1070 receive inpatient care, and 10 day care, by a paid staff of 250 and 20 volunteers.

226 (Twycross) Dr. Michael Minton, M.R.C.P., F.R.C.R., is now Consultant in Palliative Medicine at Sobell House. Dr. Twycross is at present Macmillan Reader in Palliative Care, Oxford University, based at Sobell House.

(PRN) "As needed"—in other words, the patient must "earn" drugs by suffering rather than having pain prevented by sufficient and regular dosage, as in good hospice care.

(Ten Commandments) Even so, Dr. Twycross has provided me with a recent revision of his rules, as follows:

1. Thou shalt have clearly defined medical leadership.
2. Thou shalt not assume that every symptom is caused by the malignant process.
3. Thou shalt remember that many symptoms are caused by multiple factors.
4. Thou shalt explain simply the patient's symptoms to him and together determine appropriate treatment.
5. Thou shalt explain the treatment to the patient's relatives.
6. Thou shalt not limit treatment simply to the use of drugs.
7. Thou shalt use drugs prophylactically for persistent symptoms.

8. Thou shalt not be afraid to ask a colleague's advice.

9. Thou shalt never say "I have tried everything" or "There is nothing more I can do."

10. Thou shalt have an air of quiet confidence and cautious optimism.

229 (Kingsbury) By permission, private communication, June 25, 1990.

230 (Appropriate therapies) U.S. and U.K. hospices have also drawn closer in style in that there are now more home care teams, proportionately, in the U.K. and more inpatient units in the U.S. Of 400 "hospice services" now in Britain and Northern Ireland, 277 are, or have, home care teams, with 145 inpatient units and 115 day care units: *Directory of Services: U.K. and Republic of Ireland* (London: St. Christopher's Information Service, 1990). St. Christopher's itself had a home care team as early as 1969, and this, too, has been enlarged.

231 (West) St. Christopher's Hospice: Annual Report, 1987–1988, p. 2.

232 (Mount) Private Communication, August 8, 1977. Used by permission.

233 (Lo-Yi Chan) From "Designing a Better Place to Die" by Joan Kron, *New York,* March 1, 1976, p. 49.

234 (Mount) "Changes in Palliative Care," keynote address, First Annual American Conference on Hospice Care, June 1984, *American Journal of Hospice Care,* Nov./Dec. 1985, p. 25.

(Peck) Op. cit., p. 231.

235 (Mount) Op. cit., p. 28.

237 (Thomas) Op. cit., p. 110.

242 (For-profit chain) The *Chicago Tribune* reported: "For-profit corporations are relatively rare in the hospice field. Ninety-five percent of U.S. hospice organizations are small, not-for-profit, community-based groups which usually must raise donations to make ends meet. HospiceCare, which was founded by several leading hospice organizers who were instrumental in lobbying the federal government to pay for hospice care through Medicare and Medicaid, actively mar-

kets its program" (Aug. 27, 1990, Chicagoland section, p. 4). The same newspaper reported on Sept. 9, 1990: "HospiceCare is under investigation following disclosures to the Tribune that employees of the company issued directives to hospitalize patients to boost the company's revenues" (Chicagoland section, p. 1).

243 (Medicare benefits) "To qualify for coverage under the Medicare hospice benefit, the patient must meet four criteria: he or she must be terminally ill with a life expectancy of six months or less, be unable to benefit from further aggressive (curative) therapy, be able to receive most (80 percent, by law) of his or her care at home, and have a care-giver (relative or friend) who will assume the responsibility for custodial care of the patient and be the decision maker in the event the patient becomes no longer competent to make decisions": "Rx for Dying: The Case for Hospice," by Wilma Bulkin, M.D. and Herbert Lukashok, M.S., *New England Journal of Medicine,* Feb. 11, 1988, p. 376.

244 (Pat Newby) Pat was formerly executive director of Gallatin Hospice. The present director is Don Leonhardt.

246 (Concept of care) "Developing a Community-Based Hospice Program," paper by Mary Runge, R.N., n.d. Used by permission.

250 (Watson-Williams) "Developing a Hospice Program: Educating the Physician," by E. J. Watson-Williams, MB, MRCP, FRC. Path. Address presented at Los Angeles Regional Meeting of the National Hospice Organization, April 19, 1979.
(Student reactions) "Caring From The Heart, by Kathryn Garvey, in *The U.C. Davis Physician,* Spring, 1980, pp. 12–14.

252 (Hospice nurse) Margaret Wolters, R.N., Hospice of HealthEast Program Director, St. Paul, Minnesota.

253 (Letter) Private communication with Carole B. Klein, director of Hospice Volunteers of Hilton Head, Hilton Head Island, South Carolina. Used by permission.

254 (Most like a single cell) Thomas, op. cit., p. 5.

255 (MacDonald) "Hospice, Entropy, and the 1990's: Toward a Hospice World View," *Am Journal Hospice & Palliative Care,* :7:4:40–42; 7:5:42; 7:4:47; 7:4:46.

258 (Soul-making) This lovely phrase is borrowed from the *Letters* of John Keats (1819) by way of *Soul Making: The Desert Way of Spirituality,* by Alan W. Jones, San Francisco: Harper & Row, Publishers, 1985.

Chapter 14

259 (Mary Kennedy) By permission, private communication, Aug. 2, 1990.

(Sue Bingham) By permission, private communication, Sept. 1988.

265 (Judaic law) For further development of this idea, see Cynthia Ozick's excellent book of essays, *Metaphor and Memory* (New York: Alfred A. Knopf, 1989).

(Yeshua) In *A Walker in the City* (New York: Harcourt Brace Jovanovich, 1951) Alfred Kazin writes: "Yeshua, our own long-lost Jesus, speaking straight to the heart and mind at once. . . . Yeshua my Yeshua! What had he to do with those who killed his own and worshipped him as God? Why should *they* call him only by that smooth Greek name of Jesus? He was my Yeshua, my own Reb Yeshua, the most natural of us all, the most direct, the most enchanted . . . (pp. 161–2).

(All the wrong people) M. Scott Peck writes: "I do not think that Jesus walked vulnerably among the outcasts and crippled of the world purely as a sacrificial act. To the contrary, I suspect he did so because he preferred their company": *The Different Drum* (New York: Simon & Schuster, 1987), p. 231.

(Maggie Ross) Op. cit., p. 1.

268 (Africa) World Health Organization spokesman Michael Merson says: "By the year 2000 we expect 80 percent of the [AIDS] cases to be in the developing world. . . . Today AIDS is the leading cause of death among young adults in many African countries" (AP release by John Edlin and Didrikke Schanche, Sept. 30, 1990).

269 (Engelcke sermon) Church of the Holy Cross, Kahuku, Oahu, Hawaii, Sept. 16, 1990.

271 (Parade) "So why am I concerned [writes Bobbie Earle of Darien, Connecticut]? I think that those of us committed to hospice have become older but not necessarily wiser, and must return periodically to our roots and to the original simplicity of the concept. As my mother used to say, 'We know the words but we have forgotten the music' ": private communication, Oct. 23, 1988. Used by permission.
(Peck) Op. cit., pp. 93, 68.

281 *(The New York Times)* p. C1.

282 *(Nova Law Review)* "AIDS Discrimination: Its Nature, Meaning and Function." 12:3, 1113ff.

285 (Hospice of St. John) It should be noted that this hospice, like most others, does not include patients using aggressive treatment for AIDS such as AZT.

287 (Hospice and AIDS) By permission, private communication with Pat Kelley, June 1989.

294 (Message from Sue B. used by permission)

295 (Should share its attitudes): We now see hospice techniques and attitudes being applied, to the great benefit of patient and families, in certain chronic care situations as, for example, at the Rush Alzheimer's Disease Center (a division of Rush-Presbyterian–St. Luke's Medical Center) in Chicago. The line between hospice care and chronic care, though medically and psychologically distinct, is, in the moral sense, a fine one. Clearly, the overarching moral imperative in our world today is *care.*
(Lynn) "Ethics in Hospice Care," in *Hospice Handbook: A Guide for Managers and Planners* (Rockville, Md.: Aspen Systems Corp., 1985), p. 320.

296 (Variations) The theme being explored here from varying points of view is the creation of a more ethical human community in the process of caring for members of society who are gravely or chronically ill. In the *Nova Law Review* article previously cited, Schulman called for religious and federal financial support of education for chronic care in the home, by volunteers, of such long-term conditions as AIDS, Alzheimer's, and ALS. (See also his articles, "Rethinking

the Way America Takes Care of Its Chronically Ill," *Los Angeles Times* [Sept. 17, 1989], and "Stopping AIDS Euthanasia," *Tikkun* [July/Aug. 1987].) My proposal, from a hospice rather than a chronic care perspective, has been that professional hospice teams should teach and demonstrate palliative AIDS care techniques on site in the inner cities; and I have suggested that government would do better to support such teams rather than investing exclusively, or primarily, in costly facilities capable of serving only a few patients. (See my keynote address, Annual Meeting of the National Hospice Organization (Nov. 18, 1988) in *The Journal of Palliative Care,* pp. 10–19, and the U.S. Congressional Record (Feb. 7, 1989). For further philosophical and bioethical perspectives on hospice care, chronic care, and the development of community, see works previously cited by Balfour Mount, Douglas MacDonald, and Joanne Lynn. Also, Deborah Allen Carey, *Hospice Inpatient Environments: Compendium & Guidelines*, Introduction (New York: van Nostrand Reinhold Company, 1986); and David J. Roy, "Humanity, The Measure of an Ethics for AIDS," *Proceedings,* Fifth International Conference on AIDS, June 1989, from which the quotation on this page is taken.

298 As this book goes to print, ten months after my interviews with William, he is still active in giving care to others; and, despite increasing debilitation, is involved in the planning of a place of respite for AIDS care-givers.

Chapter 15

305 (Apocrypha) *The Apocryphal New Testament,* tr. Montague Rhodes James (Oxford: Clarendon Press, 1924), pp. 253–4.

307 (Medical professionals volunteer) In 1990 the Hospice Care Association of Singapore had twenty volunteer doctors, one hundred volunteer nurses, and eighty lay volunteers.

309 (Catherine Bateson) Mary Catherine Bateson, *Composing a Life* (Boston: Atlantic Monthly Press–Little, Brown, Inc., 1989).

319 (Tigers, British troops) *Singapore,* 1988–89 ed. (Lausanne, Switzerland: Editions Berlitz), pp. 14–23.

320 (Flag) My hospice friends in Singapore have kindly informed me that the red stripe on the nation's flag stands for universal brotherhood and equality; the white stripe stands for purity and virtue; the crescent refers to a young nation on the ascendant; and the five stars are for democracy, peace, progress, justice, and equality.

326 (Gregory Bateson) *Angels Fear: Toward an Epistemology of the Sacred* (New York: Bantam, 1988), pp. 170–71.

329 (Bal Mount) Dr. Balfour Mount, op. cit.

331 (Eastern tradition) Dr. Tam points out that Chinese traditional medicine is particularly helpful with palliative care because its emphasis is upon the symptoms as presented (subjective) rather than the objective signals often held to be of sole importance in traditional Western medicine. He continues: "When you understand that the Chinese have come to use their right brain more, you will not scorn them for not being so 'advanced' in scientific research, nature-disrupting mining and oil extracting, the formation of colonies. Four inventions of the Chinese—magnetic compass, paper, gunpowder, and printing—were tools used centuries later by colonizing countries to conquer others by sea, thus changing world history. It has been claimed that Chinese medicine is not modern, updated, since few new findings have been added over the centuries. But others have shown that the *system* of diagnostic labeling was so good that it was hard to improve significantly upon the Nei Ching [Canon of Medicine, written 475–221 B.C.] over the last few millennia."

338 Biblical quotations on this and the following page are from Luke 4:21, 1 Corinthians 15:51, and Revelation 21:4.

339 (Many . . . laboring) In a television broadcast (Aug. 29, 1990) of her visit to the fortieth anniversary of the United Nations, Mother Teresa said, "Holiness is not something unusual. Holiness is a simple duty for you and me—it is what we were born for."

SELECTED BIBLIOGRAPHY

Abel-Smith, B. *The Hospitals, 1800–1948.* London: Heinemann, 1964.

Ainsworth-Smith, I., and P. Speck. *Letting Go: Caring for the Dying and Bereaved.* London SPCK, 1982. (U.S. distributor: Abingdon Press, Nashville.)

Amenta, M. O., and M. L. Bohnet. *Nursing Care of the Terminally Ill.* Boston: Little, Brown, 1986.

Aries, P. *Western Attitudes Toward Death.* Baltimore: Johns Hopkins Press, 1974.

Bateson, G., and M. C. Bateson. *Angels Fear: Towards an Epistemology of the Sacred.* New York: Bantam, 1988.

Billings, J. A. *Outpatient Management of Advanced Cancer.* Philadelphia: J. B. Lippincott, 1986.

Blake, J. B. *Public Health in the Town of Boston, 1630–1822.* Cambridge, Mass.: Harvard University Press, 1959.

Bluebond-Langner, M. *The Private World of Dying Children.* Princeton: Princeton University Press, 1978.

Bowlby, J. *Attachment and Loss.* 3 vols. New York: Basic Books, 1984.

Brieger, G. H., ed. *Medical America in the Nineteenth Century.* Baltimore: Johns Hopkins Press, 1972.

Carey, D. A. *Hospice Inpatient Environments.* New York: Van Nostrand Reinhold Company, 1986.

Clay, M. R. *The Medieval Hospital of England.* New York: Barnes & Noble, 1966.

Comper, F.M.M., ed. *The Book of the Craft of Dying and Other Early English Tracts Concerning Death.* New York: Arno Press, 1977.

Corr, C. A., and D. M. Corr, eds. *Hospice Care: Principles and Practice.* New York: Springer Publishing Company, 1983.

Feifel, H., ed. *The Meaning of Death.* New York: McGraw-Hill, 1969.

Frankl, V. E. *Man's Search for Meaning.* New York: Washington Square Press, 1963.

Gorer, G. *Death, Grief and Mourning.* New York: Doubleday, 1965.

Habenstein, R. W., and W. M. Lamers. *Funeral Customs the World Over.* Milwaukee: Bulfin, 1963.

Hume, E. E., ed. *Medical Work of the Knights Hospitallers of St. John of Jerusalem.* Baltimore: Johns Hopkins Press, 1940.

Jolly, J. *Missed Beginnings: Death Before Life Has Been Established.* (The Lisa Sainsbury Foundation Series.) London: Austin Cornish Pub. Ltd., 1987. (U.S. distributor: Essex, Conn.: Hospice Education Institute.)

Jung, C. *Memories, Dreams, Reflections.* New York: Random House, 1965.

Kaye, P. *Notes on Symptom Control in Hospice & Palliative Care.* Essex, Conn.: Hospice Education Institute, 1989.

Kübler-Ross, E. *On Death and Dying.* New York: Macmillan, 1969.

Larking, L. B., ed. *The Knights Hospitallers in England.* New York: AMS Press, 1968.

Lugton, J. *Communicating With Dying People and Their Relatives.* (The Lisa Sainsbury Foundation Series.) London: Austin Cornish Pub. Ltd., 1987. (U.S. distributor: Essex, Conn.: Hospice Education Institute.)

Lynn, T. "Ethics in Hospice Care" in *Hospice Handbook: A Guide for Managers and Planners.* Rockville, Md.: Aspen Systems Corp., 1985.

Mannes, M. *Last Rights.* New York: William Morrow, 1972.

McCaffrey, M. *Nursing Management of the Patient With Pain.* Philadelphia: J. B. Lippincott, 1979.

McDannell, C., and B. Lang. *Heaven: A History.* New York: Vintage Books. 1990.

Neuberger, J. *Caring for Dying People of Different Faiths.* (The Lisa Sainsbury Foundation Series.) London: Austin Cornish Pub. Ltd., 1987. (U.S. distributor: Essex, Conn.: Hospice Education Institute.)

Nouwen, H. *Beyond the Mirror.* New York: Crossroad, 1990.

————. *Reaching Out.* New York: Doubleday, 1975.

————. *The Wounded Healer.* New York: Doubleday, 1972.

Ozick, C. *Metaphor and Memory.* New York: Alfred A. Knopf, 1989.

Parkes, C. M. *Bereavement: Studies of Grief in Adult Life.* Middlesex: Penguin, 1975.

Peck, S. M.: *The Different Drum: Community Making and Peace.* New York: Simon & Schuster, 1987.

Peters, T., and N. Peters. *A Passion For Excellence.* New York: Random House, 1985.

Riesman, D. *The Story of Medicine in the Middle Ages.* New York: Hoeber, 1935.

Risley, M. *House of Healing.* New York: Doubleday, 1961.

Rosen, G. *A History of Public Health.* New York: MD Publications, 1958.

Ross, M. *The Fountain and the Furnace.* New York: Paulist Press, 1987.

Sarton, M. *After the Stroke.* New York: Norton, 1988.

Saunders, C., ed. *Hospice and Palliative Care.* London: Edward Arnold Ltd., 1990.

Saunders, C., ed. *The Management of Terminal Malignant Disease.* London: Edward Arnold Ltd., 1986. (U.S. distributor: William & Wilkins.)

Saunders, C., D. H. Summers, and N. Teller, eds. *Hospice: The Living Idea.* London: Edward Arnold Ltd., 1981. (U.S. distributor: William & Wilkins.)

Shilts, R. *And the Band Played On.* N. Y.: St. Martin's Press, 1987.

Snow, L. W. *A Death With Dignity: When the Chinese Came.* New York: Random House, 1974.

Solzhenitsyn, A. *The Cancer Ward.* New York: Dial, 1968.

Speck, P. *Being There: Pastoral Care in Time of Illness.* London: SPCK, 1988. (U.S. distributor: Nashville: Abingdon Press.)

Spilling, R., ed. *Terminal Care at Home.* New York: Oxford University Press, 1986.

Stedeford, A. *Facing Death: Parents, Families, Professionals.* London: Heinemann, 1984. (U.S. distributor: Butterworth & Co.)

Thomas, L. *The Lives of a Cell.* New York: Viking, 1974.

Thompson, J. D., and G. Goldin. *The Hospital: A Social and Architectural History.* New Haven: Yale University Press, 1975.

Tolstoy, L. *The Death of Ivan Ilych and Other Stories.* New York: New American Library, 1960.

Twycross, R. G. "Relief of Pain" in C. Saunders, ed., *The Management of Terminal Malignant Disease.* London: Edward Arnold Ltd., 1986.

Twycross, R. G., and S. Lack. *Therapeutics in Terminal Cancer.* London: Pitman, 1984. (U.S. distributor: Baltimore: Urban & Schwarzenberg.)

Wall, P. D., and R. Melzack, eds. *Textbook of Pain.* 2nd ed. New York: Churchill Livingstone, 1989.

Worcester, A. *The Care of the Aged, the Dying, and the Dead.* Springfield: Charles C. Thomas, 1935.

Worden, J. W. *Grief Counselling and Grief Therapy.* New York: Springer Publishing Company, 1982.

Zborowski, M. *People in Pain.* San Francisco: Jossey-Bass, 1969.

Zimmerman, J. M. *Hospice: Complete Care for the Terminally Ill.* 2nd ed. Baltimore: Urban & Schwarzenberg, 1986.

FOR FURTHER INFORMATION

On hospice care:

Hospice Education Institute
5 Essex Square, Suite 3B
Essex, CT 06426
(800) 331-1620

Foundation for Hospice and Homecare
519 C Street, NE
Washington, DC 20002
(202) 547-6586

National Hospice Organization
1901 North Moore Street, Suite 901
Arlington, VA 22209
(703) 243-5900

St. Christopher's Hospice
51–59 Lawrie Park Road
Sydenham, SE 26 6DZ
London, England
Tel: 081-778-9252

On AIDS:

National AIDS hot line, U.S.A.:
English-speaking: (800) 342-AIDS, 24 hours a day, 7 days
week.
Spanish-speaking: (800) 344-7432, 7 days a week, 8:00 A.M. t
2:00 A.M., and recording.
Hearing-impaired: (800) AIDS-TTY, 10:00 A.M. to 10:00 P.M
Monday–Friday, and recording.

National AIDS Information Clearinghouse
P.O. Box 6003
Rockville, MD 20850
(800) 458-5231

On Alzheimer's disease:

National Information Service: (800) 621-0379
Illinois: (800) 572-6037

INDEX

ABOUT THE AUTHOR

Sandol Stoddard is the author of many widely-translated books for people of all ages, and her articles have appeared in professional journals here and abroad. An early interest in the hospice concept brought her, in 1977, to St. Christopher's Hospice, London, as a volunteer. Since then she has become a leading advocate of the international hospice movement, and has participated in the founding of several U. S. hospices. A magna cum laude graduate of Bryn Mawr College, Ms. Stoddard has lived in Alabama, New England and the San Francisco Bay area as well as in Europe. She now lives on the Kona Coast of Hawaii.